Asia-Pacific Environment Monograph 2

BOATS TO BURN: BAJO FISHING ACTIVITY IN THE AUSTRALIAN FISHING ZONE

Asia-Pacific Environment Monograph 2

BOATS TO BURN: BAJO FISHING ACTIVITY IN THE AUSTRALIAN FISHING ZONE

Natasha Stacey

ANU
THE AUSTRALIAN NATIONAL UNIVERSITY

E PRESS

ANU E PRESS

Published by ANU E Press
The Australian National University
Canberra ACT 0200, Australia
Email: anuepress@anu.edu.au
This title is also available online at: http://epress.anu.edu.au/boats_citation.html

National Library of Australia
Cataloguing-in-Publication entry

Stacey, Natasha.

Boats to burn: Bajo fishing activity in the Australian
fishing zone.

Bibliography.
ISBN 9781920942946 (pbk.)
ISBN 9781920942953 (online)

1. Bajau (Southeast Asian people) - Fishing. 2.
Territorial waters - Australia. 3. Fishery law and
legislation - Australia. 4. Bajau (Southeast Asian people)
- Social life and customs. I. Title. (Series:
Asia-Pacific environment monograph; 2).

305.8992

Cover design by Duncan Beard.
Cover photographs: Natasha Stacey.

Table of Contents

List of Tables

List of Maps

List of Figures

List of Plates

Foreword

This book, Natasha Stacey's *Boats to Burn*, is a study of considerable importance for an understanding of maritime relations in the Arafura and Timor Seas. The Arafura and Timor Seas link Australia and Indonesia. These seas provide more than just a source of shared resources; they also offer a common history of maritime involvement. This book explores this critical, but little known maritime history and considers its implication for the present.

Boats to Burn focuses on the role of a distinctive population, the Bajo or Bajau Laut, who are remarkable for their sailing and fishing traditions. Known as the 'sea nomads' of the region, the Bajo have established themselves throughout eastern Indonesia searching out marine resources — trepang (or sea-cucumber), shark fin, turtle and trochus shells — and feeding these products back into a trade network linking island Southeast Asia to the Asian continent.

Bajo migration has been integral to the maritime development of eastern Indonesia. In the seventeenth century, the Bajo were primarily established on many of the small islands of the Sulawesi region; by the 18th century, they had sailed southward and had reached Roti, the southernmost island of the Indonesian archipelago. Records of the Dutch East India Company from May 1728 report a Bajo fleet of some 40 small family boats searching for trepang first along the southern coast of Roti and then in the Bay of Kupang. The Bajo thus sailed as the advanced scouts for other Macassans, particularly the Bugis, searching out new areas for gathering trepang.[1]

By 1750, Dutch Company officers began issuing formal letters of permission to Macassan boats to allow them to gather trepang without hindrance. These letters covered not just the Timor coast but also the coasts of northern Australia, which was then referred to as New Holland.

Describing the situation in northern Australia in the first years of the nineteenth century, Matthew Flinders sketches the beginning of this trepang-gathering industry:

> The natives of Macassar have long been accustomed to fish for trepang … upon a dry shoal lying to the south of Rotee but about twenty years before, one of their prows was driven by the northwest monsoon to the coast of New Holland, and finding trepang to be abundant, they afterwards returned; and have continued to fish there since that time.[2] (1814, II: 257).

[1] See Fox, James J., 'Notes on the southern voyages and settlements of the Sama-Bajau' in *Bijdragen tot de Taal-, Land- en Volkenkunde* 133:459-65. 1977.
[2] Matthew Flinders, *A Voyage to Terra Australis … in the years 1801, 1802 and 1803*. 2 vols. London. 1814.

If we accept Flinders' account and recognise the "dry shoal lying to the south of Rotee" as Ashmore Reef, then it follows that the Bajo arrival on the northern coast of Australia was roughly contemporaneous with the arrival of Captain Cook in Botany Bay. What is remarkable, however, is not these early dates, but the fact that Bajo sailing patterns at least to the seas in and around Ashmore Reef continue to this day.

One of the great values of Natasha Stacey's research has been to trace the historical continuity of Bajo sailing patterns and demonstrate their continued presence in Australia waters even in times when little attention was paid to the area of Ashmore Reef, Cartier Island and the smaller reefs further to the south.

For the contemporary period, Dr Stacey focuses on a group of Bajo who originate from two villages in the Tukang Besi Islands of Southeast Sulawesi but have settled at a site, Tanjung Pasir, in the village of Pepela at the eastern end of the island of Rote. While still maintaining close contact with their origin villages in Sulawesi, these Bajo fishermen now regularly sail into Australian waters in search of shark. They form part of a much larger group of eastern Indonesian fishermen who are permitted to fish within an area delimited by the 1974 Memorandum of Understanding agreed upon by Australia and Indonesia.

Whereas the Bajo have been doing this for centuries, the majority of other Indonesian fishermen are relative late-comers to shark fishing, particularly shark-fishing in Australian waters. These various fishermen, however, have been able to take advantage of the terms of the MOU that defines 'traditional fishing' by the use of a sailing technology rather than by the continuity of recognised historical traditions – a situation that has greatly disadvantaged the Bajo.

Dr Stacey's study raises a range of critical policy issues in regard to the rights of access to fishing. These issues have become even more complex as resources in the area defined by the MOU have diminished and many fishermen from Pepela, including Bajo, have turned to the use of small, motorised *bodi* rather than sailing *perahu* to penetrate deeper into Australian waters in pursuit of shark. This has been met by concerted apprehension efforts in the past few years, forcing further shifts in the dynamics of this 'traditional' fishery.

Dr Stacey's research relates to the period prior to these latest developments. She did her fieldwork in 1994-1995 with further follow-up research in 1997. Her study is nonetheless particularly relevant to an understanding of small-boat – so-called 'traditional' – fishing in the region. The explorer-navigator, George Windsor Earl, described the Bajo as a 'singular people'. He encountered the Bajo when they visited Port Essington in 1840 and wrote of his plans, which he never succeeded in carrying out, of sailing with them in eastern Indonesia.[3]

By contrast, Dr Stacey has done what Earl never managed to do. She has lived with Bajo in their villages and sailed with them over long distances; thus she has come to know them intimately and appreciate the dilemmas they face. Her book is a plea for the recognition of these 'singular' people whose world has been radically altered by international regulations, large-scale commercial fishing, and ever-diminishing resources for small-boat fishermen.

Ultimately this is a book in which good ethnography raises critical questions for public policy. The impoverishment of the coastal communities in eastern Indonesian whose previous livelihoods depended, in part, upon access to Australian waters calls for efforts at redress. The absence of alternative livelihoods for these fishermen leaves them with few options but to continue to sail into Australian waters, taking greater risks in the process. This situation is particularly acute for the Bajo who have little access to land. Each apprehension only increases the impoverishment that has prompted the problem in the first place.

We may all hope that this book will serve as a catalyst for further cooperation between Indonesia and Australia in addressing the problems of the Bajo and other poor fishermen of eastern Indonesia.

James J. Fox
Research School of Pacific and Asian Studies
The Australian National University

---

[3] See Earl, G. W., p. 335 in *The Eastern Seas, or Voyages and Adventures in the Indian Archipelago in 1832-33-34*. London. 1837 and p. 65 in *Enterprise, Discoveries and Adventures in Australia. London. 1846*.

Acknowledgments

I would like to thank many people who have assisted my work from its beginnings as a doctoral research program in 1993. Professor James Fox, from The Australian National University (ANU) in Canberra, Paul Clark from the Museum and Art Gallery of the Northern Territory, and Dr Ian Walters from Charles Darwin University (formerly the Northern Territory University) have all provided ongoing enthusiasm, support and advice at various times. I am also very grateful to Drs Colin Filer and David Lawrence of the Resource Management in Asia-Pacific Program at the ANU for the editorial assistance they have provided in turning my original thesis into a book.

I received financial assistance from Charles Darwin University; the International Federation of University Women in Geneva; the Northern Territory Branch of the Australian Federation of University Women; the North Australia Research Unit of the ANU; the Australian Centre for International Agricultural Research (ANU Eastern Indonesian Fisheries Project); and the Commonwealth Department of Employment, Education and Training (Asian Studies Library Award).

In Indonesia, field research was carried out under the auspices of the Indonesian Institute of Sciences (Lembaga Ilmu Pengetahuan Indonesia) (LIPI) and the sponsorship of Haluoleo University in Kendari, Southeast Sulawesi, and I should like to thank the Rector and staff of that university for their support.

I wish to express my gratitude to people in the communities of Mola and Mantigola in the Tukang Besi Islands and in Pepela on Roti Island, who permitted me to live in their villages and supported my research during between 1993 and 1997. I am particularly indebted to Pak Akmad, Ibu Mambi and their children in Mola, and Pak Hassan and his family with whom I lodged in Pepela. I would also like to thank Pak Kasmin from Mola Selatan who provided translation assistance during periods of fieldwork in Mola.

There were dozens of people from Mola, Mantigola and Pepela who patiently provided their time and offered information during my field research. Particular thanks are due to Pak Sahrulla, Pak Gunda, Pak Mbaga, Pak Bilaning, Pak Pallu, Pak Harun, Pak Gudang, Pak Panghasi, Pak Mahating, Pak Mpeno, Pak Kiramang, Pak Nurdin, Pak La Ode Ndoke, Pak Subbung, Pak Badolla, Pak Talla, Pak Kaharra, Pak Kariman, Pak Acing, Pak Mudir, Pak Dudda, Pak Goseng, Pak Idrus, Pak Hasim, Pak Usman, Pak La Musa, Ibu Runnia and Ibu Muna. In many parts of this book, I have used pseudonyms to protect the identities of my informants, especially the Bajo boat captains and crew who were operating in 1994, so I cannot identify the real names of many people whom I would like to thank in person. I am grateful to Pak Sahrulla for allowing me to sail on his *perahu*; to Pak Nasseng of Sulamu for offering information on Bajo history, and to the captains and crews of apprehended boats in Darwin and Broome who allowed me to interview them during such stressful times.

Pak Alimaturahim, Director of Yayasan Sama (a non-government organisation) and his family and staff in Kendari provided considerable support, information and assistance. I would also like to acknowledge the assistance provided by the Director of PT Sumberguna Makasarnusa in Ujung Pandang regarding the trade in marine products in Indonesia. On a number of occasions during fieldwork in Indonesia, Gwen and Peter Deacon in Kupang, and Allaster Cox and Susila Selvaraja in Jakarta provided hospitality. In Jakarta, Allaster Cox and Andreas Vecchiet from the Department of Foreign Affairs and Trade at the Australian Embassy supplied me with copies of maps and publications. They also allowed me to accompany an official Australian-Indonesian delegation during an educational meeting concerning illegal Indonesian fishing activity in the AFZ in Southeast Sulawesi in January 1995.

I would also like to acknowledge the assistance provided by the following individuals and organisations during the course of my research: Professor Pim Schoorl in Holland for providing copies of his published and unpublished material on Southeast Sulawesi; Nick Burningham, formerly of the Western Australian Maritime Museum, for information on Indonesian watercraft technology and for correcting many technical errors in the manuscript on *perahu* construction and design; Dan Dwyer for information on Indonesian fishing activity in the AFZ; Gus Bottrill for access to his unpublished material; Dr Ian Crawford for access to his Ph.D. thesis; Dr Greg Acciaioli and Ester Velthoen for providing copies of unpublished papers; George and Virginia Hilliard in Sydney for information on Robin Hilliard; CSIRO Division of Fisheries in Hobart for providing me with a copy of the 1949 Warreen Survey Log; Alan Pearce of the CSIRO Division of Marine Research in Perth for going out of his way to locate and provide copies of visual material associated with that survey; Bruce Wallner and Kevin McLoughlin of the Bureau of Rural Sciences in Canberra for copies of their unpublished report; Dr Mark Donohue for some basic Sama language training in Mola; Silvano Jung for his technical assistance; and staff of the Australian Surveying and Land Information Group's Maritime Boundaries Program in Canberra (now part of Geoscience Australia) for providing some of the maps.

In Darwin, staff from the Foreign Fishing Operations Branch of the Australian Fisheries Management Authority (AFMA) — especially Colin Mellon, Mick Munn, Roy McKay and Raymond ('Doc') Doherty — have at various times over the course of the study provided information on Indonesian boat apprehensions and allowed me to interview Indonesian boat crews held in Darwin Harbour. Daryl Rolf and Nigel Scullion of Barefoot Marine Security provided me with transport to visit these fishermen on their boats. Des Pike from Parks Australia in Darwin provided extensive information on Indonesian activities at Ashmore Reef National Nature Reserve. Pak Argus Sardjana, Pak Mochtar and Ibu Tien of the Indonesian Consulate in Darwin also provided information on Indonesian apprehensions. Staff from the Northern Territory Legal Aid Commission also supplied information at various times.

In Broome, Les Garbellini, Greg Gaynor, Mike O'Dea, Michael Ferris, and Colin Ossel from the WA Fisheries Department provided information on Indonesian boat boardings and apprehensions. They also provided me with office space during a visit to Broome and took me to visit Willie Creek Detention Centre. Volunteer staff at the Broome Historical Museum went out of their way to assist in my inquiries and allowed me access to their files. In Perth, the WA Australian Customs Service located a file from 1957 and generously supplied me with a copy, Philip Vincent supplied information on cases dealt with by Broome magistrates. fishing cases, and Chris Majors provided information on Bajo communities resident at Sampela and LaHoa in the Tukang Besi Islands. In Canberra, Stuart Fitch from AFMA and staff from the Department of Foreign Affairs and Trade in Canberra supplied information on Indonesian fishing activity and the maritime borders between Australia and Indonesia.

Finally, my gratitude goes to Didier Rouer and my family for their encouragement and support during the many years over which this study was conducted.

Natasha Stacey
Charles Darwin University
April 2007

Abbreviations

AFMA	Australian Fisheries Management Authority
AFS	Australian Fisheries Service
AFZ	Australian Fishing Zone
ANPWS	Australian National Parks and Wildlife Service
AusAID	Australian Agency for International Development
CSIRO	Commonwealth Scientific and Industrial Research Organisation
MAGNT	Museum and Art Gallery of the Northern Territory
MOU	Memorandum of Understanding
NT	Northern Territory
PFSEL	Provisional Fisheries Surveillance and Enforcement Line
RAAF	Royal Australian Air Force
RAN	Royal Australian Navy
UNCLOS	United Nations Convention on the Law of the Sea
WA	Western Australia

Conventions

In this study different typefaces are used to indicate different languages. Words in *italics* are from Bahasa Indonesia, the Indonesian national language; those in a **bold** typeface are from Baong Sama, the Sama-Bajau language.

Chapter 1: Contested Rights of Access

This study considers contested rights of access to fisheries resources between Indonesian fishermen and the Australian government in the Timor and Arafura seas. The imposition of international maritime borders between Australia and Indonesia has created a situation of conflict between various groups of Indonesian fishermen seeking access to traditional fishing grounds and the sovereign integrity of Australia's border regime. This conflict is exemplified by the many Indonesian fishing vessels apprehended for illegal incursions into Australian waters each year.

This book is an ethnographic study of the sailing and fishing voyages undertaken by one group of eastern Indonesian maritime people who operate in waters now claimed by Australia. It concerns Bajo people (also known as 'Bajau' or 'Bajau Laut' and by the generic terms 'sea nomads' or 'sea gypsies') who originate from the villages of Mola and Mantigola in the Tukang Besi Islands, Southeast Sulawesi, as well as Bajo from these communities who have recently migrated and settled in the village of Pepela on the island of Roti in East Nusa Tenggara. These Bajo belong to a much larger ethno-linguistic group known as the 'Sama-Bajau' who are found in scattered settlements in Indonesia, the Philippines and Malaysia.

For at least three centuries diverse groups of fishing peoples from islands now part of the archipelagic nation state of Indonesia have engaged in seasonal voyages to fish in the plentiful coastal and offshore waters, reefs and islands in the Timor and Arafura seas off northern Australia. This activity is focused on the collection of a range of marine products including trepang, shark fin, turtle shell, trochus shell and reef fish, some of which command high prices on international markets in Southeast Asia.

Since the early decades of this century, but particularly since the 1950s, Australia has successfully carried out a series of maritime territorial expansions culminating in the establishment of a 200 nautical mile Australian Fishing Zone (AFZ), legitimated under the 1982 United Nations Convention on the Law of the Sea (UNCLOS). These claims have gradually encroached on the traditional fishing grounds of a number of distinct groups from Indonesia and turned Indonesian sailors of the open seas into trespassers and illegal fishermen. [1]

The Australian government has taken measures to recognise some form of prior fishing rights and to regulate ongoing access for Indonesian fishermen in offshore waters now under Australian control. Under a Memorandum of Understanding (MOU) signed with Indonesia in 1974, Australian authorities

---

[1] All voyages to Australia are undertaken by males. Thus the term 'fishermen' is used in preference to the term 'fishers'.

allow traditional Indonesian fishermen to operate within an area incorporating a number of offshore reefs and islands in the western region of the Timor Sea, located in the outer part of the AFZ. According to the minutes of a bilateral government meeting held in 1989, access to the area is limited to 'Indonesian traditional fishermen using traditional methods and traditional vessels consistent with the tradition over decades of time, which does not include fishing methods or vessels utilising motors or engines'. However, this arrangement has largely failed to address issues of marine resource management, recognition of fishing rights and prevention of illegal activity outside the permitted areas.

Australia's response to these illegal incursions has been to adopt a series of policy strategies aimed at deterring Indonesians and protecting fisheries resources. These policies take the form of: apprehension of boats and crew found operating illegally in the AFZ; prosecution; confiscation of boats, catch and equipment; jail terms for repeat offenders; and repatriation of fishermen to Indonesia at Australia's expense. Complementary to this approach, a series of educational visits by Australian officials to provinces of eastern Indonesia has been undertaken to inform Indonesians of the maritime boundaries existing between the two countries and the areas where Indonesian fishing is permitted inside the AFZ. This response costs Australian taxpayers millions of dollars each year. However, more controversial than the cost is the burning of the confiscated Indonesian fishing boats by Australian authorities (Fox 1998). Despite these strategies, Indonesian fishing continues.

The issues are part of a complex, tangled web of legal, political, economic and historical trajectories. Since the late 1980s, the problem has at times posed a serious impediment to diplomatic relations between Australia and Indonesia (Campbell and Wilson 1993: 6). It will continue to pose a serious challenge for both countries until a suitable and appropriate policy and management response is devised.

For some years a number of Australian commentators have argued that the shortcomings of Australia's policy and treatment of Indonesian fishermen are due, at least in part, to a lack of culturally sensitive insight and understanding (Campbell and Wilson 1993; Van der Spek 1995; Fox 1998). This argument has been supported in the report of the Joint Standing Committee on Foreign Affairs, Defence and Trade: 'if there are deficiencies in some aspects of Australia's handling of the problem of illegal fishing they were probably caused in part at least by a lack of knowledge about complex social and economic situations in eastern Indonesia' (JSCFADT 1993: 129).

Commentators have suggested that there is a limited acknowledgment and understanding of the diversity of ethnic groups fishing in Australian waters. Generally, Indonesian fishermen 'assume an inherent, inalienable Indonesian identity' in Australia (Pannell 1993: 72). They are categorised as one homogeneous group and all prosecuted in the same fashion without any regard to their historically specific activities in northern Australia (Fox 1998: 134). In fact, Campbell and Wilson (1993) demonstrated that at least five different Indonesian fisheries were operating in the early 1990s. These involve a number of ethnically distinct populations using a range of technologies with differing historical antecedents.

It has further been argued that there are serious problems with the MOU arrangements and the definition of traditional fishing encapsulated within it. This definition restricts access to the allowed areas based on 'traditional' technology and ignores the dynamic aspects of culture change (Campbell and Wilson 1993; Fox 1998). Furthermore, Australian authorities continue to develop and enforce their policies without a clear understanding of the complexities of the situation, the social and economic impacts of the policies themselves, and the relationship of these to continued legal and illegal fishing activity (Campbell and Wilson 1993; Fox 1995a, 1998).

The issue of traditional Indonesian fishing has been further complicated since the late 1980s by a series of waves of illegal fishing activity involving a number of opportunistic groups of people from Indonesia who generally do not demonstrate a history of fishing activity in the Timor and Arafura seas. Consequently, the Australian Government's focus since the mid-1990s has been on the 'problem' of illegal fishing, 'solutions' to minimise or prevent illegal intrusions (Fox 1992; Reid 1992; JSCFADT 1993; Wallner and McLoughlin 1995a: 33), and the current impact of Indonesian fishing on Australia's marine resources (Wallner and McLoughlin 1995a, 1995b). While over-exploitation of some resources in the Arafura and Timor seas is a matter of concern, the problems faced by the fishermen have generally been ignored. Attention has focused on surveillance, apprehensions, prosecution and boat forfeiture, rather than on alternative management responses.

Alternative approaches involving both short- and long-term strategies are required (Russell and Vail 1988; Campbell and Wilson 1993; JSCFADT 1993; Fox 1998). These include identification of different groups of Indonesian fishermen in order that individual arrangements and treatment can be devised for each group, since the different fisheries 'present separate problems for which different measures are needed' (JSCFADT 1993: 117). Such an approach calls for investigation of the historical, social, cultural and economic organisation of each fishery active in Australian waters (Campbell and Wilson 1993: 193; JSCFADT 1993: 117; Fox 1995a: x). The absence of detailed ethnographic research has continued to mar Australian policy decisions (Van der Spek 1995). This study will begin to fill the gap by examining 'what is actually happening on the water' (Cordell 1989: 5) with regard to Bajo fishermen from Southeast Sulawesi.

The aim of this study is to examine the social, cultural, economic and historic conditions which underpin legal and illegal Bajo activity in the AFZ. It presents an analysis of the history and economics of voyaging, identifies elements of continuity and change in the patterns and organisation of voyaging, examines the material culture of fishing, and illustrates Bajo world views and rituals associated with boats and fishing. It also considers issues arising from Australian maritime expansion and Australian government policies regarding the treatment and understanding of Indonesian (especially Bajo) fishing activity.

The first question posed in this study concerns the effect of Australian maritime expansion and the 1974 MOU on Bajo fishing activity. As a result of area restrictions, Bajo fishing activity underwent considerable change from the late 1980s. However, the changes did not happen in isolation. This dynamism is examined through analysis of the interrelationship between Bajo responses to Australian maritime expansion and the wider impacts of the domestic and international trade in marine products. The Bajo are now firmly tied to the wider maritime economic patterns in Southeast Asia. They have adopted new technology and interact with the wider domestic and international economies in a creative and enterprising fashion.

Marcus and Fischer have stated the need for anthropology to embed local cultural worlds in larger impersonal systems of political economy. They argue that '"outside forces" are integral to the construction and constitution of the "inside", the cultural unit itself, and must be so registered' (Marcus and Fischer 1986: 77). The Bajo are a people attempting to accommodate cultural continuity within broader processes of influence (ibid.: 78). Transformations in material culture provide insights into issues of encapsulation and culture change among peoples previously categorised as ahistoric (Wolf 1982), Oriental (Said 1979), or 'traditional'. A central theme of this study is the opposition of 'tradition' to 'modernity' in relation to Bajo fishing activity in the AFZ, because access to the 1974 MOU area for Indonesian fishermen is defined by the use of 'traditional' technology.

The second question posed in this study is thus about the immediate and long-term consequences of this concept of 'traditional' fishing contained in the 1974 MOU. While Australia and Indonesia continue to enforce policies towards 'traditional' fishermen as if they were people frozen in time, the Bajo are in fact demonstrating a form of cultural dynamism in response to a range of local and international forces. Because of changes in Bajo fishing activity, an adherence to entrenched notions of 'traditional' fishing activities as static, subsistence-oriented and non-commercial means that the Bajo are no longer considered to be operating 'traditionally' but 'commercially'. Yet Bajo fishing activity in the AFZ has 'traditionally' been a commercial activity. Misunderstandings and inconsistencies have thus arisen in Australia's treatment of Indonesian fishermen. Furthermore, it appears that this has hindered attempts at providing solutions to the issues concerning traditional Indonesian fishing activity in the AFZ.

This leads us to the third question, which is why the Bajo continue to fish both legally and illegally in the AFZ. For as long as illegal fishing continues, the effectiveness of the Australian policy of deterrence is minimised. The apprehension and prosecution of Bajo fishermen, and the confiscation and destruction of their boats, not only fail to deter illegal fishing, but through the creation of indebtedness, result in further illegal fishing activity. There are also other historical, socio-cultural and economic motivations for continued fishing and sailing despite the loss of access to traditional fishing grounds, and despite technological restrictions, boat apprehensions and confiscations. The evidence counters claims that fishing activity is driven only by the prospect of monetary gain and the fact of resource depletion in Indonesian waters (JSCFADT 1993: 128).

A final question concerns future management of Indonesian fishing activity in the AFZ. Previous research by social and natural scientists, working in both academia and government, agrees that the most suitable options for sustainable management of marine resources and equitable arrangements for traditional fishermen in the MOU area rest on a re-negotiation of the MOU itself, a revised definition of traditional fishing, and more appropriate ways of regulating or licensing access for the different groups of traditional fishermen (Russell and Vail 1988: 139–43; Reid 1992: 8; Campbell and Wilson 1993: 186; Wallner and McLoughlin 1995a: 34, 1995b: 121; Fox 1996: 174, 1998: 130). The first step in this process involves identifying the fishermen 'who can demonstrate an historic interest in these waters' to whom 'priority access rights should be granted' (Wallner and McLoughlin 1995a: 34). This study therefore asks whether the Bajo have an historic interest in the AFZ.

Chapter 2: Bajo Settlement History

Scattered throughout mainland and island Southeast Asia are three groups of people generally referred to in literature as 'sea nomads', 'sea people' or 'sea gypsies' (Sopher 1977). These three broad ethno-linguistic groups are the Moken, the Orang Laut and the Sama-Bajau. Each group is geographically, linguistically and culturally distinct and has adapted to the rich maritime environment and island ecosystems of Southeast Asia (Sather 1997: 320–8).

The Bajo of eastern Indonesia are a sub-group of the largest group, the Sama-Bajau. As well as being nomadic boat dwellers or former boat nomads, the Sama-Bajau are also inshore and land-based peoples:

> Sama-Bajau speakers comprise what is arguably the most widely dispersed ethnolinguistic group indigenous to insular Southeast Asia. Sea-nomadic and much more numerous strand and settled Sama speakers live scattered, and in most areas interspersed with one another, over a vast maritime zone 3.25 million square kilometers in extent, stretching from eastern Palawan, Samar, and coastal Mindanao in the north, through the Sulu Archipelago of the Philippines, to the northern and eastern coasts of Borneo, southward through the Straits of Makassar to Sulawesi, and from there over widely dispersed areas of eastern Indonesia (Sather 1997: 2).

It is estimated that there are between 750 000 and 900 000 speakers of Sama-Bajau in Southeast Asia (ibid.) (see Map 2-1). Although a comprehensive survey has never been conducted in Indonesia it is estimated that Sama-Bajau speakers number between 150 000 and 230 000 (ibid.: 3).

The Sama-Bajau languages make up a discrete sub-group of Austronesian languages within the Western Malayo-Polynesian language family. There are ten Sama-Bajau languages and numerous dialects (Pallesen 1985). The Sama language spoken in Indonesia appears to be closely linked to the Southern Sama language spoken along the coast of Sabah, on its offshore islands, and in the Sulu Archipelago of the southern Philippines (Sather 1997: 9–10). In Indonesia, there is only 'small divergence on a dialectal level' (Verheijen 1986: 26–7) and Indonesian Sama 'is only one language' (Noorduyn 1991: 6).

The term Sama-Bajau, used as a composite label to cover all the languages spoken by members of this group, not only incorporates most exonyms commonly used by outsiders but also includes terms of self-designation used by Sama-Bajau speakers themselves (Pallesen 1985: 43). Most Sama-Bajau speakers refer to themselves as Sama or A'a Sama (Sama People) (Sather 1997: 5). In the Philippines, Malaysia and Indonesia, a host of names are used by outsiders, including Bajau (and its many cognates) and Bajau Laut (Sea Bajau). In addition to these, the name Samal is used by Tagalog speakers in the Philippines to refer to land-based speakers of Sama-Bajau (ibid.).

Map 2-1: Area in which Sama-Bajau speakers are found in Southeast Asia.

In Indonesia, a number of terms have come into regular usage in the historical period. The Bugis name for these sea people was Bajo, and according to Velthoen (1997: 2), colonial Dutch observers tended to follow local usage. Thus the cognate terms Bajo and Bajau, and variations such as Bajos or Badjoos, appear in early Dutch and later English historical accounts from the late seventeenth and early eighteenth centuries (see Fox 1977a; Sopher 1977: 143–56; 158–61; 296–307; Reid 1983: 126). The name Bajau subsequently became established as a generic name for Sama-Bajau speakers among English observers (Sather 1997: 6–7).

In the Indonesian language, Bajau is the official designation as well as a general ethnic label for Sama-Bajau speakers (Acciaioli 1996: 25). As a result, this name is used by Sama-Bajau people in both Indonesia and Malaysia (Pallesen 1985: 43; Acciaioli 1996: 25; Sather 1997: 5).

In this study, the name Bajo is preferred to Bajau or Sama for a number of reasons: it is still the more commonly used exonym for Sama-speaking peoples in eastern Indonesia, and in particular in Sulawesi and East Nusa Tenggara; it is the name most commonly used by scholars writing about eastern Indonesia;

and it is familiar among Australian government officials and in literature regarding Indonesian fishing in the Australian Fishing Zone. The name Sama is used to refer to the language spoken by the Bajo peoples of eastern Indonesia.

Origin and Dispersion of the Sama-Bajau

The most comprehensive work regarding the origin and dispersion of Sama-Bajau language groups is *Culture Contact and Language Convergence* (Pallesen 1985). Based on linguistic evidence, Pallesen suggested a point of origin in what is now the southern Philippines. Around the beginning of the ninth century, speakers of Proto-Sama-Bajau dialects lived in the area of the Basilan Strait between the Zamboanga area of South Mindanao and Basilan Island in the southeastern part of the Sulu Sea (Pallesen 1985: 117). A number of groups split off during this early period. By the eleventh century further dispersion began with a major group moving southwest through the Sulu Archipelago and then along the northeastern coastal areas of Borneo (Kalimantan). Here communities again split into the North Borneo and Jama Mapun groups with the 'forward wave' of the Indonesian Bajau moving further down the eastern Borneo coastline via Tawau and Tarakan (ibid.: 121). The southward movement of Sama speakers into the southern Sulu and Borneo regions was 'accelerated' by the expansion of maritime trade after the founding of the Sulu Sultanate in the fifteenth century (Sather 1993a: 218). From the eastern coasts of Borneo, or perhaps directly from southern Sulu, Sama speakers spread southward into the Makassar Straits, arriving along the coasts of Sulawesi and spreading outward into other parts of eastern Indonesia some time before the beginning of the sixteenth and seventeenth centuries (Pallesen 1985: 121; Sather 1997: 15).

Origin myths, stories and legends found among the Bajo in Sulawesi (and among other Sama-Bajau in Sabah and Sulu) cite Johore in Peninsula Malaysia as an original homeland from where the Bajo dispersed, bringing them to South Sulawesi and hence into relations with the kingdoms of Luwu, Gowa and Bone (Pelras 1972: 157; Sopher 1977: 141; Zacot 1978: 26; Reid 1983: 125; Pallesen 1985: 5; Sather 1993b: 31, 1997: 17). The Tukang Besi Bajo have versions of similar stories. One concerns a Bajo princess, or heavenly girl, from Johore, who, after being separated from her family, was washed up in South Sulawesi and later married the Prince of Makassar. She gave birth to four sons who ruled the regions of Gowa, Bone, Luwu and Soppeng. By linking their origins with a centre of power, Johore, 'the most prestigious of all Malay kingdoms', and one which preceded the powerful Sulu Sultanate, this gave legitimacy to the kingdoms of Luwu, Gowa and Bone. These myths, according to Sather, 'have more to do with political ideologies and the subordination of maritime peoples in a succession of sea-orientated trading states than they do with actual migrations or literal origins' (Sather 1997: 17–18).

The earliest evidence of the presence of Bajo in Sulawesi is the mention of a people called Bajo Sereng (Moluccan Bajo) in the major narrative epic from South Sulawesi — the La Galigo cycle (Pelras 1996: 74). This reference apparently relates to the role Bajo may have played in relations between the maritime powers of South Sulawesi and the Moluccas (ibid.: 74). According to Pelras (ibid.: 56), this text probably dates from the fourteenth century, at the time of the dominant kingdom of Luwu.

European historical records document the presence of Bajo in South Sulawesi from the sixteenth and seventeenth centuries. In an early record from 1511, the Portuguese, Tomé Pires, documented the likely presence of Bajo in the kingdom of Gowa around the city of Makassar (Pires 1944 in Reid 1983: 127; Pelras 1996: 17). The Dutch Admiral Speelman, the 'conqueror of Makassar' (1666–67) remarked that the Bajo lived on small islands off the coast of Makassar and there they collected turtle shell which they paid as tribute to the King of Makassar and 'must always be ready to go with their vessels in any direction they are sent' (Speelman 1670, quoted in Reid 1983: 126). By the late 1670s, the Bajo were reported in northeastern Sulawesi in the Manado area (Valentijn 1724–26, cited in Sopher 1977: 300).

As skilled sailors and maritime specialists, the Bajo played an important role in the rise of the State of Gowa to a political and economic power in eastern Indonesia during the sixteenth and early seventeenth centuries, and later with the powerful Bugis kingdom of Bone to the east of Makassar. In these dominant maritime states, the Bajo were useful as explorers, messengers, sailors, and harvesters of sea products that were traded to other centres in East and Southeast Asia (Reid 1983: 124–9; Collins 1995: 14).

The eastward and southward dispersion of Sama-speaking boat nomads from the southern areas of Sulawesi over the last three centuries appears to have been closely linked to Bugis and Makassarese political and commercial expansion and migration in the region, and to the development of an archipelago-wide trading network in marine products — particularly trepang and turtle shell — which spread as far as the northern coasts of Australia (Fox 1977a; Sopher 1977: 144; Sather 1993a: 218; Velthoen and Acciaioli 1993). Although boat dwelling declined after the nineteenth century, having given way to a more shore-based existence, the trade in trepang and turtle shell in eastern Indonesia was an important factor in the distribution of Bajo through the region (Sopher 1977: 144).

Sama speakers are now distributed from eastern Kalimantan and Sulawesi across to Maluku and south along the Lesser Sunda Islands. The majority of Sama-speaking communities are found in scattered settlements along the coast of Sulawesi and on its offshore islands. In South Sulawesi, settlements are found around Ujung Pandang (Makassar) and on the Spermonde Islands, along the coast of the Gulf of Bone and offshore on the Sembilan Islands (Pelras 1972), as well as on small islands in the Flores Sea such as Selayar, Tanah Jampea, Bonerate and Karompa. In Southeast Sulawesi, settlements exist on Kabaena, Muna, Buton and the Tukang Besi Islands, on islands in the Tiworo Straits, along the shores of Kendari Bay, on the island of Wowonii and to the north at La Solo. In Central Sulawesi, Bajo settlements exist along the east coast and on the Salabanka Islands (Tomascik et al. 1997: 1221), as well as on the islands of the Banggai and Togian archipelagoes. In North Sulawesi, scattered communities exist around the Gulf of Tomini and in the Gorontalo and Manado districts (Zacot 1978). It is also reported that there are communities of Sama speakers near Balikpapan in eastern Kalimantan and on islands off the east coast of Kalimantan (Sather 1997: 4; Tomascik et al. 1997: 1219). In North Maluku, Bajo communities exist on the Sula islands of Taliabo, Senana and Sular, on islands in southern Halmahera, at Gala and on Jo Ronga, Kubi, Katinawe and Dowora islands (Teljeur 1990: 204), as well as in the Bacam Archipelago, on Obit Island and the Kayoa Islands (Collins 1995: 16). In East and West Nusa Tenggara, communities can be found on the islands of Lombok, Sumbawa, Flores, Adonara, Lomblem, Pantar, Timor, and Roti, and on small offshore islands located near to these larger islands (Verheijen 1986). These communities are linked by strong bonds of kinship, marriage and language. Sama-Bajau-speaking communities are widely dispersed geographically but the Bajo people are a united ethnic minority in eastern Indonesia.

The majority of these Sama speakers in eastern Indonesia now live in pile house settlements built over the water in coastal areas, the littoral zone and on the land. Only small numbers of boat dwellers remain along the coast of eastern Sulawesi, most particularly to the north of Kendari at La Solo and around island groups in Central Sulawesi. The number of nomadic boat-dwelling people in Indonesia is unknown, but it is estimated that only a few hundred families remain (personal communication, Alimaturahim, 1994). Despite the abandonment of permanent boat dwelling and a more sedentary lifestyle, some Bajo still spend short or long periods of time at sea, living on boats while engaged in fishing activities. The degree of engagement in maritime lifestyles and pursuits varies between Bajo communities. As well as fishing and aquaculture, Bajo engage in boat building, trading, collection of forest products, and some land-based farming.

While the Sama language is the main language spoken by the Tukang Besi Island Bajo among themselves, many also speak Bahasa Indonesia with varying degrees of competency. Indonesian language reading and writing are important skills for a boat captain, who must be able to complete administrative papers such as *surat jalan* (travel passes) and other sailing papers for himself and his crew. Many Bajo speak the local Tukang Besi language (in which local market transactions are normally carried) and some speak other Muna-Buton languages, Bugis, Makassarese and trade-Malay languages. This multilingualism reflects the wide variety of people with whom they come into contact through maritime and trading activities, and also the extent of their kinship ties.

The Tukang Besi Islands

The Tukang Besi Islands are located in the northeastern part of the Flores Sea, southeast of the island of Buton. There are five main inhabited islands — Wanci, Kambode, Kaledupa, Tomia and Binongko — and a number of smaller, mostly uninhabited, islands. The islands previously formed part of the realm of the Sultanate of Buton, but since 1964 they have been part of the province of Southeast Sulawesi (Sulawesi Tenggara). The capital of the province is the sprawling town of Kendari, located on the shores of Kendari Bay. Until recently, the Tukang Besi Islands were part of the Regency of Buton, with its administrative centre at Baubau, and the region was divided into four sub-districts (*kecamatan*): Wangi Wangi, Kaledupa, Tomia and Binongko (Map 2-2).

The chain of islands is adjacent to one of the largest and most biologically diverse coral reef systems in Indonesia (Tomascik et al. 1997: 754). In July 1996 the Tukang Besi Archipelago was declared a Marine National Park by the Directorate General of Forest Protection and Nature. The Wakatobi Marine National Park [1] includes all the reefs and islands in the archipelago and covers 1.39 million hectares (13 900 km²), which make it the second largest designated marine protected area in Indonesia (Stanzel and Newman 1997).

The Tukang Besi people are well known throughout Indonesia and beyond as 'daring seafarers, shipbuilders and maritime traders' (Evers 1991: 147). The maritime economy in the Tukang Besi Islands developed because these relatively infertile islands can only support a limited amount of small-scale agriculture, mainly during the period of the west monsoon. During the dry or east monsoon season the economy focuses on maritime activities, including collecting, fishing and trading. The trading routes can range as far as Singapore, Malaysia, Java and West Papua, and the trade involves a range of cargoes including timber, salt, tubers, second-hand clothes, copra and spices. These are mostly derived from other parts of Indonesia, particularly from Maluku and Java.

---

[1] In 2004, Wangi Wangi was split in two, and the five sub-districts were combined in a new regency or district called Wakatobi. Wakatobi is an acronym derived from the names of the four original *kecamatan*.

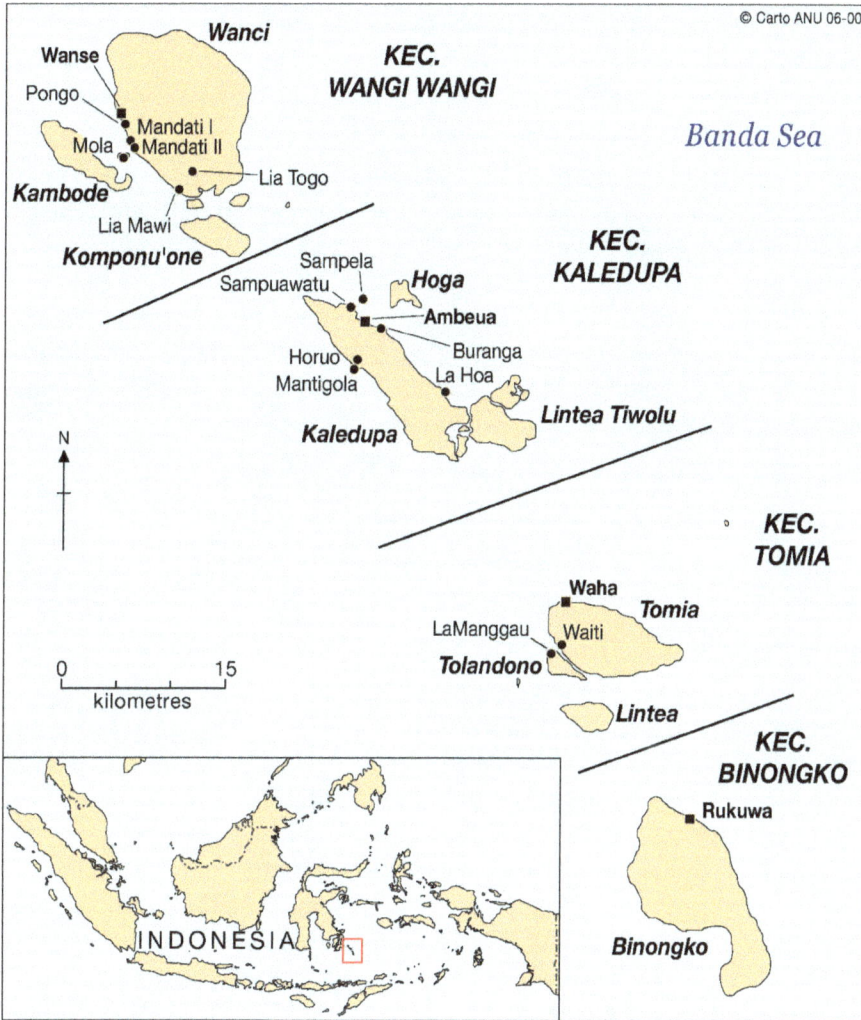

© Carto ANU 06-001

Map 2-2: Settlements in the Tukang Besi Islands, Southeast Sulawesi Province.

The major foods grown on the islands include cassava, sweet potato, corn, cocoa, cashews, peanuts, vegetables, coconuts and fruit. Rice and other seasonal foods are imported to the islands from other parts of Southeast Sulawesi. Fish is a staple part of the local diet and economy. The Tukang Besi Islanders engage in local fishing activities for both consumption and sale.

A 1994 government census counted a total population of 73 251 in the Tukang Besi Islands. The *kecamatan* of Wangi Wangi had the largest population with 34 081 inhabitants (see Table 2-1). It incorporates Wanci and Kambode islands (see Map 2-2), and smaller uninhabited islands on the east and south sides of Wanci Island. [2] There are 16 villages (*desa*) within the *kecamatan*. Kambode Island has three communities: two *desa*, Kapota and Kabita, and the *dusun* (hamlet) of Kolo, with a total population of about 3000. The largest number of people is concentrated on the western and central part of Wanci Island.

Table 2.1: Population of the Tukang Besi Islands, 1994.

Kecamatan	Wangi Wangi	Kaledupa	Tomia	Binongko
Population	34 081	14 379	12 948	11 843

Sources: Kabupaten Buton 1994a: 8; 1994b: 1; 1994c: 1; 1994d: 17.

The main town of Wanci is located in the metropolitan Wanse-Pongo area. Government departments and services, junior and senior high schools, and a *losmen* (guest house) are all located in Pongo. The main market was in Pongo, but a few years ago was shifted to the village of Mandati I, which is the closest land village to Mola Utara. [3] Wanci can be reached by a number of routes, all involving long and arduous journeys. From Baubau, the capital of Buton, buses travel to the village of Lasalimu on the eastern coast of Buton, which is usually a three-hour trip. From here a Wanci-based ferry, and more recently a passenger speedboat, travel daily between the islands, which is usually a two- to three-hour trip. Ferries also make a 16-hour trip directly from Kendari to Wanci, usually once or twice a week.

The old capital of the vassal state of Kaledupa was Buranga, but now Ambeua is the official capital of the *kecamatan* which includes Kaledupa Island, the nearby island of Hoga, and the two uninhabited islands of Lintea and Tiwolu. There are ten *desa* on Kaledupa. Daily transport operates between Wanse and Ambeua in a small motor boat — a trip that takes 2–3 hours. The island of Hoga was formerly uninhabited because of the lack of fresh water supply, but in 1992 the local government constructed a traditional style Butonese house on the island to attract international tourists. This venture was unsuccessful, but in 1995 the

[2] The Bajo cemetery is located on the small rocky island of Otoue located to the south of Mola.
[3] Bahasa Wanci, a local dialect of the Tukang Besi language, is the lingua franca used at the market by Wanci and Bajo people.

building was taken over by Operation Wallacea, a non-governmental organisation that invited fee-paying volunteers or students to join its two- to six-week coral reef survey expeditions (Stanzel and Newman 1997). This organisation has also been working with the Indonesian government to design and implement a management plan for the Marine Park using the data it has been collecting. [4]

The *kecamatan* of Tomia includes the islands of Tomia, Tolandono, Lintea and Sawah. The capital of Tomia is Waha and there are eight villages on the island as well as a small community on Tolandono. In 1996, the Wakatobi Dive Resort was established by foreigners on Tolandono Island (also called Onemobaa), which is located southwest of the main island of Tomia (Map 2-2). In early 2001, the resort opened a 1506 m airstrip on Tomia to bring tourists by air direct from Bali.

The island (and *kecamatan*) of Binongko is much drier and more desolate than the other islands (Burningham 1996). Aside from maritime trade, the Binongko people engage in metalworking, particularly the manufacture of *parang* blades (similar to machetes) which are regarded as some of the finest in the Sulawesi region. 'Tukang Besi' is actually the Malay term for a metalworker or blacksmith.

Bajo Settlements in the Tukang Besi Islands

There are five Bajo communities in the Tukang Besi Islands. The largest is the settlement of Mola on the island of Wanci, which is divided between two villages called Mola Utara (North Mola) and Mola Selatan (South Mola). There are three villages on the island of Kaledupa — Mantigola, Sampela and La Hoa. The village of La Manggau is located on the island of Tolandono near Tomia. It is the Bajo fishermen from the villages of Mola Selatan, Mola Utara and Mantigola who undertake seasonal voyaging to the northern Australian region. This study is primarily concerned with these villagers, and in particular with men from Mola Utara and Mola Selatan, where most of the fieldwork was undertaken.

The Bajo are a minority group in the Tukang Besi Islands, comprising only about 10 per cent of the total population. The majority ethnic group are the Tukang Besi Islanders, sometimes called 'Butonese', who speak a distinctive local language. [5] Like their land-based neighbours, the Bajo often identify themselves or are identified by others as Orang Buton or Butonese. This label can be somewhat misleading, giving an impression that the person or people in question actually come from the island of Buton rather than one of the islands in the Tukang Besi chain. This practice of identification by 'historical allegiance

---

[4] Operation Wallacea now has a four year marine science program (2004–08) to guide social and biological research in Kaledupa, with two other research centres to support its activities in the sub-district. The impact of significant numbers of researchers on the local community is unknown but Operation Wallacea boasts that supporting the community through improved management of the marine environment has a direct benefit for the Bajo who depend so heavily on marine resources (www.opwall.com).

[5] A detailed description of the Tukang Besi language can be found in Donohue (1999).

rather than ethnic identity' dates from the time of the Buton Sultanate that once claimed the Tukang Besi Islands and its residents as part of its realm (Fox 1995b: 5). The generic term 'Butonese' can thus embrace a number of sub-ethnic groups from Buton and neighbouring islands in Southeast Sulawesi.

The Villages of Mola Utara and Mola Selatan

The settlement comprising the two adjoining villages of Mola Utara and Mola Selatan is located in the shallow inshore waters on the southwest coast of Wanci Island, approximately 2 km from Wanse (Plate 2-1). Running parallel to the coast, the Mola settlement extends approximately 800 m in length and up to 400 m from the shoreline. It is the largest Bajo settlement in the Tukang Besi Islands, and possibly one of the largest in Indonesia. It was originally one village, but was designated as two villages in 1981 because of its growing population. Each village is divided into two hamlets. In 1994 Mola Utara had a population of 1963 living in 338 houses, while Mola Selatan was slightly larger with a population of 2315 living in 388 houses (see Table 2-2). In some cases there was more than one family living in a house, so the number of houses did not reflect the number of families. Mola Utara is much smaller in area than Mola Selatan (2.3 km^2 as against 6 km^2), so had a higher population density. High rates of seasonal migration mean that population numbers fluctuate over time, particularly during the east monsoon between the months of July and December, when males engage in voyaging and families and extended relatives resettle in Pepela for the duration of the fishing season. Moreover, since Bajo people often spend extended periods of time away from Mola engaged in other activities, it is difficult to obtain exact population numbers.

Table 2-2: Population and number of houses in Mola, 1994.

	Male	Female	Total	No. of houses
Mola Utara	981	982	1963	338
Mola Selatan	1158	1157	2315	388

Sources: Kapubaten Buton (1994a: 9) and 1994 field survey data.

The Mola population is predominantly Bajo, but some intermarriage has taken place with other Tukang Besi people and with other Butonese, Bugis, Makassarese and Moluccans, as well as with Bajo from other parts of Indonesia. Many Bajo living in Mola Utara originated directly from other communities or boat anchorages in Buton, whereas most of the middle-aged population of Mola Selatan were born in or originated from Mantigola in the late 1950s. Some elderly Bajo reported they were born at sea on small boats called **soppe**. This older generation had parents who were born in places like Kulingsusu, Pasar Wajo, La Goro, or Bisaya in Buton or on the island of Kabaena, west of Buton. Others have parents who were born in Oenggai (on Roti Island) or in Kabir (on Pantar Island). Most Bajo of the younger generation were born in Mola.

The Mola settlement consists of rows of houses built either directly on coral rock foundations or on wooden piles over the water, with each row generally separated by waterways or canals of various widths. Individual houses and village sections are connected by tenuously placed wooden planks or lengths of bamboo above the water or raised bridges between coral foundations. Some of the older village sections have larger areas of coral rock foundation in front of the houses. The settlement is accessible from the land by two main arterial coral rock pathways, one near a village office (*kantor desa*) and one near the mosque. There are also arterial footpaths running parallel to the main waterways. Every house in the settlement has direct access to the sea. Older residents claim that Mola was originally built over the water and quite a distance from the land, before permanent walkways were built in the 1960s, so as children they had to swim or travel by dugout canoe to attend school. Nowadays, Bajo travel around the settlement by foot or canoe, but some of the more recently constructed houses to the north and south are accessible only by canoe. Travel by canoe is often the fastest and easiest method of moving around the settlement and is competently undertaken by skilled Bajo of all ages (Plates 2-2, 2-3 and 2-4).

Tidal movements range up to 2.5 m, periodically flushing out household rubbish and personal waste, but during low tides, particularly neap tides, a profound stench permeates the settlement. At times of very high tides and stormy weather, the rock foundations may be submerged in some locations.

Plate 2-1: The villages of Mola Utara and Mola Selatan, Wanci Island.

Plate 2-2: The mosque and houses along the main canal in Mola Selatan.

Plate 2-3: Houses lining a narrow canal in central Mola Utara.

Plate 2-4: Recently built houses on the northern end of Mola Utara.

The Mola Bajo have no territorial right or claim to the body of water in which they build their houses. Only the coral rock foundations and the houses are privately titled. Houses are constructed from a variety of materials — wood, brick or thatched palm leaf panels, with roofs of asbestos, tin and thatched palm. Many of the wooden houses are actually built of materials purchased from Tukang Besi people, especially from Kaledupa. A thatched hut, with a wooden or bamboo slat floor, is normally built at the back of the house to serve as a cooking area. Since it is often the coolest part of the house it is used as a general-purpose living area, but in smaller houses the sleeping rooms and cooking area are contained in the one structure. Some houses have small toilet huts built on piles over the water, and one toilet is often used by a number of families. Bathing is most commonly conducted outside, using fresh water stored in ceramic jars or jerry cans. Some houses have a separate hut for use as a washing area, while the newer brick houses have a bathroom.

Since 1989 fresh water has been pumped from tanks on the mainland through pipes to a number of satellite holding tanks. Some houses in the central part of the settlement have water pumped directly to their houses. More commonly, women and children have to either collect water from a well located in Mandati I, or buy water from others, or travel by canoe to Kapota village on Kambode Island to collect good quality drinking water. Women spend long hours each day collecting water in plastic containers and then transporting it in canoes to their houses.

While many parts of the settlement have electricity, it is only available from late afternoon until around 6.00am and on Sunday afternoons. Not every household has its own television but communal TV viewing is a popular pastime, and about four houses, notably those belonging to Haji, had satellite by 1995 and were able to access international television channels.

There is a primary school (Sekolah Dasar Mola Utara) located on land in Mandati I. Bajo children's attendance at school is irregular so there is a high level of illiteracy in the community. Few complete junior and senior high school, and even fewer go on to tertiary education. Parents who place a high value on education and have the necessary financial means or family contacts often send their children to school in Baubau or Kendari to receive a higher standard of education.[6] In 1995, around 20 young Mola Bajo adults had completed some form of tertiary education at universities in Baubau, Kendari and Ujung Pandang, but even these young people found it hard to secure formal employment.

---

[6] Tukang Besi people from Kaledupa have had a tradition of sending children away for purposes of education to other parts of Indonesia for centuries (Donohue 1999).

Other Bajo Settlements

The *dusun* of Mantigola is built on sandbanks and reef flats in shallow waters on the western side of Kaledupa island, approximately 400–500 m from the mangrove-lined strand area of Desa Horuo and only accessible by boat. Desa Horuo is approximately 1 hour's walk from Ambeua. Mantigola, with a population of around 600–700 people, is officially part of Desa Horuo, which had a total population of 1342 in 1994. Like Mola, the settlement experiences fluctuations in population with males sailing on seasonal trading and fishing voyages during the east monsoon.

Evidence of a larger population residing at Mantigola in the past can be inferred from a series of coral foundations further out to sea and from the fact that houses are now placed at some distance from each other. Mantigola is favoured by the Bajo because a large lagoon situated in the centre of the village serves as a deep-water anchorage. However, unlike Mola, there are only a few walkways around Mantigola and it is necessary to travel around the village by canoe at high tide. Houses are similar to those in Mola, constructed of a variety of materials such as bamboo, nipa palm, timber and roofing iron, and built either on wooden piles directly above the water or on coral rock foundations (see Plate 2-5). There is no electricity. Water must be collected from a well on the land at Horuo and transported in jerry cans by canoe. The isolation of Mantigola makes it difficult to obtain fresh food and household goods, and women usually buy food from Horuo or walk to the main market area in Ambeua. The Mantigola Bajo bury their dead on the land to the right of Horuo.

Dusun Sampela is located approximately 400 m from the mainland on the northeastern side of Kaledupa Island. Administratively it is part of Desa Lau Lua. The population of Sampela (around 1200 people) live in about 210 houses built of temporary material (personal communication, Chris Majors, 1998). Most of the village is accessible by foot over walkways and bridges. There is no electricity nor any local supply of fresh water, which therefore has to be collected from wells and transported by canoe from Kaledupa. Rates of immigration and emigration are lower for Sampela than for other Bajo villages. Sampela is reported to be very poor compared with Mola and Mantigola, but is one of the intended beneficiaries of community development projects funded by Operation Wallacea.

Plate 2-5: Low tide in Mantigola.

Dusun La Hoa is located on the eastern side of Kaledupa and is administratively part of Desa Langge, which had a total population of 1771 in 1994. La Hoa is the smallest of the Bajo communities on Kaledupa, comprising about 15 houses (personal communication, Chris Majors, 1996).

Dusun La Manggau is located on the northern tip of Tolandono Island, not far from Waha, the capital of Tomia Island, and has a population of 500–600 people. The settlement is administratively part of Desa Waiti. The hamlet comprises a small number of Bajo families as well as some Tomia people. There are 10–15 Bajo houses built above the water on the seaward side of the settlement. Their houses are accessible from the land on which the Tomia people live.

The History of Bajo Settlement in the Tukang Besi Islands

Village elders from the Bajo communities at Mantigola and Mola narrate stories of their ancestors' arrival in the Tukang Besi Islands via the island of Buton during the nineteenth century. Two respected village elders, Si Bilaning and Si Mbaga, [7] both reported that the first settlement or congregation area for boat-dwelling Bajo in the Tukang Besi Islands was on Kaledupa at Lembonga. Lembonga is located near to the present day settlement of La Hoa on the northern side of the island, not far from Buranga, the old capital of Kaledupa Island. Later, many Bajo moved to the other side of the island, to what is now Mantigola, to

---

[7] Si Bilaning, one of the oldest Bajo men in Mantigola, died in late 1994, and Si Mbaga, one of the oldest Bajo men in Mola Selatan (and a contemporary of Si Bilaning) died in May 1996.

fish during the east monsoon. They would then return to Lembonga at the onset of the west monsoon. The establishment of Mantigola came about when the Bajo asked the Sultan of Buton for a permit to build houses there because it was closer to the offshore reefs than Lembonga.

A Bajo man from Mantigola stated that the name 'Mantigola' comes from the phrase *menanti gula*, which means 'to wait for sugar' in Indonesian. The story behind its name is interesting in light of the Tukang Besi–Roti Island connections. Apparently, Binongko traders would sail to Roti to buy *gula air* (sugar from the *lontar* palm) which they then carried back to the Tukang Besi Islands and sold to Bajo and land-based people at the site of present day Mantigola. Binongko traders have a long established trading connection with Pepela and the local Rotinese population. Some of the first maritime settlers in Pepela were Binongko men.

The oral accounts provided by Si Bilaning and Si Mbaga concerning the Bajo arrival and settlement in Kaledupa may be compared with a record made by Pak Kasmin, a Bajo from Mola Utara, who graduated in 1993 from Haluoleo University with a teaching qualification. Pak Kasmin documented the story of the arrival of the Bajo in Kaledupa based on interviews with a number of elderly men in Mola and Mantigola, including Si Bilaning and Si Mbaga:

> Before the Bajo came to the Tukang Besi Islands they lived in Pasar Wajo [south coast of Buton]. Sometime in the 1850s, several *perahu* **bidu** [large wooden boats] and *perahu* **soppe** [small wooden boats] left to survey the condition of the Tukang Besi Islands. They found the islands to be in a very strategic location and with rich seas possible for development. After that, they returned to Pasar Wajo to request a permit from the Sultan of Buton; they were given a permit to move to live in the Tukang Besi Islands. The Bajo people who moved to the Tukang Besi Islands were led by two **punggawa** [leaders], Puah Kandora and Puah Doba. They sailed in groups in several *perahu* [wooden boats] with several heads of family in each *perahu*. They first stopped at Lia on Wanci Island. Not long after they moved to Lembonga in the northeast part of Kaledupa, and there they lived on their *perahu* **bidu** or **soppe** and caught fish and gathered other kinds of sea products, and at that time they still lived moving from place to place. During the northeast season they moved to the southwest part of Kaledupa, known by the name Kampung Mantigola, and they returned to Lembonga during the west season. The arrival of the Bajo people in the Tukang Besi Islands was welcomed by the Government and the local society and they asked for a permit to build houses in Mantigola in the 1850s (Kasmin 1993: 32–3).

According to Sopher (1977: 151, 268), in the nineteenth century the headman of each Bajo group had the title of **punggawa** — the customary title of chiefs or leaders amongst the Bajo-Bugis, or Bajo owing allegiance to Bugis or Makassar princes. The Bugis used the term to mean a military chief or ship's captain (Pelras 1996: 332). According to the Mola Bajo, Puah Doba, a Bugis leader mentioned in the above story, was also called Daeng Nyirrang. He married a Bajo woman and therefore there are close kinship links between the two groups. Bajo often say 'orang Bugis saudara kita' ('Bugis are our brothers').

During the nineteenth century the original capital of Wanci Island was at Lia Togo, situated atop a ridge with commanding views of the surrounding sea and islands, especially Kaledupa. The location was chosen for safety from Taosug slave raiders and pirates. Most of the Wanci population lived in the higher regions of the island, and settlement along the coast was relatively recent. The central market and commercial area previously operated from Lia Mawi on the coast. Following pacification of the area by Dutch colonial powers, a small Bajo community was established at Lia Mawi but the capital moved to the Wanse-Pongo area (Donohue 1994: 4). It is unclear whether the old Bajo settlement in present day Mola Utara was established at this time, but Si Juda from Mantigola stated that the original inhabitants of Mola came from the villages of Lagoro and Lasalimu on the eastern coast of Buton. Until the 1950s, Mantigola was the largest Bajo settlement in the Tukang Besi Islands. After this time, Bajo from Mantigola embarked on a major migration to Mola. Bajo were also driven out by rebellion and inter-community conflicts.

The Kahar Muzakkar Rebellion and Bajo Migration

Between 1950 and 1965, Kahar Muzakkar led a rebellion (gerombolan) against the national government which kept South and Southeast Sulawesi in a state of civil unrest. This was linked to the Darul Islam (Islamic State) political faction and associated with the Tentara Islam Indonesia (Indonesian Islamic Army) rebellion in West Java and Aceh. During this period, Sulawesi was divided between the followers of Kahar Muzakkar and the Tentara Nasional Indonesia (National Indonesian Army), and much of Southeast Sulawesi was under the control of the rebels (Harvey 1974: 1437). The Kahar Muzakkar rebellion, commonly referred to simply as the gerombolan by the Bajo, resulted in great upheaval for the Mantigola Bajo and was responsible for large numbers settling in Mola and other settlements in the Tukang Besi Islands. From there many dispersed around eastern Indonesia.

Older generation Mola and Mantigola Bajo recall the disorder in their lives, especially during the years 1956 and 1957. Some members of the Bajo community were active supporters of the gerombolan, but their actions were opposed by the Kaledupa people and their local government. Subsequent violent reprisals and attacks by the land people forced the Bajo Mantigola to move to Sampela. These attacks took place at the instigation of local units of the Tentara Nasional Indonesia based in Kaledupa who wished to have tighter control on the Bajo.

However, support for the rebellion continued, and about a year later, with further threats from the Kaledupa government, the Mantigola Bajo fled in their boats and canoes to Mola. This was done with the permission of the Wanci government which supported the rebellion (personal communication, Si Pallu, 1995). At that time, a small Bajo community of about 30 houses already existed in central Mola Utara.

During this period of unrest and upheaval, the majority of Mantigola Bajo moved to Sampela. A short while later some again fled from Mantigola and Sampela to other areas in eastern Sulawesi. Some Bajo moved to Langara village on Wowonii Island, close to Kendari. This community was later forced to flee to Kendari itself but eventually returned. Some people escaped to the villages of Matanga in the Banggai Islands and to Limbo on Kukkusang Island in Central Sulawesi. Others moved directly from Mantigola and Mola to Sulamu in Kupang Bay, and also to the Bajo village of Kabir on Pantar Island.[8] The community of Wuring on the north coast of Flores near Maumere was also settled by Bajo from Mantigola during the rebellion (Burningham 1993: 209). However, Si Pallu and others from Mola claim the majority of Bajo who settled in Wuring were from the island of Kabaena, east of Buton, and from Pasar Wajo on the southern coast of Buton. Suffering from similar problems, they also fled to safer areas on the outer islands.

According to the Bajo, the *kampung* (village) of La Manggau on Tolandono Island was established after the end of the rebellion. At that point, most of the Bajo living in Mola remained there, although some returned to Sampela and others went back to Mantigola because of its proximity to offshore coral reefs. However, since the late 1980s, the most significant migration of Bajo from Mola and Mantigola — not just male members of the community but also women and children — has been to and from the village of Pepela on the island of Roti.

The Village of Pepela, Roti Island

The island of Roti is located in the Timor Sea, southwest of Kupang, the capital of West Timor. It is the southernmost inhabited island of Indonesia. Administratively it is part of the province of Nusa Tenggara Timor (East Nusa Tenggara). The capital of Roti is Ba'a, which is located on the western side of the island. The village of Pepela is located on the northeastern end of Roti and on the southern side of a large sheltered bay (see Map 2-3). The bay is fringed by sandy beaches and mangroves, while coral reefs are located in its centre. At the settlement of Pepela, the sandy beach drops away steeply providing a

---

[8] One of these people, Si Saddong, was the *kepala kampung* (village head) at the time; he was descended from Bajo nobility and was the keeper of a rare and valuable Lontar manuscript which documented Bajo history.

deep-water anchorage close inshore. The bay is very attractive and provides year round shelter from the strong easterly and westerly monsoonal winds.

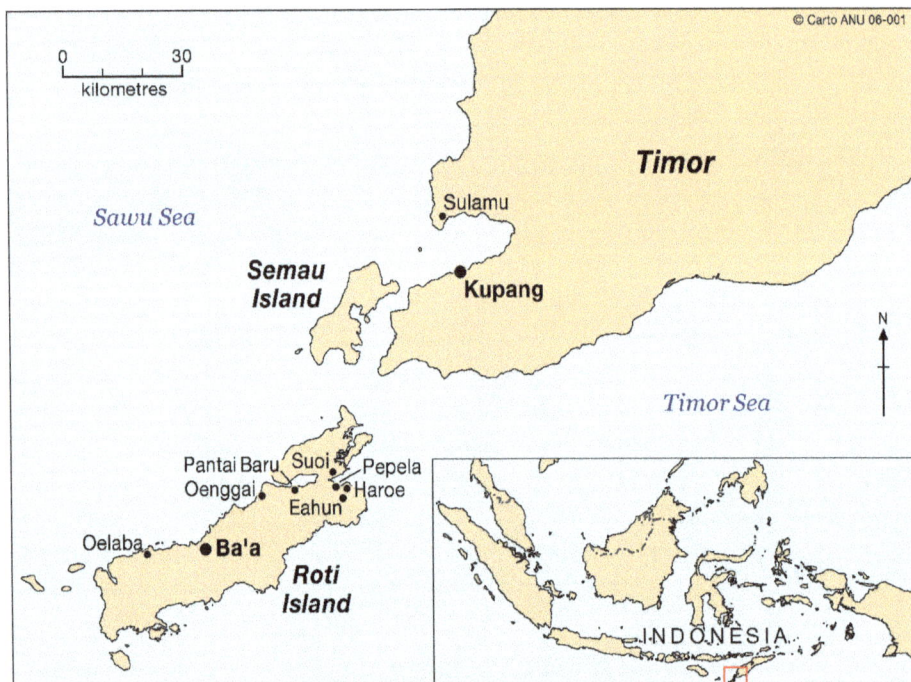

Map 2-3: The island of Roti, East Nusa Tenggara Province.

Dusun Pepela is officially part of Desa Londalusi, within Kecamatan Rote Timur, whose capital is Eahun (about 9 km inland from Pepela). In 1994, the total population of Londalusi was 2765 and the population of Pepela was approximately 800. The ethnic composition of Pepela is mixed, comprising native Christian Rotinese, descendants of Muslim Butonese immigrants from other islands (Fox 1998: 127), Bugis from Southeast Sulawesi, and Bajo from the Tukang Besi Islands. The economy of the inhabitants of Pepela is based on fishing in the Timor Sea and associated trade in marine products. Most land is owned by the native Rotinese, so the Muslim inhabitants are dependent on the sea for their income.

The native Christian population engages in agricultural activity, local strand collecting, and inshore fishing in small boats. They are 'not noted for their open sea sailing traditions' (Fox 1998: 126). The history of the settlement of Muslim maritime people at Pepela has not been documented, but Pepela was traditionally a port for the eastern part of Roti (ibid.: 127). Roti was important in the maritime trading network in the nineteenth century because the Rotinese produced cloth sails made from the *gewang* fan leaf palm (*Corypha elata*) for their own small boats and for sale (ibid.: 126). A sketch of a Macassan *perahu* off Raffles Bay in north Australia that was drawn by Le Breton in 1839 illustrates the traditional sails produced and traded by the Rotinese (see Macknight 1976, Plate 33). The Rotinese were also renowned for their cakes of crystallised sugar made from the juice of the *lontar* palm (*Borassus* sp.) (Fox 1977b). Bajo and Pepela residents state that, in the past, Binongko sailors from the Tukang Besi Islands regularly visited Pepela to purchase *lontar* palm sugar, which was then traded throughout the Indonesian archipelago. This trade continues to the present day, but vessels from Roti also sail to the Tukang Besi Islands to sell palm sugar directly to the Bajo.

This kind of maritime trading activity would account for some Muslim settlement in Pepela, possibly commencing in the early twentieth century but most probably after the 1920s. Subsequent settlement by other Muslim groups appears to be the result of fishing activity undertaken in the Timor Sea. Today the fishing population of Pepela is largely made up of migrants from other islands or their descendants, though many have intermarried with the local Rotinese population. The islands of origin most commonly mentioned by Pepela residents are Sulawesi, Buton, Binongko, Alor, Pantar, Flores and Java. [9]

The settlement of Pepela stretches inland from the coast for approximately one kilometre. A pier dominates the harbour and from here a road leads through the centre of the village up the hill. Most of the settlement is on the western side, but to the east of the main residential area is an area called Kampung Baru (New Village), which is a cluster of Bajo houses. Further to the east, and situated at the base of a ridge, is a coconut plantation and cemetery. The main Bajo settlement is located away from the main part of the village on Tanjung Pasir (Sand Spit/Point), called Tanjung for short. There is a handful of small shops along the main road. There are one or two wells in the village, but most water is collected in jerry cans from a small lake and well to the west (about 1 km from the pier) and then transported in wooden carts. Houses are mainly of brick construction although a few are made from thatched palm leaf panels.

On the other side of the bay is the Christian settlement of Suoi (Dusun Suoi, Desa Dai Ama). In recent years some of the males from Suoi have joined Pepela *perahu* in fishing activities in the Timor Sea. To the east of Pepela is a small Rotinese settlement, Dusun Haroe (Desa Hundi Hopo), the last point that boats pass by before sailing into the Timor Sea.

A passenger ferry operates daily between Kupang and Pantai Baru, a small mangrove fringed bay on the northwestern side of Roti. A motor boat also travels

---

[9] For example, two residents, Hassan La Musa and Haji Saman La Duma, now both in their 60s, came from the village of Popalia on Binongko as young men when they were on trading voyages. They married local Rotinese women and settled in Pepela, bringing with them *perahu* technology. Both their fathers had previously sailed to Pepela and engaged in trade with the local population.

twice a week between Pepela and the village of Namosain in Kupang. The trip takes around six hours depending on the weather conditions.

Bajo Settlement at Pepela

In the past, Bajo from Mola and Mantigola sailed from their home villages to Pepela and used it as a base for fishing voyages into the Timor Sea. While in Pepela waiting for suitable weather conditions, the men lived on their *perahu* and re-provisioned with firewood and freshwater. A Mantigola villager, Si Suleyman, was the first Bajo to settle in Pepela, having married a local Pepela woman in the 1950s. The main period of Bajo settlement did not begin until the late 1980s, when a number of them moved permanently from Mola, Mantigola and La Manggau villages and built or rented houses at Pepela. This migration was the result of economic, political and cultural changes in the practice of shark fishing.

In late 1994 there were 42 houses in the Bajo community on the Tanjung. Of these, three were unoccupied and one was being used as a *warung* (small food stall). In addition, there were seven Bajo houses in Kampung Baru, and five in the main part of Pepela. In total, the Bajo occupied 50 homes in Pepela with a population of about 292 people (134 adults and 158 children). Of all the households surveyed, the majority of Bajo living in Pepela came from Mola Selatan (28 households), with lesser numbers originating from Mola Utara (8 households), Mantigola (10 households) and La Manggau (2 households).[10] The village of origin for two houses was unknown. Most families in the survey said they had been living in Pepela for a period of 1–3 years, with a minority having lived there for 4–5 years.

The Bajo settlement on the Tanjung consists of two main rows of houses facing the sea (Plate 2-6). These homes are very basic in construction, most of them raised off the sand and made of panels of thatched palm. Some structures amount to little more than one room shacks. This reflects the temporary function they serve for the Bajo. Some houses in Kampung Baru are not raised off the ground and have dirt floors. The few Bajo houses in the main part of the village are generally better constructed and consist of larger wooden homes on stilts.

---

[10] These data should only be taken as an estimate because the number of people living in a house changed from day to day. The population was highly mobile, and in the week following the survey more men, women and children arrived from Mola and Mantigola. Some transient boat owners, captains and crew members sleep and eat in the homes of extended family members, while others may live on their *perahu* while in Pepela between fishing voyages.

Plate 2-6: The Bajo settlement at Tanjung Pasir.

At high tide, the Tanjung is partly separated from the main part of the village by a channel which cuts through the sandy beach and winds around in an arc behind the Bajo settlement. This channel allows small boats to enter behind the village and provides added protection from weather conditions during the west monsoon. A small walkway has been placed over this channel to allow pedestrian access to the Tanjung at high tide, but even this is under water when the tides are very high, and it is then necessary to travel a short distance by canoe to reach the main village.

There is no fresh water supply on the Tanjung, and this is a major problem for the Bajo. The office of the local *camat* (sub-district) is hesitant to provide any services because it has no assurance that the Bajo will stay permanently. The argument is that the Bajo could easily leave Pepela if the fishing situation changed. Consequently, those Bajo who report to the local *desa* office are only given visitor status, and only a few Bajo have decided to take up permanent residency.

The Bajo women and children have found it difficult living on the Tanjung, and although the conditions are similar to those in the Tukang Besi Islands, the general environment is poor. There are no toilets, fresh water must be purchased from local traders, and the women usually have to walk a kilometre or so even to wash their clothes. Only a few children attend the local primary school. The women reported that fish and marine products are scarcer around Pepela than in the Tukang Besi Islands, and there is a general shortage of food in Pepela in contrast to Mola and Mantigola, particularly during the dry season, which is the main fishing season and hence the period when the population is at its highest. The nearest market is a 20-minute bus ride away. Vegetables are sold by local Rotinese from house to house and fish caught locally are sold directly on the beach. Often there is competition among women to purchase the catch. During the east monsoon, dried shark meat and dried reef fish brought back from fishing trips in the Timor Sea form a staple part of the Bajo (and local Pepelan) diet.

Chapter 3: The Maritime World of the Bajo

The Bajo are a landless people who live in a physical landscape dominated by sea and islands (Sather 1997: 92). In the words of one Bajo, '*laut merupakan dasar hidup*' ('the sea forms the basis of their life'). The marine environment also constitutes 'living spaces' (Chou 1997: 613) for the Bajo since they spend their entire life in the vicinity of the sea, living either in pile houses built over the water or on boats. Their connection to the sea is more than physical: they also have a marine cosmology based on belief in, and causal relationship with, the spirits who inhabit the sea. The Bajo depend almost exclusively on exploitation of the marine environment and associated maritime activities for their subsistence needs and economic livelihood. Bajo commonly recite the following statement to illustrate their economic dependence on the sea: '*kita punya kebun di laut*' ('our garden is the sea'). They hold an intimate knowledge of the various maritime zones and coastal ecosystems, as well as the seasons, winds, currents and tides, the lunar cycle, stars and navigation. They have specialised boat building knowledge and skills, and different types of types of watercraft are essential to the way in which they interact with the marine environment. The social and economic domains of the Bajo extend well beyond the Tukang Besi Islands to other regions of Indonesia and the neighbouring countries of Southeast Asia. These domains are constructed through networks that link the Tukang Besi Bajo with other Bajo communities in eastern Indonesia.

Bajo World Views

Bajo religion is a syncretic system in which elements of Islam are fused with Bajo indigenous cosmology and ritual practice. This syncretism can be observed in various manifestations of Bajo 'practical religion' — in their cosmology, their life cycle rituals, and other rituals to do with boats, fishing, housing, and health (Pelras 1996: 197). Some Bajo are more 'syncretically inclined' (Acciaioli 1990: 217) than others. The Bajo follow Sunni Islam but adhere to the faith with varying degrees of observance, both while at sea and in their villages. During Ramadan, the fasting month, some fishing and sailing activities are still undertaken but most Bajo prefer to rest in their home villages and fast. [1]

Supernatural Beings

The sea is the home of **mbo madilao** (the ancestors of the sea), who are believed to be descended from the prophets (**nabbi**). There are seven original **mbo**

---

[1] In 1995 there were 10 *haji* (including 3 women) living in Mola who had made the pilgrimage to Mecca. *Haji* are usually the wealthiest and most highly respected members of the village, owning large numbers of boats, providing financial capital, and buying and trading in marine products.

madilao: Mbo Janggo, Mbo Tambirah, Mbo Buburra, Mbo Marraki, Mbo Malummu, Mbo Dugah, and Mbo Goyah. The leader and most powerful is Mbo Janggo. These ancestors are considered to be like humans and each possesses a different power. According to the Bajo, at some time in the past, the ancestors were all on one boat that somehow became lost at sea and were never found again.

The word **mbo** also means grandparent, and is a term applied to senior village members both living and dead. In this latter sense, the notion of an ancestor is not a genealogical one (Sather 1997: 316). The ancestors are considered to be sacred and the Bajo are generally reluctant to speak of them outside the appropriate time or place; it is generally forbidden to mention their names in casual conversation.

The Bajo have sought to incorporate their own cosmology into their Islamic faith. The position of the ancestors is ranked lower than the prophets, and the ancestors are said to work with and for the prophets. One village elder stated that the prophets gave the ancestors the control over the sea and described the ancestors as 'assistants to the prophets' (personal communication, Si Mbaga, 1995). In the political hierarchy of Malay societies, 'Allah whose domain is the universe is superior to the prophets ... [who are] lords of the ... natural realms, [and] who in turn rule the more localized spirits within those realms' (Endicott 1970: 177). Si Kiramang, a ritual expert, provided a more detailed version of how the ancestors came to be lost at sea. It is a Koranic version of the Flood Myth, where indigenous cosmology is combined with Islamic teachings.

> At the time Nabbi Nuhung [Noah] built a boat on the top of the mountain. Mbo Janggo, Mbo Tambirah, Mbo Buburra, Mbo Marraki, Mbo Malummu, Mbo Dugah, and Mbo Goyah did not believe that it was possible that the boat could descend to the sea. Afterward, the big water came up to the top of the mountain and the boat entered the water. Maybe because they did not believe it could happen, they were cursed and thrown into the sea and became lost.

Ritual experts in Mola say that each prophet is associated with a particular domain: Nabbi Hilir rules over the sea and fish for all Muslim people, but **mbo madilao** rule over the sea for the Bajo people alone. In the scale of things, the ancestors have a direct line to God through the prophets and therefore act as intermediaries between God and living Bajo (Sather 1997: 314). Further insight into the role of the ancestors was explained by Si Kiramang:

> **Mbo madilao** have control of the universe of the sea and all the creatures in it for Bajo people, for it is their place. **Mbo madilao** are like the rulers of the sea.... Because it is known by Bajo people that **mbo madilao** have authority over the sea, the sea is the property/possession [*milik*] of Bajo

people as the place where they live and as their place where they search for their livelihood. **Mbo madilao** live wherever there is sea, and wherever Bajo people search for a living, even if outside the country of Indonesia, they will be accompanied by **mbo madilao**.

This description provides a powerful insight into how the Bajo perceive their marine world. It also highlights some differences between indigenous and Western perceptions of the marine environment, for the latter 'tend not to recognise these spaces as culturally defined' but as 'watery voids' (Pannell 1996: 28). For the Bajo, the marine environment is not just the source of economic bounty. The belief is that guardian ancestors are not confined to any particular location but live 'wherever there is sea'. Given the wide geographical area in which they fish, the spiritual maritime domain of the Bajo has no boundaries; it is infinite. It therefore encompasses the whole of the Timor and Arafura seas and the Australian Fishing Zone.

The Bajo cosmic world is also one populated by diverse groups of spirits (**jeng/jin**). Spirits manifest themselves in many forms — as human beings or as land or sea animals. They may be visible or invisible, resident in one place or wandering around. They may dwell in the sea or on the land, or they may inhabit specific localities such as an island, a reef, a rock, or a tree. They may talk or appear in dreams, and some can enter people's bodies. Most of the spirits are generally evil or malevolent (**setang**) and can cause illness or misfortune. Usually, relationship with spirits is through propitiation by prayer (**baca doa**) and offerings (**rempo-rempo**/*kasih turun pinang*). Protection from evil and sorcery by spirits and humans can be sought through the wearing of amulets and charms. Each house and *perahu lambo* (long-distance sailing boat) has a bottle filled with water (**sampa**) hanging just inside the entrance that offers protection from evil spirits and acts of sorcery. There are also invisible spirits (**duatta**/*roh halus*) that may come to the aid of Bajo in times of need, especially to help find lost kin. Communication with these beings requires the service of a spirit medium (**sandro**).

Magic and Ritual

Interactions with the spirit world and ritual activity require the use of magical or esoteric knowledge (**pangatonang**/*ilmu*) (Southon 1995). A number of different categories of knowledge are found among the Bajo, including knowledge of sickness and healing, life cycle rituals and spirit mediumship (**pangatonang sandro**), sorcery (**pangatonang bebelau**/*ilmu jahat*), construction of houses (**pangatonang ruma'**/*ilmu rumah*) and boats (**pangatonang lambo/bidu**/*ilmu perahu*), sailing, controlling the marine world and fishing (**pangatonang a'nakoda/pangatongang punggawa**/*ilmu juragon*). Not everyone can acquire knowledge. It can be passed down through generations or acquired through study from a teacher. Esoteric knowledge is considered to be secret, thereby maintaining its power. Those with *ilmu* are afforded status and prestige within the community.

The basic elements of Bajo ritual are the recitation of prayers to spiritual entities by a ritual officiant or a person with *ilmu*. Prayers are not fixed in form and vary depending on the ritual. They can be in the form of propitiation (**malaku poppor**/*minta doa*) to apologise or ask for forgiveness, or a request to enlist the assistance of the spirits to avoid misfortune or escape danger (Sather 1997: 267). Depending on the particular ritual, accompanying items and the composition of offerings may vary. The basic offering (referred to generally as **pinah** or *sirih* after the components) consists of four folded leaves (**leko**/*sirih*) from the betel pepper vine (*Piper betle*), each containing a piece of betel nut (**pinah**/*pinang*), with lime or tobacco inside, placed on a plate. This can be accompanied by four hand-rolled cigarettes and sometimes coins. For more complex rituals, particularly boat and healing rituals, there are more substantial offerings of food, such as coloured rice, bananas, chicken and cakes. It is believed that the spirits 'partake in the spiritual essence of the offered foods' (Acciaioli 1990: 215).

Concepts of the Soul

In many Southeast Asian societies 'the navel is associated with ideas about the soul' (Southon 1995: 103). Three main terms — *semangat, nyawa, roh* and their cognates — are widely used in Indonesian and Malay societies to refer to different aspects of the soul (Endicott 1970: 48). There is a commonly shared concept of 'a vital force which suffuses and animates the universe' (Waterson 1990: 115), which is variously referred to in the literature as a 'vital principle' (Endicott 1970: 47), or 'cosmic energy' (Errington 1983: 545), or 'invisible force' (Southon 1995: 136), and is associated with notions of 'potency', 'soul-stuff' and 'spirit' (Errington 1983: 545). In Malay and Indonesian languages, the concept is commonly represented by the word *semangat* and its cognates. There are local variations in the meaning and usage of this word, but there is general agreement 'about a pervasive life-force which may attach itself in differing concentrations not only to living things but also to inanimate objects' (Waterson 1990: 115).

Endicott (1970: 48) draws on previous work by Wilkinson (1901: 400) to distinguish between *semangat* as 'the spirit of physical life' or 'vitality' and *nyawa* as 'the immortal essence or soul' or 'the breath of life'. Verheijen's (1986) dictionary of the Sama language defines **sumangaq** (equivalent to *semangat*) as 'spirit' or 'zest' and **nyawa** as 'life' or 'soul'.

Sumangaq and **nyawa** are both thought to be attached to the navel of the human body. In Mola, at the moment of birth, a child's **nyawa** is said to travel from the placenta, along the umbilical cord, to enter the stomach and live permanently at the navel. After the birth of a child in Mola, one local midwife said that while the placenta and umbilical cord are still moving, the **nyawa** is still in the process of entering the child. Once it has ceased moving, the **nyawa** has entered, and it is then safe to cut the umbilical cord of the newborn. While it was not clearly stated at what moment **sumangaq** attaches itself to the navel, Endicott (1970: 51) noted that 'the *semangat* of a person makes its appearance at the moment the umbilical cord is severed'.

An important aspect of Bajo spiritual life is the idea of a sibling represented by the placenta of a newborn child. After a child is born, the placenta (**tamuni**) is washed and wrapped inside a woven mat with salt, tied to a rock, and with the recitation of prayer, thrown in the water next to the house by the midwife.[2] The **tamuni** is said to be received by three prophets. The Bajo believe the **tamuni** becomes Kaka, the child's supernatural twin brother or sister, depending on the sex of the child, who inhabits the sea along with other spirits and accompanies the Bajo on their travels.

If at any period during the precarious early months or years of a child's life, or at any time during adulthood when a person suffers from ill health or sickness, it is believed that the person has lost their **sumangaq** because it has detached itself from the navel.[3] As a result, the person becomes sick with hot or cold fevers, or a headache, or a condition of weakness, faintness, exhaustion, or lack of enthusiasm (**maluntu**). A person who is **maluntu** is said to be lacking in **sumangaq** (*kurang ada semangat*). In this case, it is necessary to call on a healer to perform a healing ritual to restore the person's **sumangaq** and hence their health and well-being. This ritual is directed at Kaka and is called *kasih makan Kaka* or *pengobatan Kaka*. In Mola the ritual was performed by the **sandro**, and consists of a series of prayers and offerings beginning in the house, followed by an offering with prayers to Kaka in the sea. Here, a half coconut shell, filled with rice, betel nut (**pinah**), nine lit candles and a cup are lowered into the sea. As the coconut receptacle sinks, and the cup fills with water, the **sandro** removes the cup. Inside, the cup of salt water is believed to hold **sumangaq** which is caught using a thread (*di pancing semangat dengan benang*). Back in the house, further prayers are made and this thread is later tied around the wrist of the sick person and the **sumangaq** is restored in exchange for 'food' (see Plate 3-1).

---

[2] The concept of a sibling symbolically represented by the placenta, which protects a child throughout its life, is widespread in Malay and Indonesian societies (Warren 1993: 38). Amongst land dwelling communities, the placenta is most commonly disposed of by burial or stored in the house. Some groups, such as the Bugis of Luwu in South Sulawesi, occasionally dispose of it by sending it out to sea (Errington 1983: 551). Amongst Sama-Bajau speakers in the Southern Philippines and eastern Borneo, the placenta may either be buried on land or set adrift at sea (Nimmo 1990: 184–5; Bottignolo 1995: 225; Sather 1997: 276). The Tukang Besi Bajo dispose of the placenta exclusively in the sea.

[3] The same belief is found amongst the Bugis of Luwu in South Sulawesi (Errington 1989: 52). Among Bajau Laut it is said that this is a result of a person being shocked or startled (*kaget*) (Sather 1997: 294–5).

As we shall see, rituals conducted during phases of a boat's construction liken it to the conception and birth of a child, and boats are given 'ritual navels' (**bebol**) which act as the point of attachment for their *semangat*. Houses, kinship groups and kingdoms also have navels which are a source of power that must be guarded and protected from harm (Errington 1983: 547).

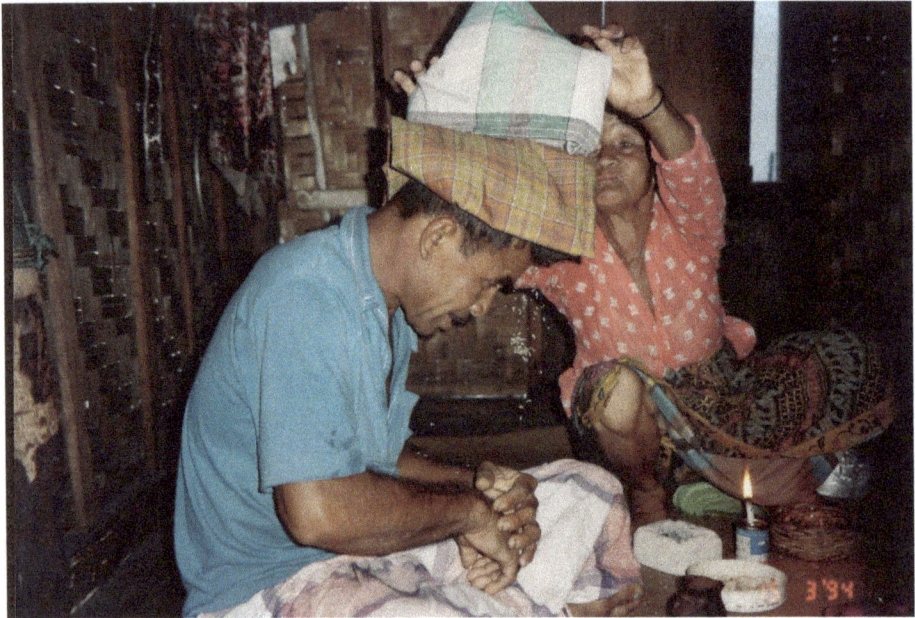

Plate 3-1: Healer restoring the sumangaq of a sick person.

'Custom' (*Adat*)

Bajo voyages and fishing activity are governed by *adat* practices. The meaning of the word *adat* varies considerably between ethnic groups in Indonesia, and there is an extensive anthropological literature on this subject (Acciaioli 1985; Warren 1993). However, *adat* has become the generic term for describing local customary practice and institutions throughout the Indonesian archipelago. Its conventional translation as 'customary law' fails to convey the vision of a necessary correspondence of cosmic and human relationships towards which it is directed (Warren 1993: 3), or its capacity to encompass 'the entire governance of society' (Acciaioli 1985: 151). For the Bajo, *adat* encompasses more than just customary law; it embraces institutions and rituals that are connected with customary practices, as well as social norms, rules, and sanctions that apply to almost every aspect of life and provide a complete code of behaviour. When Bajo talk about 'following the custom of our ancestors', they include all forms of behaviour associated with sailing and fishing. *Adat* is passed down from one generation to another and younger crew members are instructed by their elders on fishing voyages.

Maritime Livelihoods

Mobility underlies Bajo social and economic life. People move regularly, and may spend short or extended periods of time in different settlements. Strong kinship ties exist between all Bajo villages in the Tukang Besi Islands as well as with other Bajo communities in eastern Indonesia. A crew sailing from Mola to Pepela (on Roti Island) is likely to stop at the village of Wywuring in Adornara, or at Sulamu in Kupang, to get supplies, rest, and visit relatives. The wider Bajo community provides 'fixed points of localized reference' (Nadjmabadi 1992: 340) which facilitate the migration and movement of Tukang Besi Bajo around the eastern Indonesian archipelago.

Although there are five Bajo communities in the Tukang Besi Islands, it is predominately fleets of boats owned by Bajo from the villages of Mola Selatan, Mola Utara and Mantigola that seasonally engage in fishing and sailing voyages to the northern Australian waters. However, because of the close kinship ties between all Bajo communities in the Tukang Besi Islands and with other Bajo communities in eastern Indonesia, *perahu* crews are often drawn from other Bajo villages. In Sampela, most of the population are engaged in locally based fishing activities around Kaledupa and on the outlying coral reefs. In 1994, the majority of watercraft in Sampela were canoes, with only a few small motor boats. Because there was only one *perahu lambo,* the Sampela Bajo were less inclined to voyage to the Timor Sea, but some men would join Mola and Mantigola *perahu* as crew members. The small Bajo community at La Hoa and La Manggau was also predominantly engaged in local fishing activities. There were no *perahu lambo* from La Hoa or La Manggau engaged in long distance voyaging to the Timor Sea, but a number of families from La Manggau were some of the earliest Bajo from the Tukang Besi Islands to settle in Pepela with their *perahu* in the 1980s.

The Monsoon Regime

Bajo sailing and fishing activities are dominated by the east and west monsoon wind regimes. The monsoonal weather patterns produce periods of strong and light wind conditions and dry and wet seasons.

The east monsoon (**salatang**/*musim timur*) begins in April and ends in November. The beginning of the east monsoon is characterised by strong easterly winds (**sangai banga'**/*angin timur kencang*) lasting until July. These winds bring light rain between the months of May and July. This is followed by a period of light south easterlies and then a period of calm or no winds (**sangai teddo/sangai matai**/*angin mati/angin teduh*) between September and November. The latter part of the east monsoon is the best time to fish in the Timor and Arafura seas. At the end of the east monsoon there is a transitional period of changing wind directions (**sangai taputar**/*angina pancaroba*) that leads to the beginning of the west monsoon (**barra'**/*musim barat*). The west monsoon starts in late November or sometimes early December and lasts until March. It is a period of strong westerly winds, heavy rains, high seas, storms and squalls. The end of the west monsoon in March is another transitional period with winds that may blow from the southwest, northeast or northwest. This is followed by the doldrums, a period of light variable winds and smooth seas usually lasting for a week or two, which is ideal for fishing, but there is still the possibility of intermittent squalls or cyclonic activity in the waters of northern Australia. Then the strong easterlies return and the cycle begins again.

The Local Fishing Economy

The ecologically rich inshore, coastal, and offshore ecosystems, and deep open waters of the Tukang Besi Archipelago are fertile grounds for the high marine biodiversity that provides a life support system for the Bajo. Modes of exploitation of these habitats are diverse. Technology ranges from simple hand-made gear such as traps, hooks and lines, and spears, to more costly store-bought equipment such as nets and longlines. Diving with *hookah*, a relatively inexpensive form of breathing apparatus, has become popular in recent years. This enables men to fish at greater depths for reef fish, lobster, trepang and trochus. Blast fishing, involving the use of dynamite on coral reefs, was fairly common in the past but the authorities have made it illegal and regular patrols of the marine park appear to have reduced the practice.

Bajo build and use a range of types of watercraft to carry out their diverse fishing activities and to transport people and cargoes. This includes a number of types of dugout canoe (**lepa/lepa kaloko**/*sampan*) propelled by paddle, a simple sail, or sometimes with an outboard motor (**jonson**); small 5–10 tonne planked boats (**soppe**/*sope*); small planked wooden boats with engines (**bodi/motor**); sail-powered and motorised *perahu* (*perahu lambo, perahu layar motor*) and larger motorised boats (*kapal layar motor*) (see Plates 3-2 and 3-3).

Bajo classify their fishing activities into four main types: **nubba** (gleaning), **pali libu** (inshore coastal fishing), **pongka** (reef fishing), and **lama** (long-distance, nomadic fishing). The distinctions between these activities depend on the environment fished, the technology used, and the distances travelled. The first three of these are mentioned briefly here, while **lama** is discussed in more detail in a later section.

Women and children undertake **nubba** in order to meet domestic needs. This activity covers the beach and the littoral zone, including sandflats, shallow waters and fringing reefs, during daylight hours. The products include trepang (**bala**), sea urchins (**tetehe**), edible seaweed, shellfish, crustaceans, hard corals and sponges.

Plate 3-2: A *perahu lambo*.

Plate 3-3: A *perahu layar motor*.

Pali libu refers to fishing in coastal waters near the village, or in offshore open waters and on coral reefs, but still returning home on the same day. This type of activity includes handlining (**missi**), trolling (**tonda**), and spearing (**sapa**) from canoes to catch reef fish or pelagics such as tuna, mackerel, squid and octopus. Various netting methods are used, some of which involve small groups of people using different types of throw net (**ringgi, tokong, jalla**) or engaging in fish drives (**ngambai**). Spear gun fishing (**pana**) for lobster and fish is also undertaken either in the night or during the day. Women also fish from canoes using handlines, often go netting with family members, and accompany their husbands on nocturnal spear fishing expeditions.

Pongka refers to fishing in the sea or on a reef for a few days or a week, or sometimes several weeks, with a day or two travelling to reach a destination or return home. In the past, **soppe** or *perahu lambo* were the main craft used to carry out this activity, but nowadays small motorised vessels are also used. These expeditions can be all male affairs when they involve fishing for shark fin using longlines, netting reef fish, or collecting turtles around the Tukang Besi Islands. However, voyages may include whole families — even extended families — travelling to the offshore reefs in the Tukang Besi Archipelago and staying either on their boats or in small pile huts built over the reef. These huts are used as sleeping areas and as places to dry and process trepang, clams or reef fish.

Marine products are utilised in three main ways: for food and domestic use; to supply the local market through sale or barter; or being sold to traders who supply external domestic and international markets. Local fishing is conducted all year round, weather permitting. At certain times, notably during the west monsoon and rainy season, it is restricted by poor weather conditions and this results in a general shortage of fish for home consumption. The best time for harvesting the offshore reefs is during the latter months of the east monsoon when weather conditions are calm and the sea is like glass.

Although fishing is the basis of the Bajo economy, income is also derived from other maritime activities. Men engage in boat building and the associated trade in timber and canoe blanks. Both men and women trade in marine products other than fish, including the collection of coral rocks from local fringing reefs for sale as building material. Women engage in daily economic activities to help with the household income, and in some cases they provide a more regular income than their husbands and sons. Small-time trading — especially the buying and reselling of goods from homes or kiosks — is the activity most popular with village women.

Distant Shore Fishing Activities

Tukang Besi Bajo also engage in nomadic fishing expeditions further afield. The term 'nomadic' here relates to the regular seasonal migration of individuals and households to distant regions (Lenhart 1995: 245). A large proportion of the male population of Mola and Mantigola spend weeks, months or years living on boats, making voyages around Indonesia and beyond to search for a living (*mencari nafkah*). The acquisition of sea-going watercraft enables Bajo to engage in long-distance voyaging to fish for a range of marine products including shark fin, trepang, trochus shell, turtle, and tuna. This kind of long-distance economic activity is called **lama**.

Lama is both a noun ('sail') and a verb ('to sail'). The verb refers to sailing voyages or journeys made in boats to destinations both within and outside Indonesia for the purposes of fishing, carrying cargo, or buying and selling goods. These voyages can last for periods of months or even years. **Lama** includes fishing voyages to the waters of northern Australia but other destinations include West Papua, Maluku, Bali, Malaysia and Singapore. Nowadays, the term **lama** is also applied to voyages made with motorised vessels.

Shark fishing was traditionally conducted with handlines (**koelangan tansi**) consisting of a length of nylon line with a wire trace, a lead weight and hook, connected to a wooden reel with a flat wooden base. This inexpensive equipment, costing only a few thousand rupiah to make, is assembled by the fishermen themselves. Sharks are attracted with rattles called **gogoro** or **gorogoro**. These are made from a length of bamboo split at one end. Six half coconut shells are then threaded onto a piece of bamboo fitted horizontally into the split end of the stem. Shaken in the water continuously, the noise of the clacking coconut shells attracts shark to the surface. They are then caught using a baited line and hauled onto the deck. The fins are removed and laid out to dry in the sun and in some cases the carcass flesh is retained, cut into strips, salted and dried.

In addition to shark fin fishing in the Timor and Arafura seas during 1994–95, men from Mola and Mantigola also undertook voyages of one to three months, in motorised boats with minimal sailing power (both *perahu layar motor* or *kapal layar motor*), to collect green turtle (**bokko**) (*Chelonia mydas*) from various other locations. These expeditions took them to the islands in Maluku (including the Aru Islands), to the coast of West Papua, and to some atolls and reefs in the Flores Sea. The turtles were brought back in the hull of the boat, transferred to holding pens, and then loaded onto a large motor boat and transported to the market at Benoa in Bali where they were finally sold. [4] Another alternative activity was tuna fishing, which might be regarded as a newer form of larger-scale commercial fishing for the Bajo, but is still essentially based on their flexibility and mobility. A number of motor boats from Mola worked for a Kendari-based Japanese fishing company. These vessels travelled to Kupang twice a year, using it as a base from which to catch tuna with hook and line in the Savu Sea in East Nusa Tenggara. Around the same time one or two Mola boats embarked on a trading trip to the Banggai Islands in Southeast Sulawesi to sell a load of cassava. Some men from Mola also joined vessels belonging to Tukang Besi Bajo on trading voyages to Singapore and Malaysia to buy second-hand goods which were then resold in Wanci.

Distant shore fishing activity is undertaken all year round. Travel is undertaken when there are breaks in the weather during the squally west monsoon months and the beginning of the east monsoon that also brings strong winds, but there is always a higher risk associated with sailing at these times. [5] Distant shore voyaging is commonly undertaken from July through December, although some voyages also occur at the end of the west monsoon. With the advent of larger motor boats such as those used to collect turtles, there is less restriction on travelling during unfavourable monsoonal wind conditions. The danger is partly due to the fact that no life-saving equipment is kept on board.

Most adult Bajo males have participated in a fishing or trading voyage to various destinations in Indonesia or beyond at some time in their life, and some from an early age. Sailing is almost a rite of passage for many young males. However, not all men voyage each season, nor do they necessarily travel to the same destination. Some men alternate between various activities. Shifts in

---

[4] Turtles are eaten by the Hindu population of Bali but generally not by Muslims in eastern Indonesia.
[5] In January 1995, two motor boats laden with turtles and travelling back to Mola from Karompa in the Flores Sea were caught in a storm. Only one boat crew survived. With a failed engine, and pushed by winds to the southeast, they eventually ended up at Wetar Island, north of East Timor, seven days later. The crew of the other boat were never found despite search efforts throughout the southern Maluku region.

voyaging patterns can be the result of available finances, market prices and demand, restrictions on access to particular fishing grounds, and changes in social and cultural circumstances.

Amongst the Mola and Mantigola Bajo some broad distinctions are evident in modes of livelihood. There is a specific core group of Bajo from Mantigola, Mola Selatan, and to a lesser extent Mola Utara, who embark on voyages regularly every year. However, some prefer to remain in Mola and fish the local coastal waters and offshore coral reefs for their main source of income, only occasionally joining a *perahu* on a fishing expedition outside the region to pay off debts or because of lack of other local alternatives.

An indication of the diverse maritime activities and differences between the types of fishing activities pursued by Bajo from Mola Selatan and Mola Utara is given in Table 3-1. This shows three main types of boats and their distribution by ownership in Mola Utara and Mola Selatan.

Table 3-1: **Number of boats according to type in Mola Selatan and Mola Utara, 31 May to 5 June 1994.**

Boat type	Mola Selatan	Mola Utara	Total
perahu lambo	37	7	44
perahu/kapal layar motor	27	22	49
soppe	24	2	26

These results show that nearly all *perahu lambo* and **soppe**, and even a majority of motorised vessels, are owned by people living in Mola Selatan. [6] They also indicate a general distinction between the types of fishing activities pursued by the two communities. Mola Selatan Bajo generally still use **soppe** to fish around the Tukang Besi Islands, whereas Mola Utara Bajo do not. It would appear that Mola Utara Bajo used to own just as many *perahu lambo* as their counterparts in Mola Selatan, but they decided to adopt motorised vessels to pursue other activities such as turtle collecting, carrying cargo, and tuna fishing. The majority of the Mola Selatan Bajo originally came from Mantigola, have been voyaging to the north Australian region for many decades, and are said to have a preference for sailing to Australian waters. In contrast, the original Mola Utara Bajo generally do not have a documented history of voyaging.

Ngambai Net Fishing

Bajo from Mola and Mantigola have been using a net fishing technique known as **ngambai** on reefs in the Timor Sea since the early decades of this century, and this is probably the earliest type of gear which they used in that area. While

---

[6] One *haji* in Mola Selatan owns 10 motorised vessels.

long-distance fishing methods and target catches have changed in recent years, this netting technique is still practised by Bajo from Mola Selatan and Mola Utara on outlying reefs in the Tukang Besi Islands to collect fish for local sale. In 1995 there were five **ngambai** fishing groups operating out of Mola, and when I visited Pepela in 1994, I found that one *perahu* had used **ngambai** gear at Scott Reef after engaging in shark fishing and returned with a catch of dried reef fish which they sold to local Rotinese buyers. Occasionally, a group of Bajo from Tanjung Pasir used this gear on the reef in Pepela Bay, but the catch was relatively poor.

The technique can be described essentially as a fish drive requiring around 8–11 people and requires a range of equipment: two lengths of rope (**tali ambai**) (300–500 *depa* in length) with pieces of wood (**tangkal**) attached along the rope at intervals; up to seven nylon nets (**ringgi ogah**) joined together, with floats (**patau**) made from foam and old thongs attached at intervals along the top, and tiger cowrie shells (**bolleh**) spaced at intervals along the bottom; another type of drawstring net (**bandong**); wooden stakes (**ballas**); a scoop net (**bandre**); at least two canoes (**lepa**); spearguns (**panah**); and goggles (**kacamata**). According to Akmad, a full set of **ngambai** nets and ropes costs approximately Rp 1 500 000.[7]

A **ngambai** crew will depart Mola in a small motor boat around three or four o'clock in the morning and travel for two or three hours to Kapota or Kaledupa reef. On arrival there, a fishing spot is chosen, usually in about 1–2 metres of water, the boat is anchored and all the gear is loaded into the two canoes. Both canoes, with half the crew in each, row to the place chosen under the guidance of the leader and set up the gear. The fish are scared towards the net and eventually trapped. All the gear is then disassembled and transported back to the boat. The entire procedure takes around two and a half hours and is usually undertaken twice in a day. The fish species caught in this way include *Scaridae* (parrot fish), *Labridae* (wrasse), *Acanthuridae* (surgeon fish), and *Siganidae* (rabbit fish). On the trip back to Mola the captain supervises the division of the fish catch on the deck of the *perahu*. On arriving in Mola women sell the catch either in the village or at the market.

According to Si Akmad, an unidentified species of timber (**kayu pijarang**) was formerly used instead of thongs and foam to make the floats on the nets, while the bark of another tree species (**bagu**) was beaten, treated and made into twine to weave the nets themselves.[8] Since the **bagu** tree is not found on the Tukang Besi Islands, the material was purchased from traders or from other Bajo

---

[7] Similar types of fishing gear are apparently used among the Bajau Laut in Semporna, Sabah (Sather 1985: 201, 203) and by Sama people from Sitangkay Island in the southern Sulu Archipelago in the Philippines (Nagatsu 1995: 7).

[8] Verheijen (1986: 47) identifies **bagu** as *Agave sisalana* on the basis of information supplied by a Bajo man from Wuring in Flores.

living in Southeast and Central Sulawesi. The drawstring net (**bandong**) has only been used to take the fish from the net-pole encirclement since the 1970s; before that, the Bajo used **tuba** (*Derris* or *Milletia* spp.) to stupefy the fish. [9] According to Si Akmad, the catch from **ngambai** fishing in the Timor Sea was divided in much the same way as it is today: one share for each crew member, one share for the owner of each piece of net (**ringgi**), one share for each rope (**tali ambai**), half a share for each canoe and three shares for the *perahu*.

Maritime Technology

Bajo fishing voyages to the Timor and Arafura seas are undertaken in unmotorised wooden hulled craft known as *perahu lambo*. The term *perahu lambo* refers to a number of similar types of Indonesian sailing vessel which feature design elements influenced by and derived from small European fore-and-aft rigged vessels (Horridge 1979: iv; Burningham 1996: 9). The Bajo *lambo* are of the Butonese type.

The class of vessel that has become known in the literature as the Butonese *lambo* is built and sailed by a number of ethno-linguistic groups from islands in the region of Southeast Sulawesi and as far west as the Taka Bonerate atoll and smaller neighbouring islands in the Flores Sea. The Tukang Besi Islands, Buton and Bonerate are regarded as the 'centre' of the *lambo* building tradition (Nooteboom 1947: 220; Burningham 1989: 179). Over much of the past century the *lambo* has facilitated the migration of people from Southeast Sulawesi, particularly from the Tukang Besi Islands, to other areas of eastern Indonesia. Thus *lambo* are built and sailed in many of those areas where Butonese and Bajo have settled, including parts of of Maluku and Irian Jaya, and on many of the islands in East Nusa Tenggara, including the village of Pepela on Roti Island (Horridge 1979: iv, 1985: 69; Burningham 1989: 179).

The defining features of Butonese *lambo* are a straight stem and stern post set at an angle to a straight keel, with a median rudder and gunter sail rig (Burningham 1989: 179). In contrast, the stem and stern posts of the traditional Indonesian hull form are curved end to end into the keel (Horridge 1985: 12), while traditional Indonesian sail layouts for craft larger than canoes are generally rectangular (*layar tanja*) or lateen (*layar lete*) (Horridge 1979: 10) (see Figure 3-1). While the *lambo* hull exhibits European design elements, the method of building follows the traditional Indonesian method of shell construction, where short planks of timber carved to shape are fitted edge to edge with wooden dowels and the ribs are fitted afterwards. This is in contrast to the Western method of boat building, where planking is added after the rib frame is constructed (Burningham 1989: 181; Horridge 1985: 69). Nevertheless, *perahu lambo* have

---

[9] These plants are widely known by this or some cognate term in Indonesia (Hickey 1950: 5).

been described as 'the most westernised and amongst the most recently evolved trading sailing vessels in Indonesia' (Burningham 1989: 179).

Perahu lambo are generally between 10 and 40 tonnes in weight (Horridge 1985: 66) and between 10 to 16 metres in length. Three types of stern can be distinguished on *perahu lambo*, and some *lambo* building communities show a preference for a particular type.[10] In the past, *perahu lambo* were either gaff or ketch rigged (single or double masted). The gaff and ketch rig (**lama cangking**) was replaced by the gunter sloop rig (**lama sande**/*layar nade*) from around 1960 (Horridge 1985: 10). According to Hughes (1984: 155), who carried out fieldwork in the Tukang Besi Islands in 1982, there were no more two-masted *lambo* left in Wanci or Kaledupa in 1982. Hughes (1984: 156, 162) also reported that by the early 1970s, all *lambo* in Wanci had been converted from gaff to gunter rig. Since the 1970s many *lambo* have had auxiliary diesel engines installed, and some *lambo* have undergone structural modifications, transforming them into *perahu layar motor* (motorised sailing boats).

Figure 3-1 shows six different combinations of hull and rigging: (a) *perahu pajala* with the traditional Indonesian hull form and *layar tanja* rig; (b) *perahu lete lete* with similar hull form and another version of *layar tanja* rig; (c) *perahu lambo* with gaff rig; (d) *perahu lambo* with ketch rig; (e) *perahu lambo* with counter-stern and gunter rig; (f) *perahu lambo* with double-ended stern and gunter rig.

---

[10] The most common form is the distinctive elliptical counter-stern (**pantat bebek**). Counter-sterned vessels are steered with a tiller connected to a single rudder hung on a stern post in the European style. The rudder stock passes through the stern of the vessel. Some *perahu lambo* are also built with transom sterns (**pantat puppa**), but these are less common. The other style of *perahu lambo* is double-ended with a wooden platform built upon beams laid across the stern. This form of stern is called **pantat kadera**, where **kadera** comes from the Portuguese word for chair and **pantat** means buttocks (Horridge 1985: xvi). On double-ended *perahu*, the rudder is hung externally and connected directly to the stem post. Members of the trading community at Lande in Buton (Southon 1995) appear to build and sail only *lambo* with counter-sterns, whereas in Mola *perahu* with all three types of stern are built and sailed.

a

b

c

d

e

f

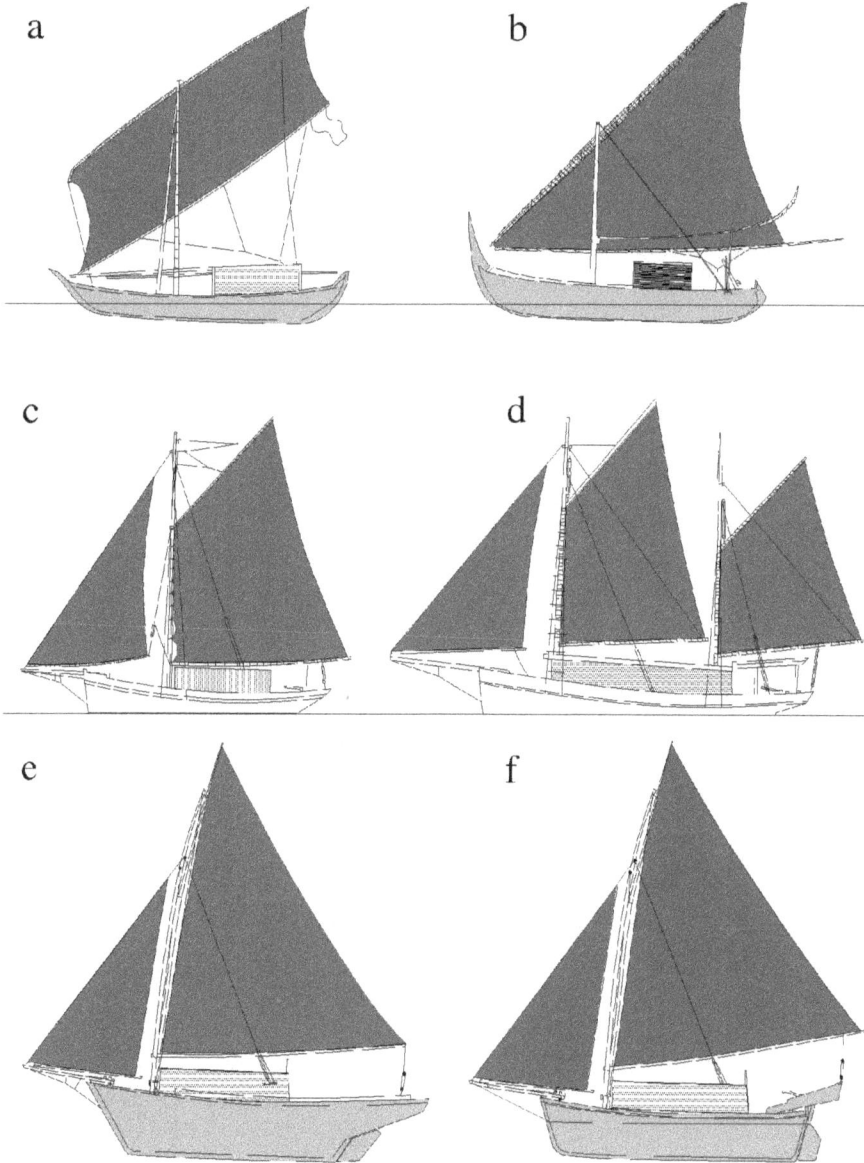

Figure 3-1: Types of Indonesian *perahu* hull forms and rigs.

Sources: Hawkins 1982, Burningham 1996.

Many of the newer *lambo* are designed for shark fishing. In the case of the Mola *lambo*, vessels were normally built with a hatch located in the middle of the aft deck. In more recent years, some of the newer *lambo* have hatches closer to the end of the stern or to the entrance of the cabin so that the deck is flush and there is greater working space to process newly caught sharks hauled onto the deck (Burningham 1996: 141). The hulls of *perahu lambo* built for Mola Bajo appear to have less beam than other *lambo* in Southeast Sulawesi since they are not engaged in cargo carrying activities. Platforms replacing the traditional toilet box are now added to the stern as an additional space for cooking and storing fishing gear, and the toilet box is then built into one corner. This appears to be related to the adoption of longline fishing gear (ibid.: 51). The design of the counter-sterned *lambo* is an Indonesian version of a small European trading sloop or cutter (Horridge 1979: iv). The counter-sterned *lambo* only appeared in the twentieth century (Burningham 1996: 11), but the European prototype from which the *lambo* was copied is still the subject of conjecture. The design could have been copied from a number of European boat types found in Southeast Asia towards the end of the nineteenth and the beginning of the twentieth centuries (Horridge 1979: 7–8; Horridge in Southon 1995: 40–1; Burningham 1996: 15, 111). The first modern usage of the word *lambo* found in records so far is recorded by Kriebel (1920: 217), who listed the types of trading *perahu* (including *lambo*) built and used by the people of Bonerate (Burningham 1996: 15). The Bonerate villagers were noted as expert builders of *lambo* in the 1930s (Collins 1936: 147; Nooteboom 1947: 220) and 1940s (Gibson-Hill 1950: 133). By the late 1930s, the *lambo* was already quite widespread throughout eastern Indonesia and was slowly replacing earlier trading vessels such as the *perahu palari* (Nooteboom 1947: 219, 220).

Much of the discussion in the literature has focused on the history and design of the counter-sterned *lambo* rather than the double-ended *lambo*. Burningham (1996: 11) says that 'some of the double-ended *lambo* from the Tukang Besi Islands have a hull form that is more closely related to that of an indigenous type called *sope* or *soppe* than to any western model', and claims that double-ended *lambo* may have been the 'original type' of *lambo* in the Buton region (ibid.: 21).

It is possible to determine when the Bajo living at Mantigola in the 1930s and 1940s first adopted the *lambo* because the oral history of past voyages to the Timor Sea through much of the twentieth century indicates the range of that were boats used. Dating from sometime in the first two decades of the twentieth century, Bajo sailed to Ashmore Reef in a double-ended *perahu* that carried a tilted rectangular sail (*lama tanja*). By the 1930s and 1940s, voyages to the Timor Sea were undertaken in *perahu lambo*, some double-ended and some with counter-sterns, with a single rudder and gaff rigged in the European fashion.

The majority of *perahu lambo* in eastern Indonesia are used as cargo carriers or trading vessels. Studies of changes in their design focus almost exclusively on their use in trading activities, and Horridge (1979: iv) goes so far as to say that the *lambo* 'was brought into use as a trader and was never a fishing boat' (see also Hughes 1984; Horridge 1985; Evers 1991; Southon 1995; Burningham 1996). However, the Bajo of Mola, Mantigola and Pepela use *perahu lambo* almost exclusively for collecting trepang and trochus, and for shark fin fishing voyages to the Timor and Arafura seas. This suggests that the *lambo* was adopted by the Bajo as a fishing vessel some time before the middle of the twentieth century.

The unmotorised *lambo* used primarily for fishing purposes in eastern Indonesia belong to Mola and Mantigola Bajo and the mixed Bajo/Rotinese population of Pepela and Oelaba on Roti Island. One reason for the continued use of unmotorised *perahu lambo* in the area permitted to Indonesian craft within the Australian Fishing Zone is that the regulations under the 1974 Memorandum of Understanding state that boats must be 'traditional vessels', which means that engines are not permitted. These regulations have contributed to the continuing use of *perahu lambo* by the Bajo and certainly stalled the widespread adoption of engines. However, most other Indonesian fishing populations, such as other groups of Bajo, Butonese and Bugis fishermen, use motorised boats to engage in illegal fishing activities in the northern Timor and Arafura seas. [11]

We have already noted that there were 37 *perahu lambo* owned by Bajo from Mola Selatan, and seven owned by Bajo from Mola Utara, in 1994 (Table 3-1). Another ten were owned by Bajo from Mantigola. Of these 54 vessels, 20 were located in Pepela at the time of the survey. A few boats from Mola and Mantigola were not used for shark fishing voyages in the Timor and Arafura seas in that year because they were not fully operational and could not put to sea when the fishing season began in August. Some Bajo had by then borrowed *perahu* from other areas, some of the boats had been sold in Pepela, some Bajo had purchased new vessels and some *perahu* were apprehended over the course of the following months.

The provenance of Bajo *perahu lambo* enables us to distinguish those which have been inherited from those purchased second-hand, either locally or from other parts of Indonesia, and those new *perahu* built in Mola, Mantigola or in other villages such as Langara. The average cost of having a new average-sized counter-sterned *perahu lambo* built by a boat builder in Mola or Langara is in the range of Rp 7–10 000 000. Smaller *lambo,* including double-ended vessels, are considerably cheaper to build. In the Tiworo Islands a new double-ender can be purchased for approximately Rp 4 000 000. The time taken to build a

---

[11] Other exceptions would be the Madurese who sail *perahu leti leti* and commonly remove their engines in Kupang before sailing south to enter and fish in the MOU area (personal communication, Dan Dwyer, 1999),

lambo can vary from a few months to a few years, depending on the pace of work fand the availability of money and timber. Second-hand *perahu*, depending on their condition, can cost Rp 2–5 000 000. In many cases a second-hand boat will require some repairs before it can be sailed. Depending on the condition of the vessel, these can cost another Rp 1–5 000 000.

A *lambo* may last for many decades if it is well maintained. Most boats undergo minor and major repairs to the hull to keep them workable during their lifetime, and after 20 or 30 years very few parts of the original hull remain. The oldest remaining working *perahu* from Mola are those built in Mantigola prior to the migration of Mantigola Bajo to Mola during the Kahar Muzakkar rebellion in the 1950s.

Rituals of Boat Construction

Perahu lambo have a particular cultural value and symbolic significance within the Bajo community, and there are a number of specialist boat builders (**sandro**/*tukang perahu*) in Mola who are also recognised for their ritual expertise. These men have acquired the esoteric knowledge that permits them to conduct the various rituals associated with different phases of boat construction — the joining of the stem and stern posts to the keel, the drilling and regular strengthening of the navel in the keel, as well as the final launching of the boat. A series of rituals is also conducted before a crew embarks on a fishing voyage and moves the *perahu* from the confines of the village to the harbour. All human actions must be synchronised with the cyclic phases that underlie the movement of nature or the cosmos (Southon 1995: 134), and on all such occasions, ritual experts consult lunar and other calendars (**nginda allau**/*kotika*) to determine auspicious times and days on which to conduct the rituals. However, 'knowledge is not uniform' and in Mola there are 'different versions of the meaning of a ritual and different understandings of how a ritual should be performed' (ibid.: 132).

One of the most respected **sandro** was Si Gunda from Mola Utara who died in 1996. A head boat builder with a number of men working for him, Si Gunda learnt the skill of boat building from his father and grandfather. He had recently built two *perahu lambo* that were still being used in shark fishing — Tunas Muda and Berkat Nelayan — and performed rituals for a number of boats departing Mola on fishing voyages in 1994. Si Adam, from Mola Utara, was also a well-regarded *tukang perahu*, and during 1994–95 he was engaged in building large motor boats for Mola and Wanci clients. Si Adam was skilled in boat ritual, but because Si Gunda was senior to Si Adam, it was Si Gunda who was called upon to conduct the rituals for boats built by Si Adam. This was common practice in Mola. Si Mahating, a *tukang perahu* from Mola Selatan, was recognised for his ritual knowledge but was generally thought to have poor craftmanship and not to be as skilled at boat building as Si Gunda. Si Mahating worked on his own with some assistance from his son, building *lambo* for his own use or for later sale, but rarely working for a wage or commission. Si Nurdin, a *tukang perahu* from Mola Selatan had built a number of boats in Mola. He had then been living in Pepela for some years and was engaged in shark fishing, but in 1996 he returned to Mola and in January 1997 began to build a new boat.

There was also a handful of older men, former boat builders, in Mola who were still summoned to carry out rituals associated with fishing fleet departures from the village. Si Mbaga, from Mola Selatan, was usually called on to conduct the ritual for *perahu* departing Mola on fishing expeditions, but by 1995 he was too ill to continue and he died in late 1996. Another man, Si Gudang, was usually called on to perform the same ritual but he also died in 1996. This meant that younger boat builders such as Si Adam, Si Mahating and Si Nurdin would have to be called upon to perform such rituals more often.

Joining the Keel, Stem and Stern Posts

The construction of a *lambo* begins with the laying of a single plank of timber which is selected for the keel (**lunas**) by the builder and owner. According to Si Gunda, if the plank of timber has a knot or eye in it, this brings good luck and good fortune (**dalle**/*rezeki*).

The length of the keel is the most important dimension of the *perahu*, and is determined by the builder or owner. According to one method, starting with the right foot, the builder walks along the length of wood, placing left and right feet end to end, one after the other, until he reaches the end of the keel. But he must finish with the right foot, not the left. Where the last right foot ends, a line is drawn exactly between the base of the toenail and the first joint of the big toe, and the keel is then trimmed to this length. Any deviation from this measure can bring misfortune to the *perahu* and its owner (personal communication, Si Gunda, 1995). Si Nurdin would take a measurement from the owner's body by winding a length of string a number of times around his belly. Whatever method is used, the measurement of the keel by reference to the human body means that *perahu* are 'individualized' or 'customized' (Southon 1995: 100).

The keel, supported by wooden logs (**kalang**), is then joined to the stem post (**pamaruh munda**) and stern post (**pamaruh bulli**) with tenon and mortice joints (**lesoang**) (see Figure 3-2). According to Si Gunda, the stem post is joined first, followed by the stern post. The ritual offerings consist of a cluster of four leaves from the pepper plant, each containing a piece of betel nut with lime, four coins and four hand-rolled cigarettes. These objects are placed on a plate next to each of the two joints. According to Si Nurdin, the keel is the female and the stem and stern posts are male; the tenon joint in the stem and stern posts represents the penis and the mortice represents the vagina, so the joining of the keel with the posts represents copulation between husband and wife and conception of the *perahu*. At the same time, the *perahu* is said to be created by God, and the prophets are said to reside in the joints, so prayers are recited at the time of the offerings.

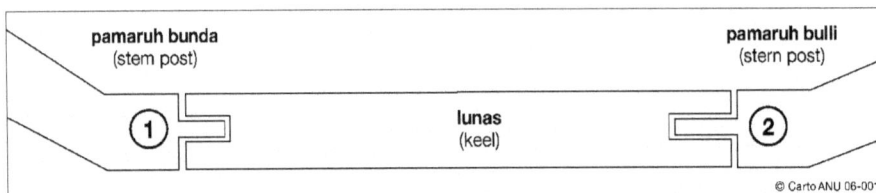

Figure 3-2: Stem, keel and stern post layout and order of joining.

It is also said that '*dua laki-laki dan satu perempuan; satu rumah tangga, satu perahu*' ('two males and one female; one household, one *perahu*'), which conveys the idea of 'the household as a metaphor for thinking about the *perahu*' (Southon 1995: 140). When the posts are joined to the keel, a small piece of gold, sometimes wrapped in white cloth, is placed inside the mortice, and a square piece of white cloth 30 cm in diameter is placed over the tenon in both joints. When the parts are joined the white cloth protrudes on all sides so that:

> the *perahu* has harmony like in the house, the *perahu* will be cold, the crew will be happy with the owner, no quarrels or disputes between the crew, and the *perahu* will always be successful (personal communication, Si Mbaga, 1995).

Gunda also said that gold and white cloth are used 'so that the *perahu* is cold, the same as a house'. During the construction of a house in Mola, a piece of gold is inserted in the mortice of the centre post. [12]

The Drilling of the Navel and Ritual Launching

Once the major structure of a *perahu lambo* is completed, a ceremony is held in which a hole is drilled in the keel. [13] The drilling of this 'navel' (**bebol**/*pusat*) is the most important moment in the boat's construction.

The day selected by the ritual expert for drilling the navel and launching the *perahu* is a time of great celebration in the village. [14] A large number of people typically assemble around the *perahu* to watch and take part in the proceedings and to help push the boat into the water after the navel has been drilled. Inside the hull, the ritual expert selects the place in the centre of the

[12] The cooling effect of metals included in house construction among the Giman of Halmahera is explained by Teljeur (1990: 70): 'cool denotes a condition that promotes health, beauty and prosperity; while hot denotes the opposite condition, resulting in illness, misfortune and a short life'.

[13] The practical function of this hole is to allow for drainage of water collected in the bilge when the boat has been beached.

[14] The following account is based on my own observation of a ceremony that took place for a *perahu motor* at 2 pm (high tide) on a Sunday.

keel to drill the navel and positions himself behind it, with a group of men around him. Three trays of offerings of 'tasty and sweet' food are placed along the inside of the hull above the keel, and a cluster of betel nut (**pinah**) is positioned at the navel itself (see Plate 3-4). A live chicken is carried into the boat and a small piece of its red comb is pulled out, producing a flow of blood that is dropped onto the place of the navel. The chicken is then left to run around freely inside the hull. [15] After prayers, the ritual expert begins to drill the hole into the keel while holding his breath (*napas*). Once the hole is drilled, it is plugged with a wooden dowel (**pasa'**) and a piece of cotton cloth. This is later replaced with a dowel made of stronger wood. The wood shavings (**sampa**) are collected on a plate situated beneath the keel, mixed with coconut oil and stored in a bottle. [16] A final round of prayers is conducted and then the men descend from the boat and prepare to launch it into the water. The ritual expert stands behind the boat with his hand on the stern to protect the *perahu* as it enters the water. The other men then push from behind or pull on a rope connected to the bow and the *perahu* finally enters the water (see Plate 3-5).

Plate 3-4: Gathering for prayers before drilling the navel for a *perahu motor*.

[15] According to Si Gunda, animals should not be sacrificed while boring the navel because that signifies death when the ritual is aimed at giving life (see Southon 1995: 104–5).

[16] This is hung inside the cabin of the boat while it is at sea, or in the owner's house when the boat is docked. It is said that the shavings offer protection from ill fortune and can also be used as medicine for a sick crew member during a voyage.

Plate 3-5: Preparing to launch the boat into the water.

At the moment the **bebol** is drilled, the *perahu* is given life by the expert. As in the case of the human body, the navel is the point of attachment for both the spirit (**sumangaq**) and the soul (**nyawa**) of the *perahu*.

> If a *perahu* doesn't have **nyawa** or a navel [**bebol**], then there isn't a place where you can ask for good fortune, the *perahu* can get into danger at sea, or the *perahu* will not have enthusiasm or **sumangaq** to search for a living. In Sama language [the consequence of] this is called **maluntu** (personal communication, Si Mbaga, 1995).

Nyawa is permanent but **sumangaq** can be precarious, fleeting and even threatening. On the other hand, **sumangaq** is the source of a boat's zest, enthusiasm or vitality. A *perahu* without **sumangaq** is **maluntu**, it has lost its vitality and must search for a living. A strengthened navel means a strong vital force which in turn is a source of good fortune. The navel of the *perahu* must be ritually restored and strengthened regularly in order ensure good fortune.

Si Nurdin observed that *'perahu di anggap sebagai anak sendiri oleh pemilik'* ('the *perahu* is the child of the owner') and *'di rawat dengan baik'* ('it must be taken care of'). He also compared its parts to those of the human body: *'perahu seperti manusia ada tanganya, ada kepalanya, ada mulut, ada matanya, ada kaki'* ('a *perahu* is like a person, it has hands, a head, a mouth, eyes and feet').[17] The

---

[17] The Butonese people of Lande make very similar comparisons (Southon 1995: 119–20).

perahu participates in a voyage as if it were a 'person', or more specifically three people, for when the costs and profits of the voyage are divided between the crew, the *perahu* (or its owner) has shares equivalent to those of three crew members.

If the *perahu* is conceived of as a living thing, what happens to its vital energy if it is destroyed? What of a *perahu* burned by Australian authorities? It is said that the boat builder and/or owner of a boat can feel if something bad has happened to a *perahu*. When asked what happens when a *perahu lambo* is apprehended and destroyed by burning, Si Gunda stated:

> When a *perahu* is apprehended and burnt until destroyed the builder experiences the feeling that the *perahu* is dead, it cannot return home since its **nyawa** has vanished. [18]

It must be assumed that the **sumangaq** is also extinguished at this time. The destruction of a boat is effectively the destruction of the owner's child.

---

[18] In an early study of Malay ritual Endicott (1970: 65) also noted that 'the removal of the *nyawa* is synonymous with death'.

Chapter 4: Bajo Voyages to the Timor Sea

The history of Bajo voyaging to the Timor Sea is well documented, and the historical record can be compared with an analysis of Bajo narratives detailing sailing and fishing voyages. It is evident from these sources that Mola and Mantigola Bajo have a long history of sailing to the Timor Sea. This is not a recent phenomenon but represents a continuation of voyaging over more than two centuries. From the outset, this **lama** fishery has been a commercial venture and Bajo have been part of local, regional and international trading economies from the beginning.

The history of Indonesian fishing activity in the region commenced with Macassan voyaging to Marege (the north Australian coast) and continues with post-Macassan fishing in the Timor Sea. The movement of European settlers into the northwest region after the 1870s, the development of a pearling industry off the Kimberley coast, and the recruitment of Indonesian labour into the industry brought about a contest for control over the marine resources of the region. This has been further driven by the expansion of Australian fishing activity in the region and the move southward by other ethnic fisher groups in Indonesia.

Australian accounts of fishing activity in the Timor Sea by maritime peoples from the Indonesian Archipelago have not revealed any source that specifically mentions or identifies Bajo activity in the region (see, for example, Serventy 1952; Bach 1955; Crawford 1969; Bottrill 1993; Campbell and Wilson 1993). Indonesian fishermen are generally referred to by generic terms, as 'Malays' or 'Indonesians', and vessels are reported to have originated from a number of different islands across the archipelago (Crawford 1969: 125). However, by examining Bajo narratives in conjunction with some of these historical sources, it is possible to identify some of these fishermen as Bajo from Mantigola and Mola, and hence to provide dates for early Bajo fishing activity in the north Australian region.

One particular account of an incident known among the Bajo as *pesawat jatuh* (the plane that crashed) concerns an encounter between the Mantigola Bajo crew of a *perahu* fishing at Seringapatam Reef and the crew of a British aircraft that crashed on the reef in the 1930s. When augmented by Australian archive and newspaper reports of the event, this provides important evidence of Bajo activity in the Ashmore Reef area (see Map 4-1). This incident has not been previously documented in the literature concerning the history of Indonesian fishing activity in the Timor Sea, and it marks a time in Bajo history remembered as a period of relatively unrestricted activity in the Timor Sea before the archipelago was occupied by the Japanese and distant shore fishing activity was restricted. Ethnographic texts concerning Bajo voyaging prior to World War II also show that it has always been primarily motivated by commercial purposes and that Bajo have sought shark fin for decades.

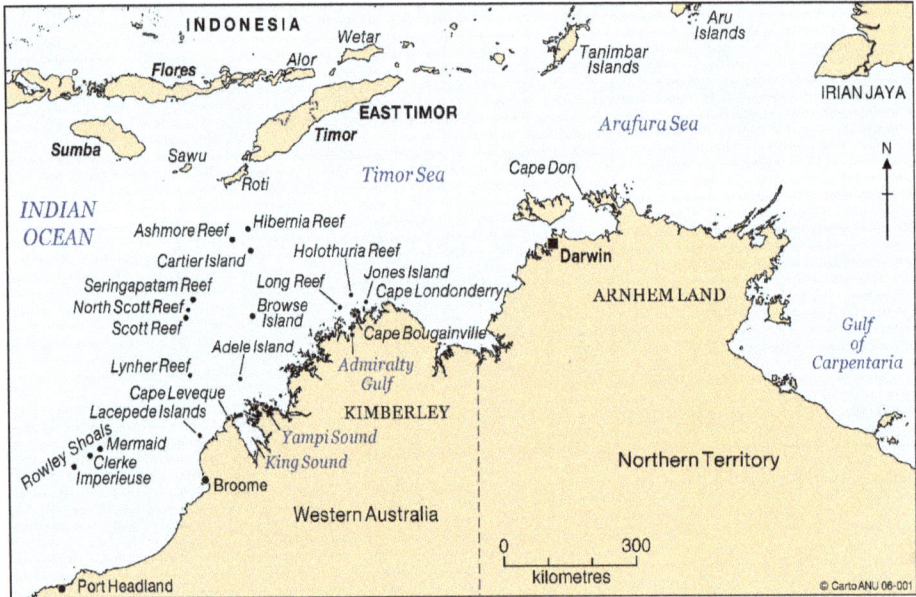

Map 4-1: Key locations in northern Australia.

Macassans, Malays and Europeans in Northern Australia

From at least the 1720s (Mitchell 1994: 56) until the early 1900s fleets of *perahu* sailed from Makassar (South Sulawesi) to the northern Australian coast each year to collect trepang or bêche-de-mer — a genus of edible holothurians found in abundance on the seabed in shallow tropical waters. Processed trepang has long been a commodity in great demand in Chinese markets, where it is considered as a culinary delicacy with potent medicinal properties. The trade soon extended to other marine commodities, including turtle shell and shark fin. This trade began well before European colonisation of the Australian continent, and involved significant contact with Australian Aborigines. The trade operated through the city of Makassar and the majority of people involved in the industry were Makassarese. As a result the term 'Macassan' is applied to the industry in the literature, but it is thought that the fishing crews included Bugis and Bajo (Macknight 1976: 18).

The Macassan fleets fished three areas: the Northern Territory coast from Cape Don to the Gulf of Carpentaria; parts of the Kimberley coast of Western Australia from Cape Londonderry to Cape Leveque and perhaps further south towards Port Hedland; and the offshore reefs and islands in the Timor Sea

(Crawford 1969: 89; Macknight 1976: 2, 27). Evidence of Macassan fishing activity is documented in Dutch archival records, in recorded contact with other Europeans, and also from the results of archaeological investigations (Crawford 1969; Fox 1977a; Macknight 1976; Bottrill 1993; Campbell and Wilson 1993; Mitchell 1994). In addition to the activity of the Macassan fleets, historical sources also document fishing activity by Bajo *perahu* travelling independently or accompanying Macassan *perahu* to Arnhem Land and the Kimberley coast in the 1840s (Macknight 1976: 18, Mitchell 1994: 32).[1]

Ashmore Reef, located 840 km west of Darwin and just 90 km south of Roti, has been regularly visited and fished by Indonesians since the eighteenth century. The area has its own Indonesian name — Pulau Pasir (Sand Island). A Rotinese narrative details the accidental discovery of Sand Island in the 1720s, and Dutch historical sources 'confirm that Ashmore was known to Indonesian fishermen in the first half of the eighteenth century' (Fox 1998: 118–9). During a visit to Kupang in 1803, Flinders obtained information linking Macassan trepang fishing activity to 'a dry shoal lying to the south of Rottee [Rote]' (probably Ashmore Reef) and met a number of Macassans on the coast of northern Australia in the same year (Flinders 1814: 257).[2] Since Ashmore Reef has a supply of fresh water and a sheltered lagoon, it has long been an important 'staging post' for Indonesian *perahu* on their voyages further south to other islands and reefs (Fox 1998: 117).

Macassan voyages to northern Australia began to decline in the latter part of the nineteenth century and came to an end in 1907. In 1882, licensing and customs duties were imposed on Macassan trepangers in the Northern Territory, and licences were not issued to the Macassans after 1906 (Macknight 1976: 106, 125). The Macassans were never licensed to fish in northwestern waters (Campbell and Wilson 1993: 31) so it is not clear why they also ceased to visit the Kimberley region (Crawford 1969: 114). All foreign fishing in territorial waters was illegal under Western Australian legislation from the 1870s, but these laws were never enforced because 'the Kimberley coast remained virtually beyond the limits of government control' (ibid.: 116–7). Although the reasons are unclear, Macknight (1976: 118) believes that those Macassans who ceased to visit Australia switched to other maritime activities within the Indonesian Archipelago.

When the Macassan fleets ceased operations in the Northern Territory and Kimberley region, fishing activity along the northwest coast of Australia and on offshore reefs was maintained by fishermen in smaller *perahu* originating from regions other than Makassar. Very little is known about these voyages and

---

[1] There is no record fishing activity by other groups operating independently of Macassan fleets along the northwest Australian coast in the nineteenth century.
[2] Flinders thought the Macassan fleets had accidentally discovered an abundance of trepang in northern Australian waters some 20 years earlier.

few records remain, but the visits are thought to have been widespread (Crawford 1969: 115, 124).

Between the early 1900s and 1924, historical sources report fleets or solitary *perahu* originating from a number of different islands across the Indonesian Archipelago. For example, vessels from Kupang sailed to Roti to take on supplies, then sailed south to Ashmore Reef and from there to other offshore reefs and islands. Vessels also sailed along the Kimberley coast, working nearby areas such as Long and Holothuria reefs, and often landed on the mainland to collect supplies of wood and water and process their catch before returning to Kupang to sell it (Crawford 1969: 124–5; Campbell and Wilson 1993: 18).

The initial decline of Macassan voyaging to Arnhem Land and the Kimberley coast in the 1870s coincided with the growth of the pearl shell industry in the Pilbara and later the Kimberley region from the 1860s, when European settlers began appropriating land under pastoral leases (Campbell and Wilson 1993: 16–18). Initially, pearl shells were mainly gathered from exposed reefs during low tide, but by the 1870s Aborigines were employed as divers and 'Malay' men from Indonesia, Singapore and the Philippines were indentured to European captains to work as seamen and divers on pearling luggers (McGann 1988: 2; Bottrill 1993: i; Campbell and Wilson 1993: 16). The first Indonesians to work in the pearling industry were recruited directly from coastal villages on the islands of Alor and Solor in 1870 (McGann 1988: 21–2). In 1874, 316 divers were recruited from Timor, and in 1875 it was reported that as many as 1000 'Malays' from Makassar, Solor, Ende, and Singapore (along with 200–300 Aborigines) would be working during the next pearling season in northwestern Australia (Bottrill 1993: 15–16). Sama-speaking Bajau from the Philippines were added to the labour force with the further expansion of the industry (McGann 1988: 42, 45).

When the underwater diving suit began to be used in 1886, Aborigines and Malays 'were considered unsuited to work with mechanical apparatus' (Campbell and Wilson 1993: 17). Coupled with later legislative changes regulating the use of Indigenous and indentured labour, this eventually led to a decline in the number of Malays and Aborigines engaged in the pearl shell industry. They were mostly replaced by Japanese workers who came to dominate the now Broome-based industry from the late 1880s until its decline after 1935 (ibid.). However, some men were still drawn from Kupang and surrounding islands to work in the pearling industry until the 1960s (Anderson 1978).

In the 1880s, the first European pearlers left Cossack for Kupang. As well as recruiting Malay labour for the northwest pearling industry, they went into partnership with Dutch, Arab or Chinese merchants and fished the northwest for pearl shell in vessels flying the Dutch flag. From Kupang, pearlers could fish waters outside of Australia's 3 nautical mile territorial waters without a licence, and there was no law preventing them from obtaining shelter and supplies along the Australian coast if needed (Bach 1955: 208). These men were joined shortly after by other pearlers from Port Darwin and Broome (Bain 1982: 187). The first pair of entrepreneurial pearling captains to skipper vessels operating out of Kupang in the 1880s were Hart and Geach Drysdale. Their place was taken by Henry Francis Hilliard who came to dominate the Kupang-based fishing activities in the Timor Sea in the 1890s. He in turn was followed by his son Robin Hilliard, W.S. Smith and Alex Chamberlain (Crawford 1969: 115; Bain 1982: 187).

The Bajo Encounter with Tuan Robin

Older Bajo men claim that their fathers or grandfathers were the first to sail to Ashmore Reef from Mantigola. At some point in the Dutch colonial period, they say that a crew of Mantigola Bajo on a *perahu* anchored at Kupang met a schooner captain known as Tuan Robin. This man asked the Bajo crew to work for him to collect turtle shell in Australia. The Bajo agreed and accompanied Tuan Robin on his schooner. They spent a number of weeks catching hawksbill turtles (*Eretmochelys imbricata*) and removing their shells at an island off the coast of northwest Australia. On their return to Kupang the Bajo were paid for their efforts and went back to their home village. These Mantigola Bajo were only employed by Tuan Robin on this one occasion.

Si Mbaga, an elder of Mola Selatan accompanied his father and grandfather and other men from Mantigola on this journey to Kupang. At that time he was an adolescent and acted as the *tukang masak* (cook). It is difficult to estimate the age of Si Mbaga, but he was probably over eighty years old in 1995. When the Bajo crew went with Tuan Robin, Si Mbaga stayed behind in Kupang and looked after their boat, so his knowledge of some of the events is based on information passed to him by his father and grandfather.

> In the old days only Raas people and Madura people went to Ashmore Reef [Pulau Pasir] and Scott Reef [Pulau Datu]. In the old days Raas people lived at Semau Island [Pulau Samahung]. Ashmore Reef was the place to cook trepang. We heard stories about Ashmore Reef from Raas people. We first wanted to go net fishing [**ngambai**] at Rote. The Raas people told my grandfather about Ashmore Reef. We obtained a sailing clearance in Kupang and followed them to Ashmore Reef. At that time, there weren't any problems [any regulations about fishing at Ashmore Reef]. We only had to obtain a clearance in Kupang if we wanted to go fishing and cook trepang at the island. This was the first time we went to Ashmore Reef. The second time [was when] we met Tuan Robin in Kupang.

> We were anchored at Tanoo [Tenau Harbour, Kupang] and wanted to go fishing for trepang at Ashmore Reef when a schooner sailing ship

came and anchored near to us. The captain of the schooner was Tuan
Robin and he had five Alor people with him. We met Tuan Robin and
he asked us to work for him. We said to him that we wanted to fish for
trepang, fish and trochus at Ashmore Reef but he said, 'if you want to,
come and work for me in Marege [Australia] and collect turtle shell'. My
father and grandfather, along with six other crew, were taken on the
schooner to Kea Island [Pulau Kea], an island off the coast of Marege,
while I stayed in Tablolong to look after the boat. I was already a youth,
already circumcised, at that time....

They were taken to Marege for 17 days to collect turtles [**kulitang**].
They collected 40 bags of turtle shell. My father said that they didn't
kill the turtles. Tuan Robin instructed them to heat up water in a drum.
After that, the turtles were pulled up onto the boat and the hot water
was poured over the turtles and the shells peeled off. Then the turtles
were thrown back in the water. Aboriginal people [*orang* Marege] took
a few of the turtles to eat.

After 17 days the schooner returned to Tanoo and they got off the boat
and called a friend of mine from Tablolong who was at Tanoo at the time
to take our *perahu* to Tanoo. The day after they returned, Tuan Robin
paid each crew member two gold coins.

Complementary to Si Mbaga's recollections are comments by Si Bilaning, a
contemporary of Si Mbaga, who also lived in Mantigola and was probably over
eighty years old.

My father was one of the first Bajo to go to the *pulau* [Australian islands].
They were taken to Marege by Tuan Robin and he had a schooner with
three layers of jib sail. There they collected turtles. From those times
until now lots of Sama people sail to Ashmore Reef, Scott Reef, and
Seringapatam Reef [Sapa Taringan]. In the old days it was open [to fish
there], then later it was forbidden.

Kupang-based Australian and British captains soon diversified into fishing
for marine products such as trochus, trepang and turtle shell traditionally taken
by Indonesians. During trips between Kupang and Cossack, these captains had
observed *perahu* from Timor and Madura returning with marine produce collected
from Rowley Shoals and the Ashmore and Holothuria reefs (Bain 1982: 184–8).
This lucrative trade passed through Dutch ports and a living could be earned
that was less dangerous than pearling.

While Henry Hilliard continued to supply men from Kupang to the northwest
pearling industry, he employed Europeans and other Indonesians to work on a
fleet of Dutch-registered schooners and cutters and locally built *perahu*. Hilliard's
fleet followed much the same sailing and fishing patterns as the Indonesian

perahu, fishing offshore reefs and various islands and reefs close to the Australian mainland where supplies could be obtained (Crawford 1969: 119–20). Vessels would stop first at Roti to obtain firewood and water and then sail south to fish the Ashmore, Scott and Seringapatam reefs, and sometimes as far south as Rowley Shoals and on to Minstrel, Clerk and Imperieuse reefs. When supplies ran low the vessels could sail to the Australian coast to re-stock and then work the reefs near the shores such as Long Reef and the Holothuria Reefs. In May, the vessels would congregate at Jones Island to catch hawksbill turtles and take their shells (ibid.). There are a number of references to Hilliard's fishing activities, over a period from 1894 through to the early 1920s, in places that included King Sound, Adele Island, Scott Reef, Ashmore Reef and Rowley Shoals (Bach 1955: 209; Bottrill 1993: 23, 28).

Around the same time as Europeans established themselves in Kupang, a number of men set up beach-combing camps along the northwest coast of Australia where they collected turtle shell, trepang, trochus and pearl shell using Aboriginal labour. These beach-combers had strong connections with the Kupang-based captains (including Hilliard) who called regularly at their camps to trade. Their camps were located near to Adele and Browse islands, the Lacepede Islands and Lynheer Reef off the Kimberley coast (Bain 1982: 188–91).

Mr H.V. Howe, a Broome-based pearling captain before World War I, published an article in *The Sydney Morning Herald* in 1952 about the Kupang-based vessels then operating in the Timor Sea.[3]

In 1910, there were 25 vessels, of which six were European-style schooners of 50 to 60 tonnes, skippered by those aged master mariners, whose eventful maritime careers were — and still are — discussed with interest in all Asiatic ports from Karachi to Shanghai. The rest of the Koepang fleet consisted of native prahus of from 10 to 20 tons, skippered by Malay 'Kungawas',[4] who, with lifelong knowledge of the coast and its winds and tides, and with the aid of more or less accurate compasses, navigated to and from various destinations with relatively few mishaps. These smaller vessels fished the coast and adjacent islands, because proximity of the mainland enabled easy replenishment of wood and water supplies. The larger schooners normally worked the six coral atolls which lie in a 500 miles-long chain about 100 miles off the Western Australian coast. From the north-east to south-west these are Ashmore, Seringapatam, Scotts, Minstrel, Mermaid, and Imperieuse Reefs.... On

---

[3] While some of Howe's comments are ethnocentric and characteristic of the time, his description of the method of turtle fishing complements that of the Bajo themselves.

[4] This is apparently a corruption of the Bahasa term *punggawa* (captain or navigator), which is widely used by the Bajo and other maritime populations in Indonesia.

each of these islets the fishing schooners set up their boilers and smokehouses for treating the trepang and trochus shell.

The usual 'take' of a schooner on a five months' trip to the reef is worth between £2,000 and £3,000.... About once a fortnight the daily routine is interrupted by a day's fishing for hawksbill turtle, which yields the tortoise shell of commerce. Nets are stretched across the seaward ends of a number of the channels crossing a reef. At low tide all hands start wading from the lagoon, beating the surface of the channel before them, and driving the turtle into the nets. The catches are taken back to the island, where bags, dipped in boiling water, are laid across their backs for a minute or two. This treatment enables the flakes of tortoiseshell to be lifted from the hard bone to which it is attached. After collection of the tortoise shell the turtle is set free to grow another crop — which it does in about two years. Cruel as the process may seem, it does not appear to hurt the turtle, which show no sign of discomfort under the bag, and when released make their way back to deep water (apparently) unperturbed by the ordeal....

Notwithstanding the hardships of the life, trips to the reefs are popular with the Timorese, who are always eager to sign on as schooner crews. With his pay of £1 a month and the smoked fish he brings back, each man earns about £20 on a trip. This is good money for in Koepang a fair average quality wife costs only 30/-, and the local equivalent of a film star can be bought for £5, which is also the cost of building a good native house.... [O]ne trip to the reefs secures the fisherman a home, economic security for life, as much domestic felicity as the average man can expect, and still leaves him £5 to spend on furniture and wedding festivities! (Howe 1952: 7)

Some time between 1900 and 1910, Hilliard was joined by his eldest son, Robin Henry Hilliard, who was born in 1888. The exact date of Robin's arrival in Kupang and entry into the business is not known, but in 1914 it was reported by Mr Stuart, the Pearling Inspector at Broome, that Alex Chamberlain, formerly a Broome-based pearler for 10 years, had gone into partnership with Robin Hilliard in a Kupang-based trading company. Together they owned a British-registered schooner, the John & Richard (Bottrill 1993: 33). [5] On 10 February 1915 Stuart wrote to the Secretary of Western Australian Fisheries about the activities of the Kupang fleet:

I found out that WA Chamberlain and R Hilliard had had an exceptionally fine year and had fished among other things £1,500 worth of turtle shell,

---

[5] Bottrill visited the village of Pepela on Roti in 1988 to collect oral histories of fishing in the northwest region, and states (ibid.: 54) that Robin Hilliard was known to the Rotinese as Tuan Robin. We also know that he married a Rotinese woman from Oenale (personal communication, George Hilliard, 1998).

Chamberlain apparently works over a large area and will work Rowley Shoals for beche-de-mer and probably the territorial waters of the north-west north of Admiralty Gulf where I believe turtles are plentiful (Bottrill 1993: 37, citing letter in Fisheries Department File 57/38, Battye Library, Western Australia).

In the same letter Stuart listed nine vessels reported to be based in Kupang and working the northwest coastal areas and offshore islands and reefs in the Timor Sea. Aside from the John & Richard, these included two schooners, Petunia and Harriet, owned by a Dutch merchant called Tiffer, the Joker owned by Ah Kit, and five schooners owned by a merchant named Toku Baru (known also as Captain China) that were managed by Henry Hilliard.[6]

In 1923, another incident concerning the activities of Robin Hilliard was reported to Stuart. In March of that year, F.H. Clark, a pearler in the lugger Emelyn Castle, came across Robin Hilliard in charge of the schooner Petina at an inlet south of Red Island off Cape Bougainville. He was processing trepang on the coast. On boarding the vessel and examining the log, Clark found that the vessel was owned by Firma Thoeng Thay Company of Kupang and had a crew of 13 Kupangers. Hilliard had been cleared by authorities in Kupang for Scott Reef and had collected trepang there (Crawford 1969: 121; Bottrill 1993: 45).[7]

The activities of the Hilliard family in the northwest region continued for around three decades. If Si Mbaga was born around 1910, the Mantigola Bajo encounter with Tuan Robin would have occurred at the very end of that period. Robin Hilliard apparently stopped working the northwest coast around the time that his father died in 1924 (Bottrill 1993: 45).[8] This may have been due to increasing Australian government control over illegal fishing activities and the Dutch refusal to issue more clearances for Scott Reef, but the beach-combers Hilliard had worked with were also growing old or had moved away and local resources were in decline (Bain 1982: 198).

After Robin Hilliard stopped fishing the northwest region he formed the Flores Pearling Company, a partnership with merchants from Broome and Makassar.

[Hilliard] proposed to H.S. Cross, an indent agent and pearl-buyer in Broome, that they move to the island of Flores, where there was

---

[6] Toku Baru is still an established shop name in Kupang, and local people commonly refer to Chinese traders by the name of their shop.

[7] Crawford (1969: 122–3; 2001) reproduces photographs of Hilliard's boat and trepang camp that were taken by Clark on 29 March.

[8] By one account Henry Hilliard is said to have died of ptomaine poisoning in Makassar in 1920 (Bain 1982: 198), but Robin's son George has confirmed Henry died of food poisoning in Kupang in 1924 and is buried in the Dutch cemetery there.

gold-lipped shell in great quantities. At Makassar, an approach was made to Gros Kamp and Drofmeyer, Dutch merchants. The Flores Pearling Company was formed and by 1929 fourteen luggers were working fifty miles off the coast and collecting large hauls of shell which was [were] sold through Osche & Co., of New York (Bain 1982: 198–9).

An advertisement appeared in the local Broome newspaper, *The Norwest Echo*, on 24 October 1926, announcing that Robin Hilliard was now pearling in the Dutch Indies, but still recruiting men for the northwest pearling industry during December-January each year (Bottrill 1993: 47). He continued to operate out of Labuan Bajo in Flores until World War II, when he and his partner, Alex Chamberlain, were interned by the Japanese. He was sent to Makassar in 1944 where he died in captivity and was buried (personal communication, George Hilliard, 1998).[9]

The Bajo Encounter with British Airmen in 1936

Si Pangasi, an elderly Bajo man aged around 75 in 1995, recalled a series of events that led to an encounter with British airmen from a plane which crashed on Seringapatam Reef in 1936.

> I was one of the crew on the *perahu* Si Gambar Bulan. At that time I had just been circumcised. I was still single, still young. My older brother, Si Tuba, was the captain and Si Tedong was the owner of the *perahu*. There were ten crew: Pangasi, Tuba, Tedong, Tidong, Jalating, Balating, Kaling, Amang, Nappa and Mpeno. Balanting is still alive and lives in Sampela. Tedong lives in Desa Bisaya, near Lasalimu in Buton. He moved there during the *gerombolan* [Kahar Muzakkar rebellion]. Mpeno lives in Mola Selatan. Jalating was lost [drowned] at Ashmore Reef.

> From Mantigola we sailed to Kupang, actually to Air Cina, to the south of Kupang. We spent three days there then sailed to Ashmore Reef, then to Seringapatam Reef [Sapa Taringan]. We ate birds' eggs on Ashmore Reef. At that time, Buton people were not yet living in Pepela and Roti people sailed *sekoci* [a type of canoe] with *layar leti leti* [lateen rig]. There were Bajo living in Oenggai [on Roti Island], but not at Sulamu [Kupang].

> We went to Seringapatam Reef to catch fish, not trepang, to salt it, to sell in Makassar. At that time we sold the fish for 4½ ringgit a kilo. The method of fishing is called **ngambai**, using nets and ropes. The nets were made from tree bark [bagu], with floats on the top and cowrie shells on the bottom, held in place with wooden stakes. Seringapatam Reef is one day and one night's sail from Scott Reef. Taringan is the name

---

[9] An interview with Pak Nasseng from Sulamu village, near Kupang, in 1994 indicates that Robin Hilliard's involvement with Bajo people from different parts of the Nusa Tenggara region continued through the final stage of his career.

of a fish [**dayah taringan**], found in great quantities at this reef. There is no island or sand there, just reef.

While we were fishing at low tide, we saw a plane run out of petrol and fall out of the sky and land on the reef. Four people from the plane walked over the reef to where we were fishing and asked for help to take them to Kupang. So we took them to Kupang on our *perahu* and on the way we met a big ship, a foreign ship, with a motor, coming from the south. The people hailed the ship and boarded it and the ship returned to Australia. It was still Dutch times, maybe five years before Japan invaded Indonesia.

When we later returned to Kaledupa, the captain received a letter telling him to go to Bau Bau to get a reward and letter for all the crew, 40 ringgit for each crew and 90 ringgit for the captain. It was my second time sailing, the first time to Ashmore Reef, the second time the plane crashed. I did not go again after that.

Si Gambar Bulan was a *perahu* with a chaired stern [*pantat kadera*] and a central rudder with gaff rig [**lama cangking**], made from cloth. This was before gunter rig [**lama sande**]. Si Gambar Bulan was built by Tedong in Mantigola but he sold it before he moved to Bisaya.

This account indicates that Mantigola Bajo sailing voyages and fishing activity in the Timor Sea were clearly commercial ventures. This particular voyage is vividly recalled by Si Pangasi and other Bajo because of the extraordinary event that interrupted their fishing activity. [10]

Si Mpeno, who was born in Mantigola and is first cousin to Si Pangasi, described the relations between the Bajo rescuers and the plane crew in more detail.

We took the men on our *perahu*. We had to use sign language, pointing with our fingers, they only knew one word — Kupang. The strange thing was, if they wanted to lie down, they didn't go inside [the cabin], they only lay on the deck. They felt sick because of the smell of the fish, and it's true the fish smelt rotten. They gave us binoculars. When they spotted the ship, they waved at it with pieces of cloth. The ship approached, and they talked with the people on it, then boarded the ship. We received a reward later from Bau Bau.

Another elderly Bajo man, La Ode Ndoke, who lives in Mola Selatan but was born in Mantigola, went on his first trip to Australian waters as a crew member

---

[10] Some of the *perahu* captains and crews voyaging to the Timor Sea in 1994 were related to the crew of Si Gambar Bulan. For example, Si Tuba, the captain of Si Gambar Bulan, was the grandfather of Samsuddin, who was the captain of Karea Baru in 1994 and the captain of another *perahu* apprehended in 1997.

on another gaff-rigged *perahu* called Asia which accompanied Si Gambar Bulan on the journey to Ashmore Reef.

> When the plane crashed, we [Asia] were at North Scott Reef [Haring Utara] and they [Si Gambar Bulan] were at Seringapatam Reef. We were quite a long way from Seringapatam Reef. The first time we saw the plane it was flying in our direction and we thought it was going to land. But maybe because they still had a lot of fuel, the plane kept going and headed in the direction of Kupang. Not long after that, the plane fell and landed on the west side of Seringapatam Reef, near to Si Gambar Bulan. At the moment the plane fell, we didn't see it because it was too far away, but our friends who were closer saw the plane fall. Then the crew of the plane joined Si Gambar Bulan and halfway through the journey to Kupang the crew were taken on board a big ship. We went to have a look at the plane afterwards and measured the wingspan — it was 8 *depa* [fathoms] long. The frame of the plane is still there to this day. After the time I encountered the plane, I went to Ashmore Reef and Scott Reef twice, so I have been three times. After that I had a rest [from sailing] for a long time, then afterwards I worked as a *romusa* [involuntary labourer] on the roads in Buton for the Japanese.

This account provides an approximate location of the remaining wreckage of the plane at Seringapatam Reef. La Ode Ndoke went on to explain that the Bajo from Mantigola sailed all the way to Ashmore Reef, Scott Reef, and Seringapatam Reef in the past to fish because

> At Scott Reef there is a lot of fish — there is more fish at Scott Reef than there is at Kaledupa Reef. There are no enemies or competitors there, it is possible to get between 1½ and 3 tonnes of fish in one trip.

Si Pangasi, Si Mpeno, and La Ode Ndoke were unclear about the nationality of the plane crew, but another surviving member of Asia's crew, Si Kiramang, thought they were from England. Mpeno and Si Panghasi could not remember much about the letter and reward, but another informant, Si Badolla, who was a young boy at the time and not actually involved in the rescue, vividly recalls this episode:

> Between Ashmore Reef and Kupang the ship came, they took the men and Si Gambar Bulan did not have to continue to Kupang. Only they said to the Bajo 'wait in Kupang'. But they went home to Kaledupa. One month later there was a letter from Bau Bau. The letter was from Australia. They were ordered to go to Bau Bau to receive their reward. In the contents of the letter it was written 3000 ringgit. But they only received 300 ringgit because the amount had been reduced because of all the offices the letter passed through, from Java to Makassar and to

Bau Bau. Maybe if they had waited in Kupang they would have received more and maybe they would have been given a *surat bebas* [free/open letter], but instead it went through Bau Bau. It was already a lot less. I saw the letter, but it was written in English. We didn't know what it said, we only understood the numbers.

Si Badolla's recollection of the size of the reward diverges from that of Pangasi. Si Badolla also thought that if the crew of Si Gambar Bulan had stopped at Kupang on the way back to Mantigola, they may have received a larger reward and a *surat bebas* — a letter stating the Bajo had permission to fish freely at offshore reefs and islands in the Timor Sea and in Australian waters as part of the reward for their rescue efforts.

Si Bilaning, who was also living in Mantigola at the time, put these seemingly unrelated events into the context of the current Bajo political situation:

> After the Bajo went with Tuan Robin to Marege [Australia], many Bajo used to sail to Ashmore Reef, Scott Reef, Seringapatam Reef; they would catch fish with nets [**ngambai**] and also take all kinds of sea products. At that time we used *perahu* **soppe** and *perahu lambo*, with sails made from tree bark, in the model of **lama tanja** [fore-and-aft tilted rectangular sail]. In former times the Bajo were free to fish there [*dulu bebas*], until later times when it became forbidden [*nanti sekarang dilarang*]. When the plane fell from the sky, the crew were taken to Kupang, but before arriving a big ship came and took the crew. The King of England [Raja Inggris] sent a letter to Kupang but the Government of Kupang sent it on to Bau Bau. Then after we met with the plane, fishing at Ashmore Reef, Scott Reef and Seringapatam Reef was not forbidden. It was free to catch fish [*bebas menangkap ikan*].

The type of sail (**lama tanja**) described by Si Bilaning is the same as that described by Si Mbaga earlier, and was the traditional sail plan used on *perahu* before the adoption of the Western-style gaff rig. Si Bilaning's comment that the letter was from the King of England was most likely a reference to official British or Commonwealth insignia. His account builds on the ideas expressed by Si Badolla about freedom to fish. The period following the rescue of the plane crew is perceived as one of relative freedom to fish the reefs in the Timor Sea, and the Bajo interpreted the letter in this light. The period of restrictions, when fishing became 'forbidden' (*nanti sekarang dilarang*), began in the early 1970s. These statements are made over and over again by Bajo in conversation about past fishing activities, and are part of a narrative invoked to legitimise their right to fish in an area that has come under increasing Australian control.

A second version of the plane crash story can be obtained from archival records and newspaper reports. The 1930s was an era of major developments in aviation, numerous attempts were made to break records for long-distance flying, and these were regularly reported in the newspapers of the day. In July and August 1936, Lord William Francis Sempill twice attempted a record flight from London to Australia in a Monospar Croydon airliner, but failed because of engine troubles and damage to the aircraft (*The Argus*, 8 October 1936). He then gave the aeroplane to another pilot, Mr H. Wood, who successfully flew from London to Melbourne in September 1936 with a crew comprising Mr F. Crocombe (designer), Mr L. Davies (engineer) and Mr C. Gilroy (wireless operator). They then attempted to break the return Melbourne-to-London record of 5 days and 15 hours, departing Melbourne on the morning of 6 October in a blaze of publicity and arriving in Darwin that same evening with a time slightly slower than their predecessors (*The Argus*, 7 October 1936). The Monospar left Darwin for Kupang at 4.50 am on Wednesday 7 October and received wireless bearings from the Royal Australian Air Force base at Darwin until 7.15 am, when wireless contact faded (*The Argus*, 8 October 1936). The plane was expected to arrive at Kupang by 8.00 am, but by mid morning, when no news had been received of the plane's arrival, it was initially assumed that the flight must have continued to the limit of its fuel range at Rembang on Java. When no further word was received, the Administrator of the Northern Territory, Colonel R.H. Weddell, ordered the government patrol launch, the Larrakeya, to proceed immediately to a position off the coast of Timor where the last wireless message was thought to have originated (*The Argus*, 8 October 1936). The Federal Minister for Defence, Sir Archdale Parkhill, asked the Civil Aviation Board to arrange for a Qantas aircraft to undertake a search of the Timor Sea, but it was uncertain when an aircraft would be available,[11] so Prime Minister Lyons sent a telegram later that evening to the British Consul-General at Batavia (Jakarta) requesting that the Dutch Government begin an aerial search and rescue attempt.[12] Two Dutch flying boats were dispatched to Kupang from their base at Surabaya in West Java on Thursday morning and began their search on Friday morning. Meanwhile, the Larrakeya was joined by the Marella, a Dutch government patrol boat based at Kupang, and an S.O.S. was broadcast to ships in the Timor Sea to alert them of the missing aircraft. On the afternoon of Friday 9 October, wireless messages were received by radio stations in Kupang, Darwin and Melbourne from the SS Nimoda, a British cargo steamer bound for Durban, reporting that the airmen had been picked up from a fishing boat near Seringapatam Reef. Their rescue made the front page of *The Argus* on Saturday morning under the headline 'Monospar Crew Found Safe, Marooned on Sandbank, Rescued by Native Craft, Now Aboard British Steamer'. The story included the observation that:

[11] A scheduled Qantas flight from Darwin to Singapore did join the search for a while.

[12] These actions are documented in Records A461/9 and N314/1/7 in the ACT Australian Archives (Prime Minister's Department).

although all the resources of modern aircraft and wireless were employed in the search for the missing machine and its occupants, it was left to natives in a fishing smack and a wandering tramp steamer to effect a rescue.

The Argus published a wireless message containing an account of the rescue by Mr Crocombe, the Monospar's designer, on Monday 12 October.

> Misled by wireless bearings from Darwin. Were assured, despite doubt on our part, that the bearings were correct as late as 6.15 am when bad atmospherics made further communication impossible. Course kept after this, but no sign of land. Forced to assume wireless bearings correct, so proceeded further for 30 minutes. Passed over coral reef at 8.00 am. Using reef as base, we reconnoitred in each direction until petrol almost exhausted. Finally proceeded down line of reefs and located native fishing-boat in lagoon. Successfully landed on rock-strewn reef without damage, but in taxi-ing aircraft out of water to higher portion of reef the tail wheel casting was fractured. Ran out wireless aerial and tried to communicate with Koepang and Sourabaya without success, although heard both stations. Managed attract attention of boat. Carried few personal effects, iron rations, and water over one mile to boat, wading through deep rocky pools infested with giant clams and occasional small sharks. Had extreme difficulty making natives understand our plight. Finally persuaded them to take us on board and to head for Koepang. Spent 55 hours on boat on short rations of food and water, and in strong odour of fish and natives. Conditions were cramped. Picked up at 3.30 pm Friday by s.s. Nimoda in weak condition. Personnel magnificent in sharing hardships. Later established aircraft landed on Seringapatam Reef. Picked up by Nimoda 100 miles north-east of reef. Bitterly disappointed untimely end of flight. Machine running perfectly.

The message hardly evokes any gratitude toward the Mantigola Bajo who had been required to stop their fishing activity and sail back to Kupang. In a subsequent interview when the airmen arrived at Durban on 1 November, they said they had used a collapsible rubber boat to carry their personal belongings across the reef to the 'Malay fishing vessel' and then 'it took them five hours to convince the fishermen that they were not making a friendly call but wanted to be taken aboard' (*The Argus*, 3 November 1936). After the initial reports there is no further mention or discussion of the 'natives' or 'Malays' in the newspapers or archival material. Statements by Si Badolla and Si Bilaning about the letter of commendation cannot be confirmed. Despite the number of different Australian and British government officials and offices involved in the search and rescue, it seems most likely that the letter came from the British Consul at Batavia or the Resident at Timor.

Given the newspaper coverage, it is perhaps curious that the incident did not give rise to claims about Malays being engaged in poaching or illegal fishing in the region, of the kind which had previously been made in the 1920s (Bach 1955: 210). One reason may be that in 1936 Seringapatam Reef, unlike Ashmore Reef, was still in international waters. Being a tidal reef awash at high tide, it was defined as part of the continental shelf. Australia only claimed it in 1953.

Bajo Fishing in the Timor Sea Before World War II

Aside from the two encounters already described, personal recollections of Bajo men aged between 65 and 80 years document a range of activities in the Timor and Arafura seas in the period before World War II.

> In Dutch times [*waktu* Balanda], black shark fin had a price of around 15 ringgit a kilogram in Dutch money. We used to sell the fin in Kupang. White *lontar* shark had a higher price, up to 50 ringgit a kilogram (Si Mbaga, Mola Selatan).

> During Dutch times, when I was still young and before I was married, I sailed to Ashmore Reef and Scott Reef. We sailed to Ashmore Reef in a *perahu* called Saniasa owned by Mbo Kandora from Mantigola. It was a big boat, 80-tonne capacity with two masts, gaff sails, one rudder. The *perahu* had no cabin only an awning made from coconut fronds. We fished using a net [**ngambai**] and used poison [**tuba**] to catch the fish. We got lots of fish and sold it in Makassar. One share was 40 ringgit per person. One time we collected trepang and cooked it in sea water, the same as the Raas people [Madurese]. At Ashmore Reef we always met Dutch and Australian people; they didn't bother us — it was permitted [*bebas*] to catch fish, trepang, trochus, and turtle shell in those times. We could sail close to the coast of Australia and it was not forbidden, we were not disturbed or apprehended; they only ordered us to return to Indonesia. At Ashmore Reef there were also lots of fishermen from Raas. One time the Raas people had run into the reef and made a hole in the hull of their *perahu*. We gave them a plank of wood to repair the damaged one. One time we sailed from Mantigola to Dobo [Aru Islands] to fish for shark using shark rattles and handlines. From Dobo we sailed for one and a half days until we reached our fishing grounds. We sold the shark in Makassar for 5 rupiah per kilo. After the Japanese period I did not go sailing to Ashmore Reef or Scott Reef again (Si Kiramang, Mola Utara).

> During Dutch times we went net fishing at Scott Reef. We could fill eight canoes with fish in one go. At the edge of the reef we used to fish for shark with shark rattles [**gorogoro**]. We still fished there after Japanese times. At that time people from Pepela used to fish at Ashmore Reef and

Cartier Island [Pulau Baru] in *sekoci* [a type of small *perahu*] for trochus and trepang — they were divers (Si Subung, Mola Selatan).

Even in Dutch times we exchanged **balur** [salted strips of dried shark meat] with Pepela people for sugar [*gula air* made from *lontar* palm]. So while net fishing we would also take sharks at the reef but the price of fins was not very high — fish had a much better price. We used longlines [**pissi borroh**] with 10 hooks, 5 *depa* long, made from tree bark [**bagu**] on the edge of the reef for shark. Like trochus, shark did not have a price then. We used to take cassava instead of rice and use poison to stun the fish (Si Pallu, Mola Selatan).

We used to fish at Ashmore Reef, Scott Reef, Adele Island [Pulau Haria], Rowley Shoals [Pulau Bawah Angin] for fish, trochus, trepang, from before the time Japan invaded Indonesia, when it was still Dutch times. The fishing gear used was **ngambai**, we used to catch lots of fish. In those times the net was made from tree bark before nylon. We made the net ourselves. We bought the tree bark from Buton. We pounded it until it was soft. At that time we made sails from tree bark. We made fish hooks from iron rods. At Ashmore Reef, if we went to get drinking water we used to step on the birds' eggs — there were so many. We used to collect the fresh eggs and eat them on the *perahu*, especially if we were constipated. There was water on all three islands and lots of rats. We used longlines near to Scott Reef. We also used shark rattles and when the shark emerged we caught it with a baited line. After we finished fishing we sold our catch in Kupang, Kalabahi [Alor], or Maumere [Flores]. Some people also sold their catch in Mola, Makassar, Ambon — wherever there was a town that required salted or dried fish (Si Badolla, Mola Selatan).

As well as reef fish caught using netting gear and fish poison, these narratives show that the Bajo pursued other marine products during this period, including shark, trepang, trochus shell, and turtle shell. Of particular interest was shark fin. Shark was caught around Scott Reef using small set longlines as well as handlines and shark rattles. Some species of shark commanded a higher price than others. According to Si Kiramang, during Dutch times some Bajo also undertook specific shark fishing voyages to fishing grounds located south of the Aru Islands in the Arafura Sea. The catch from these voyages was later sold by Bajo to traders in a number of towns throughout Indonesia.

Voyaging to the Timor Sea by Bajo and other Indonesians was interrupted during World War II due to the Japanese invasion of Indonesia in 1942 (Crawford 1969: 130). During the occupation, *perahu* shipping was strictly controlled and utilised by the Japanese for the war effort. Many *perahu* were lost or destroyed resulting in a shortage after the war (Dick 1975: 79). Fighting between Japanese and Australian forces in the Timor Sea also deterred any fishing activity (Crawford 1969: 130). Ashmore Reef may have been used for bombing practice, and survival equipment and food caches were stored on the island (ANPWS 1989: 13). [13] Serventy (1952: 13) made enquiries among Australian personnel operating in the Timor Sea and reported that no Indonesian fishing activity was observed during the war.

The Bajo recall *waktu* Jepang (the time of the Japanese) as a time of hardship and suffering. Some of the older men can still recite the Japanese national anthem or a few words of Japanese. Some, like La Ode Ndoke, were forced to work in road gangs on Buton. Si Nurdin from Mola Selatan recalls that he was on a *perahu* returning from Kupang, where he had been attending school, when the boat was boarded by Japanese soldiers. The crew were taken to Bau Bau, accused of being Dutch spies and sentenced to seven years jail. Si Nurdin spent 14 months in jail until he was released at the end of the war and returned to Mantigola. He still has a prisoner number branded on one forearm.

The Bajo Encounter with Australian Scientists in 1949

After the war the Bajo resumed fishing in the Timor Sea. This is documented in Bajo narratives and in European sources describing encounters between Australians and Bajo fishermen in the late 1940s. During a CSIRO fisheries survey of offshore islands and reefs in the Timor Sea in October 1949, the crew of the research vessel Warreen were surprised to encounter Indonesian boats near Scott Reef, Seringapatam Reef, Ashmore Reef and Hibernia Reef. Dr Dominic Serventy, the senior scientist aboard the Warreen, published a short article in 1952 describing some of their encounters with Indonesian vessels during the survey. This article is based on information recorded in the Biological Log, parts of which were written by Serventy (CSIRO 1949). The log is a key source of information on Indonesian fishing activity in the Timor Sea in this period.

Leaving Broome on 29 September 1949, the Warreen cruised up the northwest coast of Australia, past Cape Leveque to Yampi on Cockatoo Island, and then to Adele Island before heading to Scott Reef (Haring Selatan) and later to Sandy Islet (Pulau Datu). No sightings of Indonesian boats were made until 3 October 1949, while the Warreen was sailing between Sandy Islet and Seringapatam Reef, when 'the first official Australian contact with the present-day Indonesian fishing operations' (Serventy 1952: 13) was made at North Reef (Haring Utara). The vessel was described as:

> A sailing boat, cutter-rigged ... probably a Malay prow. Heavy black hull, square transome, bluff bow, stumpy bowsprit, gaff mainsail (ibid.).

---

[13] Although Cartier Island and the surrounding area within a 10 km radius has been a gazetted Defence Practice Area since World War II, the region has not been actively used as a testing area since the early 1990s (Environment Australia 2002: 25).

A few hours later, after sailing around Seringapatam Reef from the west side, the Warreen arrived at the northeast corner of the reef to find

> 2 Malay prows ... anchored inside the lagoon ... near a gap in the reef flat.... We saw several dinghies fishing in various parts of the lagoon but these made their way back to their mother-ship shortly after we arrived (ibid.).

On the following morning, Serventy and the Master of the Warreen, Captain Pedersen

> went by launch through the gap into the lagoon and interviewed the crew of the two Malay prows. They were unable to speak Dutch or English but the Captains showed us their papers which indicated that the prows were the 'Sinar-Karang' and the 'Si Mappe', the former's port being Broo Base (ibid.).

The Sinar Karang and Si Mappe had 'papers stamped by the Dutch "Praukontrole" at Kupang' (Serventy 1952: 13). Serventy recorded a lengthy description of the two engineless vessels in the Biological Log.

> The prows were some 40 ft. in length and 6–7 ft. draft. They were of crude construction and appointments, with rattan sails, spars of bamboo, and ropes of coconut palm. The 'Si Mappe' had 4 canoes and the other boat 3. Both had home-made fishing nets of about 3" mesh with floaters of wood and tiger cowries as sinkers and the crew were evidently spinning their own twine. Both prows had a conspicuous array of sun-dried fish, split kipper style and stacked on bamboo racks which formed an awning over the deck. The fish included North-west Snapper (Lethrinus), Cods (Epinephalus), large Trevally (Ferdauia), Red Bass (Lutjanus coastesi), marine eels, file fish and Stingray. There was no shark flesh but a few dried fins of large sharks were hung up. There was no tuna. There was a lot of clam meat and some trepang. The shells (whole-back and plates) of 15–20 Hawksbill Turtles were in each boat and there was a considerable quantity of large good quality Trochus shell. It was estimated that each boat would have about 2 ½ tons of marine products. About 10 persons were present in each boat. It was impossible to ascertain how long they were fishing in the area; the latest date on the papers of the 'Si Mappe' was September 1, 1949, and that of the 'Sinar Karang' August 13, 1949. It appeared that their course to Seringapatam Reef had been via Ashmore Reef. Their name for Seringapatam Reef was 'Saringang' and for Scott Reef 'Poelodatoe'. They were asked about tuna occurrences and they recognised the Northern Bluefin from illustrations. It was abundant, they said, near Koepang but not plentiful in the Sahul Shelf. Each boat had a couple of immature

Brown Boobies and one pair of Lesser Frigate-birds, tethered by the leg. Apparently they were kept as pets. Our relations with the Malays were friendly and some of our men gave them presents of clothing, etc. When our launch left the 'Warreen' for the first interview the 'Si Mappe' ran up a white flag to her masthead (CSIRO 1949: 42–3).

This is the most detailed historical record of 'Malay' fishing activities in the area between the 1920s and the 1960s. It documents the methods used and the diverse products collected. However, the ethnic identity of the fishermen is not recorded, nor is their home island. Without more ethnographic information, it could be assumed that the boats came from Kupang. The only major port in eastern Indonesia with a name similar to 'Broo Base' is Bau Bau on Buton.

Si Akmad, a *perahu* owner from Mola Utara, confirmed that the Sinar Karang was indeed a Bajo *perahu* and Si Mappeh was a village elder from Mola.[14] It was a counter-sterned, gaff-rigged vessel owned by Si Lenang who died in 1996. The captain at the time of the encounter with theWarreen was Si Saran, who died a few years ago. He was the father of Si Hader, the owner of Nurjaya, a *perahu* apprehended for fishing illegally inside the Australian Fishing Zone, forfeited and destroyed in Darwin in 1994. Si Saran's wife lives in Mola Selatan and recalled hearing of the encounter from her husband.

According to Si Akmad, about ten vessels had left Mantigola for the offshore reefs and islands in the Timor Sea in 1949 to fish with **ngambai** gear and collect other marine products for later sale.

The cost [ongkos] of the voyage was not much in those days, for example 50 ringgit per person.... We also took cassava with us to eat, we would soak it and dry it and take it for food, especially if there was no money to buy rice. After we sold the fish, then we could buy rice. In those days, we used to store water in ceramic jars from Singapore and China.

On entering the Timor Sea, the fleet encountered strong easterly winds. Some vessels lost their direction (*jatuh haluan*) and were forced to return to Pepela. From there they started out again for Ashmore Reef. However, two vessels in the fleet, theSinar Karang and the Bunga Rosi captained by Si Mappeh, had already made it to Seringapatam Reef.

Si Kaharra, one of the most respected and knowledgeable Bajo captains in Mola Selatan, had been a young crew member on the Sinar Karang and remembered having his photo taken during the encounter with the crew of the Warreen. In the Biological Log, Serventy only notes the taking of photographs and movie footage of some of the *perahu* later encountered at Hibernia Reef

---

[14] Si Mappeh died some time ago but his son lives in Mola Utara and owns a motorised *perahu* used for turtle collecting expeditions.

(CSIRO 1949: 47–8). Some of the photographs taken by the Australians have been reproduced (Crawford 1969: 132), but others have not been located. CSIRO staff have located four movie films marked 'Fishing around W.A.' in the possession of the daughter of Bruce Shipway, one of the technical officers serving on the Warreen in 1949. [15] One of the films contains a short section of footage recording a stopover at Cockatoo Island off the Kimberley coast (CSIRO 1949: 38), which is followed by footage of a double-ended *perahu lambo*, laden with various kinds of marine produce, and a bird tethered to the awning frame. This boat appears very similar to the Bajo *perahu* described in detail by Serventy at Seringapatam Reef. The footage, lasting only about 45 seconds, pans slowly along the length of the *perahu* showing some men wearing Muslim *songkok* (black fez hats) standing on the deck and in canoes tethered to the stern. The film footage ends with a young boy lowering a white flag from the top of the mast.

On 5 October, having departed Seringapatam Reef, Serventy counted '23 prows … some of them 2-masted boats' in the vicinity of Ashmore Reef, and then '12 prows near East Island' (CSIRO 1949: 44). Having anchored north of East Island, the Australian party visited 'one of two Malay prows anchored near the shore' (ibid.: 45).

> Embarked on the 'Pintoe Doea', a 2-masted boat, registered at Koepang and recorded in its book as from Waha Tomia. It had no fish on board, only a quantity of trochus shell. The only fishing gear seen was a trolling line, fitted with a single barbed 8-0 hook, the lure being a piece of sugar cane leaf…. This part of the lure is tied around the end of the hook and trace. Though no one of the 10 persons aboard understood English or Dutch, we were able to ascertain that tuna were not considered to be plentiful in these waters but that they were abundant at Koepang, Roti and Flores. They denied that they ate any birds of the island. From the prow's book, S. Halfweeg [deckhand] ascertained that it had been trading as a carrier (cement and petrol) earlier in the year (ibid.).

This description of the Pintoe Doea does not indicate whether the crew were Bajo, but the *perahu* had come from or previously visited the town of Waha on the island of Tomia in the Tukang Besi Islands. Even though it is not possible to identify the ethnic origin of the crew, who may have been Butonese from Pepela, it shows that the *perahu* and crew had alternated between trading and fishing at certain times of the year. The Warreen spent two days at Ashmore Reef. Serventy and the crew found evidence of human activity on East and Middle Islets and West Island, including fish drying racks, piles of dried fish, and the remains of lesser frigate birds, and also noted the existence of two graves on East Islet (CSIRO 1949: 45–7; Serventy 1952: 14). These observations are less

---

[15] These films have since been donated to the Battye Library in Perth.

detailed than those made at Seringpatam Reef, but the presence of drying racks could indicate net fishing operations by Bajo or Rotinese fishermen.

The Warreen then left Ashmore Reef and travelled to Hibernia Reef where '4 Malay prows were at anchor, but made sail as we approached' (CSIRO 1949: 47). About an hour later, the Australian boat caught up with the *perahu* under sail on the southwest side of the reef:

> One boat was called the 'Bintati Moer'. On board one 11 men were counted. Hailed one crew and were informed they were going to Roti. Some dried fish was seen aboard and dried clam (ibid.: 47–8).

This is the moment at which Serventy noted that photographs were taken. Thereafter, the Australians visited Cartier and Browse islands but saw no further signs of Indonesian fishing activity.

During the survey those aboard the Warreen had seen a total of 30 vessels in the area (Serventy 1952: 13). At the same time another vessel, the FRV Stanley Fowler, was surveying the central and eastern parts of the Timor Sea along the Sahul Shelf but the crew did not sight any Indonesian *perahu* (ibid.: 14–15). Since the crew of the Warreen had not sighted any *perahu* at Rowley Shoals, Serventy thought that they were

> too distant to attract, as yet, the enterprise of the Indonesians.... It is felt that the only reason these shoals have not been fished is because the Indonesians have not yet found them (ibid.: 15).

But he was wrong. Indonesian voyaging to Rowley Shoals prior to the CSIRO survey is well documented from oral history.

Bajo Fishing Activity in the Northwest, 1950s–1970s

The late 1950s and early 1960s — the height of the Kahar Muzzakar rebellion (1950–65) — was a period of relative instability for the Tukang Besi Island Bajo. In 1956–57, the Mantigola Bajo were forced to flee their settlement and most re-established themselves in Mola. According to Si Pallu, however, some Bajo from Mantigola (and after 1957 from Mola) continued to sail long distances on fishing and trading voyages around the Indonesian Archipelago and to the north Australia region, while others fished locally, not far from their settlement.

The following accounts of sailing and fishing activities in the period from the 1950s to the early 1970s are from men in their late forties to mid-sixties.

> The first time I sailed to the region of Australia was to catch fish during the 1950s. I went with the old people to **ngambai**. At that time we still lived in Mantigola, it was before the rebellion. We carried 1 tonne of salt, that's a lot of salted fish! We fished all day long and our bodies ached because there was so much work to salt and dry the fish. We

caught so much fish we could fill the entire hold of the *perahu* with salted fish. After that I sailed all over, transporting goods to different places (Si Kariman, Mola Selatan).

After we moved to Mola, between 1959 and 1969, I sailed all over, transporting copra to Gresik, Surabaya [Java], Singapore, Tawao [Sabah], Sarawak. At that time we sailed *perahu lambo*, but we still used gaff sails [**lama cangking**]; it was before [the adoption of] gunter sails [**lama sande**]. The first time I sailed to Ashmore Reef was in 1970. Before this time, from before I was born, Bajo people sailed to Ashmore Reef to fish with nets [**ngambai**]. I heard many stories from my parents and old people. My father had a *perahu* he finished building in 1955, and after launching it he sailed to Ashmore Reef. But before my father had a *perahu*, my father's brothers sailed with my grandfather's *perahu* and went net fishing at Ashmore. Formerly, at Ashmore Reef there were coconut trees owned by Bajo from Mantigola. But after white people started living there, they chopped down the trees. Actually, in the past, those coconut trees marked the location of Ashmore Reef; from a long distance we could see Ashmore Reef. There are still a few tall coconut trees left (Si Acing, Mola Selatan).

In the late 1940s and early 1950s, we carried copra to Java, but in 1957 we couldn't go out because of the rebellion. Sometimes we carried copra in the 1960s and 1970s. I also carried asphalt once during the rebellion period. But then, in the 1970s lots of motor boats became engaged in the trade in Maluku and we stopped carry copra. Around this time we went fishing for shark, not reef fish, with shark rattles and handlines (Si Kaharra, Mola Selatan).

In 1962, during the time of the PKI [Indonesian Communist Party], I carried copra. In 1972–73, I sailed to the Timor Sea and fished for shark and collected trochus shell (Si Nurdin, Mola Selatan).

My father used to sail a *lambo* with gaff rig and counter-stern to Ashmore Reef and fish using nets. Between 1969 and 1971, I carried copra from Maluku to Surabaya and in 1972 I went shark fishing in the Timor Sea (Si Mudir, Mola Selatan).

My father had three *perahu* and each *perahu* did different work; we sailed them and other people borrowed them too. After 1957 we sailed *perahu lambo* to carry copra from Maluku to Java. One time we carried copra to Sarawak. In the past when we sailed to Surabaya we could sail three times during the east monsoon. We also sailed to Singapore. I went to Singapore in 1982 and spent eight months doing labouring work around the harbour but barely earned enough to pay for the trip. In the early

1980s we stopped carrying copra and started fishing again (Si Akmad, Mola Utara).

Between 1962 and 1965 I sailed on my uncle's *perahu* and carried copra from Maluku to Java. In 1967, we changed from gaff rig to gunter rig. In 1967, we carried asphalt between Kendari and Bone [South Sulawesi]. In 1968 I went to live in Central Sulawesi for nine years and after that returned to Mola (Si Hati, Mola Selatan).

In 1965 I carried copra. I caught turtle for Bali in 1972 and fished for shark in the Timor Sea in 1973 (Si Ntao, Mola Utara).

In the early 1980s I stopped carrying copra. Before that I used to carry copra to Surabaya which we bought on Taliabo Island [Maluku]. I could carry 5 tonnes of copra (Si Mohammad, Mola Utara).

These accounts show that the diverse fishing and trading activities of Bajo from Mantigola and Mola continued uninterrupted from 1949 until the early 1970s. The main form of fishing was still net fishing for reef fish which was dried for later sale. The use of the gaff rig provides further evidence for voyaging during the 1950s and early 1960s as the Bajo only adopted the gunter rig sail in the late 1960s.

These accounts also reveal that some Bajo became involved in new trading activities, especially in the transportation of copra from Maluku for sale at Gresik and Surabaya on Java. Copra was also taken as far as Singapore, Sarawak and Sabah. The extent of Bajo involvement in *perahu* trading prior to the 1950s is unknown. Si Badolla stated that Bajo from Mantigola engaged in carrying copra using *perahu lambo* well before World War II. It appears that during the 1960s *perahu* trading across the Indonesian Archipelago and to neighbouring countries was an important economic activity for many Mola Bajo.

Many Bajo ceased to engage in *perahu* trading activities in the early 1970s and returned to shark and trochus fishing in the Timor Sea as their main economic activity. In the early 1950s, net fishing for reef fish was commonly practised at places such as Ashmore Reef, but by the early 1970s shark fin and trochus fishing had largely replaced net fishing. The Kahar Muzzakar rebellion in Southeast Sulawesi and the migration of Bajo from Mantigola to Mola in 1957 must have had some effect on patterns of fishing. Other marine products, such as trochus shell and shark fin, were probably commanding a higher price than dried reef fish towards the end of this period. Regional economic growth in the late 1960s also stimulated increased exploitation of marine resources.

From the 1940s to the early 1980s, Bajo from Mantigola and Mola were engaged in a diverse range of activities dictated by a mix of individual preferences, weather conditions and economic factors. The latter included the availability of capital and market prices for cargoes and marine products. While some Bajo preferred trading, others focused on fishing. As in many fishing communities, people alternated between the two pursuits depending on the particular social, economic and political situation at the time, as well as the seasonal cycle. The role of Bajo from the Tukang Besi Islands in the local Butonese *perahu* trading sector, as well as in fishing activities in the Timor Sea, is already documented in the literature (Dick 1975; Hughes 1984; Evers 1991; Southon 1995: 45–9).

Trading first became popular in 1940, when the Dutch East Indies Government, following the impact of the 1930s world economic depression, began to monopolise the copra trade and fix market prices. Despite the devastating impact of the Japanese occupation on local *perahu* shipping and trading in the islands (Dick 1975: 79), the government monopoly was revived after World War II, and while copra from Sulawesi was all supposed to pass through a government trading centre in Makassar, price controls created an illegal smuggling trade which resulted in *perahu* from Selayar and Sulawesi transporting copra to Surabaya and Singapore where prices were actually much higher (Heersink 1994: 67). It would appear that Bajo from Mola may have been involved in these copra smuggling activities.

According to Southon (1995: 44), the Butonese people of Lande began building and sailing *perahu lambo* in the 1940s, partly in response to opportunities created after World War II. During the 1950s and 1960s the informal trading sector expanded throughout eastern Indonesia because of problems in the formal sector. The Koninklijke Paketvaart Maatschappij (Royal Navigation Company), which had dominated trade in previous decades, was expelled from Indonesia in 1957, and the modern shipping sector was suffering the effects of political instability and economic contraction (ibid.: 45). The informal *perahu* trade in copra and cloves remained important in the Tukang Besi economy through the 1960s and 1970s, but a formal shipping business financed by ethnic Chinese investors began transporting cargoes in large motorised vessels after 1967. The subsequent decline in the Butonese *perahu* trading sector was compounded by a dramatic fall in the price of copra in 1972, and this forced the Bajo traders back into fishing (ibid.). This is the when my Bajo informants say that they resumed fishing activities in the Timor Sea. The Bajo entry into the trade of live turtles to Bali also began in the 1970s.

Chapter 5: Australian Maritime Expansion

The developments in Australian maritime expansion, fisheries policy and legislation with regard to Indonesian fishing activity in waters now claimed by Australia are complex. While many of these developments have been analysed in detail by Campbell and Wilson (1993), any analysis of the current situation must begin with an historical perspective. The offshore islands and coral reefs located along the continental shelf in the Timor Sea have long been 'stepping stones between Asia and Australia' for both European and Indonesian mariners (Fairbridge 1948: 193). While most of the reefs and islands of the Timor Sea were mapped and named by European mariners,[1] Indonesian fishermen were engaged in regular voyages to these isolated offshore areas well before the nineteenth century.

American whalers discovered the large deposits of guano on islands in the northwest Kimberley region in the 1840s. Guano was exploited only periodically before the 1870s, when more regular exploitation was carried out at a number of offshore islands, including Ashmore Reef and Browse Island (Woodward 1917: 10). Sovereignty over Ashmore Reef then became the subject of international rivalry between American and British interests in this business. After a period of negotiation between the British Colonial Office and the US State Department, Britain annexed Ashmore Reef in 1878 and Cartier Island in 1909 (Langdon 1966: 556).[2] In 1904 the export of guano was prohibited (Woodward 1917: 9), but the crew of the British cruiser Cambrian formally took possession of Ashmore Reef in 1906. The captain, five officers, and 200 men as a guard of honour landed on the island, hoisted the Union Jack, sang the National Anthem, and fired a 21-gun salute (*Northern Territory Times*, 16 February 1906).

The status of these islands began to attract attention in the early 1900s when claims were made about illegal poaching in the region. In 1909 Henry Hilliard, who was then still a British subject, complained to the Secretary of State for the Colonies in London about boats from the Dutch East Indies fishing at Long Reef, Adele Island, and a reef near Swan Point. He reported that they were interfering

---

[1] Cartier Island was discovered by the English Captain Nash in the Cartier in 1800. Scott Reef was discovered and named by Captain Heywood of the Royal Navy while surveying the northwest of Australia in 1801 in HMS Vulcan (Fairbridge 1948: 209). Ashmore Reef was named after Captain Samuel Ashmore, who sighted and named the island in 1811. Captain Ashmore had sighted and named the nearby Hibernia Reef after his ship, the Hibernia, during an earlier voyage in 1810 (ibid.). Browse Island was named in 1838 after being sighted by a schooner captain of that name on a return journey from Roti to the Kimberley (ibid.: 210). Seringapatam Reef was sighted by the crew of the merchant ship Seringapatam in 1842 (ibid.: 211).

[2] There does not appear to have been any conflict over Browse Island since it was already a possession of Western Australia (Bach 1955: 209).

with his trepang operations (Bach 1955: 208). However, Hilliard's own activities began to arouse interest among Australian authorities who were concerned about foreign-based companies poaching in Australian territorial waters, the limit of which extended 3 nautical miles (nm) out from the low water mark (ibid.).

Further reports of poaching persuaded the Commonwealth to commission a gunboat to carry out patrols of the northwest waters, but the only arrests made at this time 'turned out to be a source of embarrassment to the Australian officials' (Crawford 1969: 117). In 1911 the gunboat arrested two schooners fishing at Scott Reef, the Harriet and the Fortuna, and escorted them to Broome. It was suspected one of the vessels belonged to Hilliard. The captains, W.S. Smith and Pebo Doro, were charged with smuggling under the Western Australian *Customs Act*, and once they had paid their fines by selling their catch of trochus shell the schooners were released. Apparently the prosecution had tendered as evidence a proclamation dating from 1900 which defined the boundaries of Western Australia to include all islands adjacent in the Indian Ocean (Bach 1955: 218). The fines had to be refunded when it was later conceded that the arrest had been illegal because Scott Reef was outside Australian waters (ibid.). Most of the files relating to the incident had by then been destroyed to hide the Government's embarrassment and only a 'bare outline of the episode had been preserved' (ibid.). The ambiguous status of Scott Reef remained until 1924 when it was finally declared to be part of Western Australian territory (Bottrill 1993: 46).

The Western Australian Government continued to receive reports about vessels from the Dutch East Indies illegally fishing along the Kimberley coast and on offshore reefs and islands, including Ashmore Reef, but was 'largely powerless to act against these incursions' (Campbell and Wilson 1993: 22) since the region 'remained virtually beyond the limits of government control' (Crawford 1969: 116). Between 1919 and 1923, state authorities made frequent appeals to the Commonwealth to provide a warship to patrol the coast against vessels from Kupang which were allegedly violating territorial waters (Bach 1955: 209).

In the latter part of 1923, Henry Hilliard petitioned the Australian Minister for External Affairs to grant him a fishing concession for Ashmore Reef. He once again complained of *perahu* from Java and Timor denuding the reef of its trepang, trochus and seabird populations, and suggested that if he could fish there he could protect the stocks from poachers (Bottrill 1993: 45), but there is reason to believe that Hilliard and his son Robin were the actual 'raiders' (Campbell and Wilson 1993: 23).

In 1923 the Western Australian Government formally complained to the Commonwealth following reports of illicit fishing at Ashmore Reef. As the Commonwealth had no authority over the islands, which were still under British control, they referred the matter to the British Government. In 1931 the British transferred the islands to Commonwealth control and in 1933 the Commonwealth *Ashmore and Cartier Islands Acceptance Act* was passed. When this came into force in 1934, the islands were transferred to Australian sovereignty. Under this legislation the Western Australian Government was empowered to make ordinances for the new territory, but it decided that there were few practical benefits to be obtained from administering the islands, so it asked the Commonwealth to take over these administrative duties. In 1938 the legislation was amended to vest control of the islands in the Administrator of the Northern Territory (Langdon 1966: 56–8).

Australian Government Perspectives in the Post-War Period

Until 1952 Indonesians were free to fish anywhere off the coast of Australia and its islands so long as they were outside the 3 nm limit of territorial waters (Campbell and Wilson 1993: 115). In 1952, the Commonwealth *Pearl Fisheries Act* came into force, making it illegal to collect sedentary species on the continental shelf.[3] In the following year Australia made a unilateral claim over the entire continental shelf in order to protect pearl shell resources from Japanese fishing activities. Although the Australian Government now had the legal powers to prosecute Indonesian fishermen as well, it did not yet have the capability to apprehend them (ibid.: 28).

One 'official perspective' on Indonesian voyaging in the 1950s and 1960s was that 'there were practically no intentional visits by Indonesian fishermen to the north-west coast' and the few that did venture onto the northwestern continental shelf were believed to be 'storm-blown' arrivals (Campbell and Wilson 1993: 35). Campbell and Wilson call this the 'myth of emptiness'. A second official perspective, which they call the 'myth of subsistence', was that all Indonesian fishermen who did fish in the northwestern region during this period were doing so to meet subsistence needs. These two perspectives influenced Australian government responses to incursions into the Australian Fishing Zone until the late 1960s, when a redirection in policy led to greater maritime surveillance and control over Indonesian fishing activity.

Encounters between Australian residents and Indonesian fishermen during the 1950s and 1960s were rare and mostly unreported. During this period:

> there was practically no surveillance ... no system for reporting and recording sightings, and the [Kimberley] area was sparsely populated. [It is reasonable to assume] that only a small proportion of visits would

---

[3] The legislation gained international endorsement in 1960 through the United Nations Convention on the Continental Shelf (UNCLOS II). It was later superceded by the *Continental Shelf (Living Natural Resources) Act 1968*.

have been sighted, with even fewer being reported (Campbell and Wilson 1993: 34, 37).

Reports of 'spasmodic sightings' of Indonesians were made by Cape Leveque lighthouse keepers in 1957 and 1960 (ibid.: 25). Their diary records that foreign fishermen were collecting water from the mainland but their identity is not recorded. Eight *perahu* were sighted at Adele Island by members of the Australian Iron and Steel Company in April 1957, and in August that year, Aboriginal people from the Sunday Island mission also sighted *perahu* off Cape Leveque. In August 1958 the Australian navy ship HMAS Cootamundra visited Ashmore Reef and found Indonesian *perahu* (reportedly from Kupang) anchored there (ANPWS 1989: 10). But only one episode around this time elicited any significant government response.

On 5 October 1957 a *perahu*, the Si Untung Slamat, sailed in and berthed at the town wharf in Yampi Sound on Cockatoo Island.[4] The captain and some crew were taken to a local office and interviewed by the Acting Customs Officer, Mr Smith. It was found that the crew had left Raas Island, near Madura, and sailed to Kupang, then south to the northwest coast of Australia where they fished for trochus shell and trepang. They were then caught in a storm at sea and blown off course. The *perahu* and crew drifted for five days to the southeast until they saw signs of habitation at Cockatoo Island. The crew were given medical attention and the vessel was re-provisioned. On 8 October the boat set sail, supposedly for Kupang.

On the next day Aborigines from the Sunday Island mission saw the crew of a *perahu* collecting trochus shell at Cleft Island. This was reported to Mr Smith on 11 October, and then to the Western Australian Fisheries Department in Perth. This time Smith was instructed by the Federal Department of Customs in Canberra to intercept the vessel and interview the crew suspected of illegal fishing. An air search found the vessel anchored off the reef off McIntyre Island, 8 km north of Cockatoo Island.[5]

On 15 October Smith and five local residents, including Ronald Lind and a woman who could speak Malay, left Yampi Sound in the launch Balga, armed with a loaded .303 rifle. The vessel was located, the captain and first mate were interviewed, and a search of the *perahu* revealed a quantity of trochus shell, trepang and dried fish. The captain could not produce any papers permitting him to fish in Australian waters, so the crew were arrested and the boat was towed back to Yampi and thence to Derby on King Sound. Customs and immigration formalities were completed, a rooster found on board was destroyed,

---

[4] This sighting and the previous sighting off Cape Leveque are both documented in Australian Customs Service file WA 57/8527.

[5] Photographs of the boat that appeared in *The West Australian* newspaper of 19 October 1957 show it to be a Madurese *perahu lete lete* (see also Lind 1994: 143).

and the crew and vessel were handed over to an inspector from the WA Fisheries Department who had flown in from Broome to investigate the matter. The captain was charged under the WA *Fisheries Act 1905* on two counts of using an unlicensed boat and illegally fishing in Australian territorial waters. He appeared in the Derby court on 23 October, was convicted on both counts and fined the minimum amount of £ 15. The Indonesian embassy in Canberra agreed to pay the fine, which was out of all proportion to the cost of apprehension and investigation. The boat and crew departed for Indonesia the following day (Lind 1994: 141–6).

This was the first time a foreign fishing vessel had been apprehended in the area since Hilliard's two schooners were arrested at Scott Reef in 1911. The gap in time illustrates the lack of any coherent maritime policing policy in the intervening years. When the issue of illegal Indonesian fishing was raised in the WA Legislative Assembly on 17 October 1957, the Minister for Fisheries admitted that this was not a new problem.

> Vague reports have from time to time reached me of Indonesian fishing and shelling activity in the rather inaccessible waters off the North-West coast. As their operations were always well off the beaten track, no opportunity has offered, in the interval between the 1949 incident written up by Dr Serventy and the present week to board any such vessel to ascertain whether it has, in fact, been engaged in unlawful practices (WA Legislative Assembly Hansard 17 October 1957, quoted in Campbell and Wilson 1993: 26).

This statement reveals the official view of the northwest as an isolated, lawless 'colonial frontier', even in the late 1950s (Campbell and Wilson 1993: 26). The Government was still uncertain about the legality of Indonesian activity, there was very little information about it, and practically no official contact between government officials and Indonesian fishermen. The minister went on to say that 'without a patrol boat little could be done to police territorial waters off the northwest' (*The West Australian*, 18 October 1957).

European commercial and political influence along the northwest coast and offshore waters increased in the early 1960s when multinational companies started looking for oil in the region (Campbell and Wilson 1993: 26). During geological surveys of Browse Island, Scott Reef and Ashmore Reef employees from the Burma Oil Company found further evidence of Indonesian activity (Crawford 1969: 133–7). In August 1965 the company installed its first drilling rig near Ashmore Reef, and the workers on the rig were regularly visited by Indonesian fishermen. One party, reportedly from Madura, visited the rig in February 1967, and another group of five vessels, some possibly originating from Timor, and with at least one woman on board, visited in October (Crawford 1969: 133–7). In February 1968, Crawford went to Ashmore Reef and spent five days living aboard a *perahu* that originated from Raas, off Madura, and documented Madurese voyages to the reefs and islands further to the south of Ashmore Reef. He also described fishing and curing activities. During this time he sighted 11 *perahu*, all of which originated from Madura or Raas. His is the first report that linked the crews and boats from Madura and Raas with re-provisioning in Kupang and the sale of marine products through the trading centre of Makassar (ibid.: 137–56). [6]

Campbell and Wilson (1993: 37) emphasise that visits to the northwest during this period were not cases of subsistence fishing nor were the boats storm-blown arrivals; they were intentional voyages that had a specific commercial orientation. Ethnographic material presented in the previous chapter showed that Bajo perspectives also emphasise the intentional and commercial nature of fishing voyages at this time. Bottrill (1993) and Campbell and Wilson (1993: 27, 37) cite oral histories from residents of Pepela that also supports this argument.

New Bilateral Arrangements with Indonesia

In 1958 and 1960, the First and Second United Nations Conventions on the Law of the Sea (UNCLOS I and II) established international standards for the delimitation of national fishing zones and territorial seas. In the following decade many countries unilaterally extended their territorial waters and extended their fishing zones from 3 nm to 12 nm. Indonesia claimed a 12 nm territorial sea in 1960 (Campbell and Wilson 1993: 116), and Australia followed suit in 1968.

Although the Australian Fishing Zone (AFZ) was reserved 'for the exclusive use of fishermen and vessels licensed under Australian Law', the Australian government decided that traditional Indonesian fishing practices in waters now claimed by Australia could continue provided that:

> The operations were confined to a subsistence level, and the operations were carried out in the Declared Fishing Zone and territorial sea adjacent to the Ashmore and Cartier Islands, Seringapatam Reef, Scott Reef, Adele Island and Browse Island (DFAT 1988: 1).

This was the 'first time since the turn of the century that Australian policy had been exclusively directed at Indonesian fishermen' (Campbell and Wilson 1993: 116–7). Nothing was said as to how it was to be legally enforced, nor was it made clear how the Indonesian Government and the fishermen themselves were to be informed of the arrangement. The official view that Indonesians engaged in subsistence, rather than artisanal, fishing appears to have influenced this decision, and this view still formed the basis of misguided policy responses towards Indonesian fishing in the following years.

---

[6] Two later reports of sightings found in Western Australian archives mention three *perahu* near Cape Bossut Creek south of Broome in May 1969 that were supposedly heading for Mermaid Reef at Rowley Shoals, and four *perahu* located off Cape Leveque in 1970 (Campbell and Wilson 1993: 36–7).

There was no regular air or sea surveillance of the northwest Australian coast before 1974, but in that year the Royal Australian Navy (RAN) and Royal Australian Air Force (RAAF) began to conduct monthly sea and air patrols. By July 1974 there were reports of large numbers of foreign boats operating off the coast of Western Australia, and as the year wore on, 'more credible' reports of Indonesian vessels targeting trochus shell in and around King Sound (Campbell and Wilson 1993: 38–9).[7] According to Campbell and Wilson, the Australian Government took this as evidence of 'a dramatic rise in incursions', and the 'myth of emptiness' was then replaced with what they call the 'myth of invasion'. This in turn prompted a further increase in sea and air surveillance of the northwest coast.[8] After 1973, claims were also made that Indonesian fishermen had now begun to visit the coast of Australia in large numbers with the deliberate intent to engage in commercial fishing instead of just fishing for subsistence (ibid.: 39, 61).

The 1974 Memorandum of Understanding

Prime Minister Whitlam met with President Suharto in Jakarta in September 1974, and officials of both governments met in November to 'discuss the specific concerns of the two Governments about the activities of Indonesian fishermen in Australian waters' (DFAT 1988: 1). The outcome was the signing, on 7 November 1974, of a 'Memorandum of Understanding between the Government of Australia and the Government of the Republic of Indonesia Regarding the Operations of Indonesian Traditional Fishermen in Areas of the Australian Exclusive Fishing Zone and Continental Shelf' (see Appendix B). This MOU, which came into force on 28 February 1975, remains the foundation of current fisheries policy in the declared zone off the northwest coast of Australia. It declared that 'Indonesian traditional fishermen' would be allowed to collect and fish certain species within a 12 nm radius of Ashmore Reef, Cartier Island, Scott Reef, Seringapatam Reef and Browse Island (see Map 5-1).[9]

[7] Some *perahu* were also seen to have dried shark fin and flesh on board.

[8] From figures tabled in Parliament in August 1975, concerning reported sightings of Indonesian vessels, and the level of air and sea surveillance between 1972 and 1975, Campbell and Wilson (1993: 39) argue for a 'strong correlation between the introduction of surveillance and the dramatic increase in reported sightings' over the period 1972–75.

[9] Adele Island, which Indonesian fishermen had access to under the previous declaration of 1968, and Rowley Shoals, which they had been visiting since at least the latter part of the nineteenth century, were not covered by the MOU (Campbell and Wilson 1993: 122).

Map 5-1: Location of permitted areas of access for Indonesian fishermen in the Australian Fishing Zone under the 1974 Memorandum of Understanding.

Traditional fishermen were defined in the MOU as 'fishermen who have traditionally taken fish and sedentary organisms in Australian waters *by methods which have been the tradition over decades of time'* (author's emphasis). Under the agreement, fishing was to be confined to offshore reefs and islands. Fishermen would be allowed to take shelter in anchorages at specified islands and reefs, but all landings would be prohibited with the exception of East Islet and Middle Islet at Ashmore Reef, where fishermen would be permitted to land for the purpose of collecting fresh water. The taking of sea turtles was forbidden. Sedentary species that were protected under the *Continental Shelf Act 1968*, such as trochus, trepang, abalone, green snail, sponges and all molluscs, could be taken only within 12 nm of the specified islands and reefs, and not from any other part of the continental shelf.

In February 1975 the Commonwealth *Fisheries Act 1952* was amended to make foreign fishing within the 12 nm fishing zone an offence *regardless of the purpose*. However, the legislation allowed that, 'as a gesture of friendship ... Australia would refrain from enforcing its fishery laws against Indonesian fishermen who complied with the limitations set out in the 1974 Memorandum of Understanding' (DFAT 1988: 2). Those who did not comply could be brought before the Australian courts and charged under the new amendments to Sections 13AA and 13AB concerning foreign fishing. [10]

Australian Enforcement of the MOU

With legislative powers now in place to deal with Indonesian fishermen operating outside the allowed areas, the Australian Government mounted a massive air and sea surveillance campaign officially named 'Operation Trochus'. It was undertaken in two consecutive years as Trochus 75 and Trochus 76. From March 1975, the RAN conducted almost continuous sea patrols of the region, and there were fortnightly surveillance flights by RAAF aircraft as well (DFAT 1988: 12). These operations formed the 'enforcement and education arm' of the MOU (Campbell and Wilson 1993: 65). Operation Trochus officially ceased in June 1976, partly because some of the surveillance aircraft were destroyed by a fire at their base in Nowra (in New South Wales), and partly because the Darwin-based naval patrol boats were diverted to deal with the arrival of Vietnamese refugees after the fall of Saigon. However, because of ongoing infringements by Indonesian vessels collecting trochus within 12 nm of the Australian mainland, regular air and sea patrols continued after that date (Campbell and Wilson 1993: 68).

Indonesian fishermen found operating along the Kimberley coast were informed of the provisions of the MOU and were forced into the permitted areas

---

[10] Prior to the amendments, the *Fisheries Act* only regulated commercial fishing and only applied to Australian residents.

to the north (Campbell and Wilson 1993: 65). Navy patrols encountering Indonesian *perahu* handed out leaflets and employed Indonesian interpreters to assist with the dissemination of information about the MOU. Indonesian officials, particularly the Governor of the Province of East Nusa Tenggara and the officers of the Provincial Fisheries Department (Dinas Perikanan), were also involved in this exercise. A sign was constructed on West Island, part of Ashmore Reef, with a map and text in Bahasa Indonesia outlining the MOU regulations (DFAT 1988: 2). [11]

Once the *Fisheries Act* had been amended, an inter-departmental committee planned to authorise the apprehension of some *perahu* to run a test case in the Australian courts. It was hoped that 'the courts would order forfeiture of vessels owned by Indonesians offending against our Fisheries Laws' (Campbell and Wilson 1993: 67). On 13 March 1975 three *perahu* were detained near Troughton Island about 16 km north of Cape Bougainville and inside the 12 nm limit. While under tow to Wyndham one *perahu* sank and so the skipper did not face charges (*The Kalgoorlie Miner*, 17 and 20 March 1975).

> 13 March 1975: HMAS ASSAIL encountered the *perahu* 'KENAGAN LAMA', Capt Mahmoud Malang denied fishing and said his boat had been damaged in a storm and was leaking badly. The 'Assail' took the vessel under tow seemingly against the advice of Mahmoud, and headed for Wyndham. During the tow the *perahu* took water and was cast off after a couple of days. It sank moments later (Bottrill 1993: 54). [12]

The other two skippers were charged under Section 13AA of the *Fisheries Act* which states that:

> A person shall not, in the Australian fishing zone
>
> (a) use a foreign boat for taking, catching or capturing fish for private purposes; or
>
> (b) use a foreign boat for processing or carrying fish that have been taken, caught or captured for private purposes with the use of that boat or another boat.
>
> Penalty: $5000.

Under this section of the Act, a captain can be charged even if the fish on board the vessel were caught outside the AFZ and the vessel is in transit through the AFZ or forced into the zone by adverse weather (Campbell and Wilson 1993: 66). In this case the captains claimed that 'they had been travelling for more

---

[11] This was a rather strange move because Indonesian fishermen were forbidden to land there under the MOU.

[12] Bottrill does not cite the source of this quotation, but it is most likely taken from WA Fisheries Department archive files held in the Battye Library in Perth.

than a month in their tiny boats and had not intended to enter Australian waters but had been blown off course by westerly winds' (*The Kalgoorlie Miner*, 20 March 1975). The captains were found guilty but Magistrate Ian Martin refused to order any punishment as he considered they had no option to argue their defence under the law. In his words:

> the men were unlucky to have been blown off course, unlucky that they had no clear indication that they were in Australian waters and unlucky to be charged under a law worded as it was (ibid.).

In a statement written in March 1976, contained in an Australian Fishing Zone file held at the WA Fisheries Department, the failure of the cases is explained as follows:

> Simply the problem is this then. Fisheries legislation can be effectively applied to keep and remove Indonesian fishermen from the Australian mainland areas, but if the same legislation is used in an attempt to persuade the courts that the fisheries offences are of such seriousness as to require forfeiture of the vessels involved, such a course may not be successful (quoted in Campbell and Wilson 1993: 67).

Officials from the WA Fisheries Department thought that the *perahu* were from Roti and were targeting trochus shell (Campbell and Wilson 1993: 174), but the magistrate observed that they had shark fin on board, and *The Kalgoorlie Miner* (17 and 20 March 1975) reported that they were from Kaledupa Island in the Tukang Besi Islands. Campbell and Wilson (1993: 68) agreed that these were 'traditional shark fishermen' from the Tukang Besi Islands. My own inquiries indicate that they were Bajo boats from Mantigola village on Kaledupa Island, and would have sailed to Pepela on their way to Ashmore Reef. Whether they were trochus or shark boats is debatable, and the fishermen may have been targeting both species. They certainly appear to be the first Bajo boats whose crews were brought before the Australian courts.

With the release of the two *perahu*, WA fisheries officers began to implement a policy of 'local justice' (Campbell and Wilson 1993: 68). Under the WA *Fisheries Act* they could legally board *perahu* operating outside the permitted areas — particularly those operating along the Kimberley coast and collecting trochus in the King Sound region — and confiscate fishing gear and catch. In some cases, gear and catch were thrown overboard. Crews were left with supplies, given warnings, and told to return to the permitted areas to the north. This program was cost effective and relatively successful, with the loss of equipment and catch providing sufficient punishment for the fishermen. But one of the outcomes of increased contact between Australian officials and diverse groups of Indonesian fishermen was a more 'realistic assessment' of the fishermen's commercial motives, and this in turn was used to legitimate the policy of 'local justice' (ibid.: 70–1).

Nevertheless, in 1980 it was decided — on recommendations by fisheries and navy officers — that stronger policy and tougher penalties should be introduced to combat repeated illegal fishing activity along the northwest coast, and so the 'local justice' approach ceased. The first of the new measures was taken in July 1980 when two *perahu* were apprehended. The Sama Biasa was detained off Gregory Island and the Jangan Tanya Lagi was apprehended off Bedford Island in the Bucaneer Archipelago near King Sound. The crews had been collecting trochus shell and had attempted to hide from authorities in the mangroves along the Kimberley coast. The captains were charged and found guilty under Section 29A(2)(b) of the WA *Fisheries Act*. The boats and all equipment were forfeited and the captains and 31 crew members repatriated to Indonesia.[13] Both boats were owned by Pepelans and the crew had planned to sell their catch to a trader. The loss of the *perahu* and equipment, and the economic hardships suffered by the crew and their families, had 'an immediate and lasting effect' on the fishing patterns of the Pepela fleet that was now forced to concentrate its fishing effort in the areas set out in the MOU (Campbell and Wilson 1993: 72–3). It was to be another eight years before *perahu* from Pepela were again apprehended and confiscated.

Extension of the Australian Fishing Zone

In November 1979, along with many other countries, Australia unilaterally extended the limits of the AFZ from 12 nm to 200 nm from the coastline, and Indonesia followed suit in March 1980 by proclaiming an Exclusive Economic Zone with the same limits.[14] To deal with overlapping jurisdictions in the Timor Sea, the two governments signed a 'Memorandum of Understanding on a Provisional Fisheries Surveillance and Enforcement Arrangement' on 29 October 1981, which came into effect on 1 February 1982. Under this arrangement, each country would refrain from surveillance and enforcement action against fishing boats licensed by the other state beyond a Provisional Fisheries Surveillance and Enforcement Line. It was also agreed that the arrangement would have no effect on the position of Indonesian traditional fishermen operating in accordance with the 1974 MOU. The provisional line would apply only to pelagic fisheries and jurisdiction over sedentary species in the region would be based primarily on the seabed boundary lines previously agreed in 1971 and 1972 (DFAT 1988: 20–25). The Australian Fisheries Service (AFS) would be responsible for enforcing the arrangement in the AFZ.[15]

---

[13] The Jangan Tanya Lagi was destroyed but the Sama Biasa, with all equipment and gear, was donated to the Western Australian Maritime Museum in Fremantle.

[14] These arrangements were endorsed by the Third United Nations Convention on the Law of the Sea (UNCLOS III) in 1982.

[15] The AFS became the Australian Fisheries Management Authority (AFMA) in 1992.

The areas now placed off limits to Indonesian fishermen included Bajo shark fishing grounds that stretched along the Sahul Shelf in a line north of Broome across to the Arafura Sea. Moreover, the new arrangements meant that they could no longer legally fish while in transit between areas permitted under the 1974 MOU (Campbell 1991: 116). But their fishing activities continued despite regular surveillance patrols, and *perahu* were routinely boarded in both the permitted areas and in other parts of the AFZ. [16] In practice, Australian authorities tolerated Indonesian shark fishing activities within the areas newly added to the AFZ throughout the 1980s, and the confiscation of boats apprehended for illegal activities did not begin until 1990.

The Ashmore Reef National Nature Reserve

Before 1978 the laws of the Northern Territory applied to Ashmore Reef and the Cartier Islands. The *Ashmore and Cartier Island Acceptance Amendment Act 1978* was passed shortly before the Northern Territory was granted self-government, and had the effect of making the islands a separate commonwealth territory under the control of the Minister for Arts, Sport, the Environment, Tourism and Territories. This was justified by the significance of the islands for Australian maritime jurisdiction (Burmester 1985) and the presence of major hydrocarbon resources in the area (Bergin 1989: 13).

In August 1983 the Ashmore Reef National Nature Reserve was declared under the Commonwealth's *National Parks and Wildlife Conservation Act 1975* to be managed by the Australian National Parks and Wildlife Service (ANPWS). This action was justified by reports that wildlife populations had been severely depleted by Indonesian fishermen acting in contravention of the 1974 MOU (ANPWS 1989: 13). Their activities were also thought to contravene Australia's international obligations under bilateral agreements with Japan and China on the protection of migratory sea birds [17] and as a signatory to the *Convention on International Trade in Endangered Species*.

The nature reserve covers an area of 583 km^2, encompassing the reef itself and surrounding waters to the 50 m bathometric (see Map 5-2). The reserve is recognised to have high nature conservation significance because of its rich and diverse marine life and a high degree of endemism due to its isolation. It is an important breeding ground for seabirds, a staging point for migratory bird populations, and a breeding and feeding habitat for endangered marine turtles (ANPWS 1989: 3).

---

[16] Patrol reports from the 1980s record the date and location of boarding, the name and origin or last port of call of the vessel, the names of the owner, captain and crew, the type of vessel; the catch and type of fishing gear, and the movements of vessel. They also indicate whether an information sheet on the 1974 MOU regulations had been given to the fishermen, and whether the crew received a warning about their fishing activities.

[17] See *Migratory Birds Ordinance of the Territory of Ashmore and Cartier Islands 1980*.

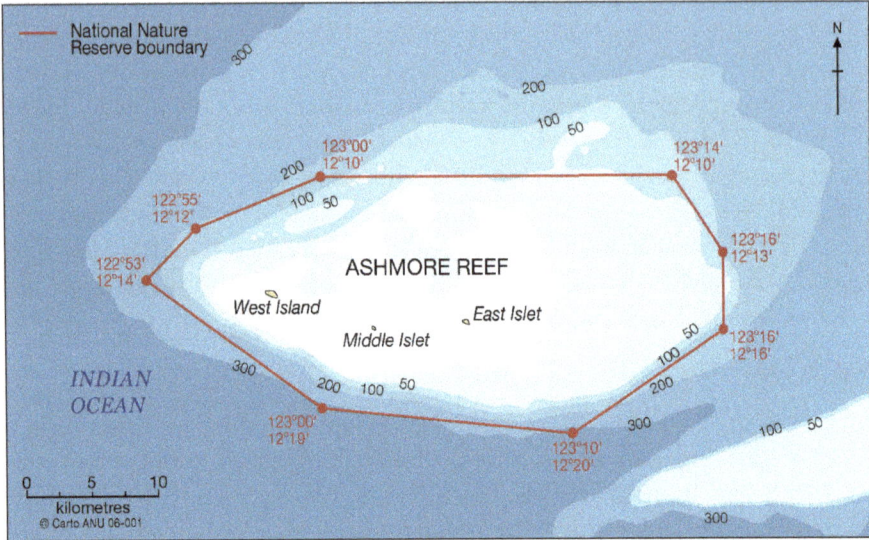

Map 5-2: Ashmore Reef National Nature Reserve.

With the declaration of the reserve, an increase in random air surveillance was instituted as part of the Civil Coastal Surveillance Program ('Coastwatch') operated by the Australian Customs Service, and regular patrols and inspections were undertaken by ANPWS and fisheries officers on navy ships or chartered boats. [18] In the ANPWS Annual Reports for the years 1983/84 and 1984/85 concerns were expressed about offences including damage to vegetation, unauthorised landings, the taking of seabirds and eggs, and the capture and killing of turtles (ANPWS 1985a, 1985b). [19]

In August 1985 a review of surveillance and law enforcement procedures at Ashmore Reef was undertaken, and the Minister for Territories announced that a significant budget increase would be granted to establish a seasonal surveillance program. In the 1985 pilot program, caretakers were based in a camp on West Island during the latter part of the fishing season with a remit to monitor Indonesian activity, warn fishermen of their responsibilities under the MOU, and prevent infringement of landing rights and the destruction of protected wildlife. For the 1986 fishing season, a chartered vessel was stationed at Ashmore Reef as a base camp for caretaking operations (ANPWS 1986: 23), while ANPWS wardens continued to operate with the assistance of RAN patrol boats, supported

[18] Officers were expected to board any Indonesian vessels in the reserve and fill out a report recording the vessel's name, type and location, the presence of a motor, the master's name and number of crew, the home port and last port of call, details of any catch on board, and the number of days fishing in the reserve. Vessels were searched for evidence of protected species, crews were given warnings and provided with notices advising of the area's reserve status (ANPWS 1985a: 15–17).

[19] It was also reported that the well on Middle Islet was contaminated with cholera (DFAT 1988: 34), but this could not necessarily be blamed on Indonesian fishermen (Bergin 1989: 15).

by additional aerial surveillance by Coastwatch, RAAF and RAN aircraft. It was at this time that comprehensive quantitative information on Indonesian voyaging and fishing activity around Ashmore Reef and other parts of the AFZ began to be collected.

In 1985/86, 85 violations of the 1974 MOU were reported and wardens searched 63 Indonesian vessels in order to ascertain the level of harvesting of marine products in the reserve. From estimated catches of trochus shell, reef fish, shark, trepang and clam meat, it was reported that although the 'crews rely on the reserve for subsistence (apart from water and rice)' the increase in the harvest of trepang recorded during the year 'may be in response to the re-opening of the markets in China rather than subsistence demand in Indonesia' (ANPWS 1986: 23–4). This statement is misleading because it implies that there was a local 'subsistence' demand for trepang, but is correct in assuming that the international market is driven by the demand for trepang in China. The statement illustrates the confused use of the term 'subsistence' and the lack of familiarity with the 'chain of custody' for certain marine products in Indonesia.

The ANPWS Annual Report for 1986/87 again reported on violations of the MOU by Indonesian fishermen and expressed concerns over the impact on bird populations. It was also stated, based on information from various patrols and surveillance of the reserve carried out that year, that the size and number of marine sedentary species was declining and that Indonesians were attempting to use 'hookah' gear (underwater breathing apparatus) to dive in the deeper waters of the reserve. The Northern Territory Museum was then commissioned to investigate the impact of Indonesian fishing activities on the reserve in order to provide the scientific evidence needed to justify a revision of the MOU (ANPWS 1987: 18).

The research consultancy report includes an analysis of *perahu* visits for the years 1986, 1987 and 1988, the results of interviews with crew of 13 *perahu*, and population data on the main marine species exploited by Indonesians based on fieldwork undertaken at Ashmore Reef in April and September 1987. The consultants considered two options for management of the marine environment: (1) a complete ban on all fishing activities; and (2) permission for a managed traditional fishery to continue (Russell and Vail 1988: 139–43). Their argument in favour of the second option was that Ashmore Reef had long been a traditional fishing ground for Indonesian fishermen, especially those from the villages of Oelaba and Pepela on Roti. [20] They said that a total ban on fishing would not only be difficult and expensive to enforce, but would also create economic hardships for the fishermen and their families. They suggested a set of

---

[20] No specific mention was made of Bajo fishermen.

management practices which would allow a traditional fishery to continue and recommended the conduct of further research.

In 1989, the ANPWS prepared its own Plan of Management for the nature reserve which came into force in December 1990 and had effect for 10 years.[21] Despite the recommendations of the consultants, the plan made no mention of allowing a traditional Indonesian fishery to operate.

> The prime objective of the Reserve is the protection of marine and terrestrial habitats and wildlife. To achieve this it is necessary to maintain so far as possible natural processes undisturbed by people (ANPWS 1989: 43).

In order to manage and protect the natural values of the reserve, contractors were to be stationed on a vessel moored at Ashmore Reef between March and December each year, and one crew member was to be appointed as a warden under the *National Parks and Wildlife Conservation Act 1975* to enforce the legislation within the reserve and inform fishermen of the regulations.[22]

Amendments to the 1974 MOU

The concerns outlined in the previous section led the Australian Government to submit a draft revision of the MOU to the Indonesian Government in August 1986 (ANPWS 1987: 18). The Indonesian Government rejected this draft in November 1987, stating its preference for more effective implementation of the existing MOU. The Indonesian Government was officially notified in February 1988 of the Australian Government's further intentions in the form of a 'Third Person Advisory Note' that outlined the developments since 1974 which made new arrangements necessary (DFAT 1988: 54–65). This included observations about the destruction of local flora and fauna by Indonesian fishermen and their use of 'non-traditional' methods of fishing.

The Indonesian Government was also informed that, as of 1 March 1988, the 1974 MOU would be enforced by Australian authorities in accordance with Australian laws, including laws related to conservation, customs and quarantine. For the Australian Government, traditional fishing did not include fishing from motorised vessels or the use of motorised fishing gear. Only fishermen in paddle-powered or wind-powered boats using lines or nets would be permitted in the MOU areas. Landing rights were withdrawn from East and Middle Islets because the wells had either dried up or were contaminated. Fishermen could only land on West Island for the purpose of obtaining water, and would be allowed safe anchorage in the channel leading to it (see Map 5-3). Fishing activity would continue to be limited to a radius of 12 nm around specified islands except

---

[21] This has since been replaced by a new plan released in June 2002 (Environment Australia 2002).
[22] The first apprehension for wildlife violations had already occurred in 1988.

at Ashmore Reef, where fishing would not be permitted inside the reserve. Any person convicted under the *Fisheries Act 1952* for taking fish or sedentary organisms outside the permitted areas could face a maximum fine of A$ 5000 or forfeiture of boat, equipment and contents. Giant clams and turtles protected under the *Convention on International Trade in Endangered Species* could no longer be taken even in the permitted areas (DFAT 1988: 54–65).

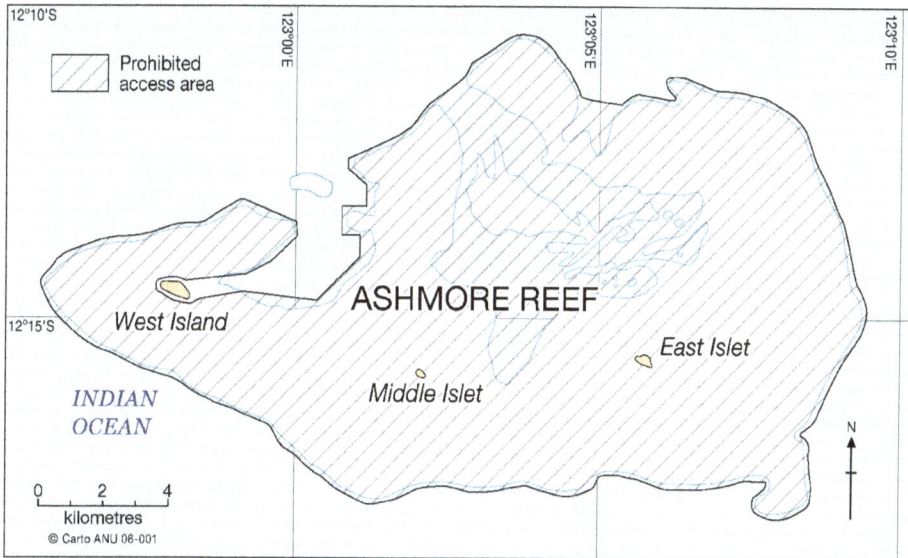

Map 5-3: Areas of prohibited access at Ashmore Reef National Nature Reserve.

During the period from 27 June to 1 July 1988, the Australian Ambassador to Indonesia visited Sulawesi and East Nusa Tenggara to inform Indonesian officials and fishermen of the new interpretation of the MOU and the ban on all fishing at Ashmore Reef (Campbell and Wilson 1993: 133). In April 1989, officials from Indonesia and Australia met in Jakarta to discuss the activities of Indonesian fishermen and review the operation of the MOU. They also discussed the activities of Indonesian fishing vessels operating in other areas of the AFZ, including 'non-traditional' vessels operating along the northwest coast and in the Arafura Sea. Following these discussions, both sides agreed to the requirements previously outlined by Australia in the Third Party Advisory Note of 1988, but allowed that 'traditional' Indonesian fishermen would be able to conduct fishing activities in a wider 'MOU box' within the AFZ (see Appendix C). Under a set of 'Practical Guidelines for Implementing the 1974 MOU', access to the expanded MOU area would continue to be limited to 'Indonesian traditional fishermen *using traditional methods and traditional vessels consistent with the tradition over decades of time, which does not include fishing methods or vessels utilising motors or engines'* (author's emphasis).

Apprehension, Detention and Confiscation, 1985–95

The Australian Government instituted a new regime to control the activities of Indonesian fishermen in the late 1980s, including specific arrangements to detain and process suspected offenders in Darwin and Broome. The key elements of this regime are still in place today.

The Australian policy response was partly motivated by a sudden increase in illegal fishing in the AFZ by a number of diverse groups of Indonesian fishermen who had not previously operated in the north Australian region. The perceived threat to Australian marine resources resulted in a policy of apprehension, forfeiture and destruction of *perahu* as a prime solution in the campaign to deter illegal activity. In the past Bajo and Pepela *perahu* found inside the AFZ had been boarded and warned but not apprehended, but these 'traditional fishermen' were now punished in the same fashion as those other fishermen who did not have a long history of fishing in the north Australian region.

The Institutional Regime

The Australian Customs Service has a mandate to provide a civil coastal and offshore surveillance and response service for a number of government agencies in order for them to carry out their portfolio responsibilities. This service is provided by a branch called Coastwatch, whose central headquarters are located in Canberra, using a variety of boats and aircraft contracted from other government agencies and private companies. In the early 1990s, the surveillance and response effort in the AFZ involved 13 privately contracted aircraft flying approximately 12 000 hours per annum, 250 hours of dedicated patrols by RAAF P3C Orion aircraft, and 1800 days of surface surveillance by RAN patrol boats (Naylor 1995: 1–4).[23]

When a suspected illegal foreign fishing boat is sighted, a report is sent to the Australian Fisheries Management Authority (AFMA) in Canberra and to regional fisheries officers in Darwin or Broome. *Perahu* found operating in Australian waters are officially classified according to 'the degree to which Western technology has influenced design' (Campbell and Wilson 1993:4). There are three main categories: Type 1 *perahu* are those with a traditional lateen rig such as *lete lete* sailed by the Madurese; Type 2 *perahu* are those with a western sailing rig, most commonly *lambo*; and Type 3 *perahu* are motorised, either with a sail and auxiliary motor (*perahu motor layar*), or with a motor only (*perahu motor*) (see Figure 5-1).[24]

---

[23] According to Campbell (1991: 61), implementation of the new policy was facilitated, if not partly motivated, by the introduction of more technologically sophisticated aircraft capable of spotting *perahu* in the outer regions of the AFZ.

[24] Type 3 includes boats or ships larger than those shown in Figure 5-1.

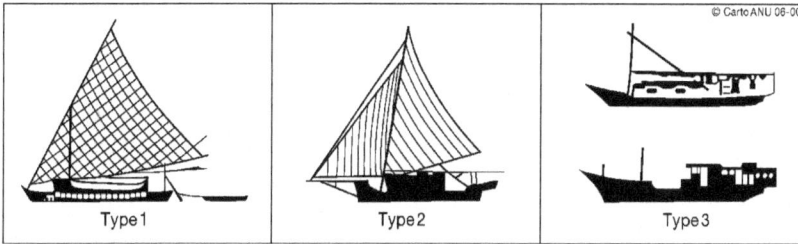

Figure 5-1: AFMA Classification of Indonesian *perahu* types found operating in Australian waters.

Source: Cowan, Mellon and Anderson 1990: 20.

The information in the sighting report is assessed to determine whether a response action is warranted. If the assessment is positive, a naval patrol boat with a fisheries officer on board is usually directed to the area. [25] The captain of the foreign vessel is questioned about his activities, often through the use of Indonesian language cards, and the fisheries officer completes a Fisheries Vessel Reporting System ('Fishreps') form and boarding report. This information is wired to Canberra for further assessment by AFMA officers and a decision is made about whether there is sufficient evidence of illegal fishing activity and whether the boat and crew should therefore be apprehended. If apprehension is approved, the captain is informed and the vessel is towed to either Darwin or Broome for further investigation and prosecution.

On arrival in either Broome or Darwin, a number of other Australian government agencies become involved in the detention, prosecution and repatriation of the fishermen. The Commonwealth provides AFMA with funds to meet the costs associated with action arising from apprehension of illegal fishing vessels, including the costs of interviewing offenders, maintaining seized vessels, housing and maintaining the crew, and court proceedings. After arrival, formal processes of immigration, health and quarantine are completed, and custody of the boat is formally transferred to AFMA. In Broome and Darwin, some of AFMA's functions, including investigations into the alleged offences, are carried out by officers of the NT and WA Fisheries Departments. The captain and crew are then charged by summons and a date is sought for the court hearing.

In Broome, the boats and fishermen are held at Willie Creek, an isolated coastal property 20 km north of the town. Boats are anchored in the bay at the mouth of the creek and fishermen are free to move between their boats and the property. The property is owned and operated by a private contractor responsible

---

[25] Under the Commonwealth *Fisheries Management Act 1991*, fisheries officers and members of the Defence Force are authorised to question and detain fishermen suspected of committing an offence under the Act.

for the care and security of the fishermen and their boats. [26] At Willie Creek, fishermen are questioned and given telephone access to the Indonesian consulate in Perth. At one stage, the WA Legal Aid Commission provided representation for the captains but did not have the resources to continue this service (Campbell and Wilson 1993: 128). AFMA supplies an interpreter used for questioning and during appearances in the Broome Magistrates Court.

Plate 5-1: The recreation building and accommodation block at Willie Creek.

In Darwin, fishermen are held on their boats anchored some 300–400 m off Stokes Hill Wharf in Darwin Harbour in a designated quarantine mooring area. Barefoot Marine, a local marine charter company under contract to AFMA, is responsible for maintaining the boats, providing security, enforcing the quarantine zone, supplying food and water to the fishermen, and transporting them to and from the shore to attend meetings, appear in court or receive medical attention if necessary. In Darwin, access to interpreters, legal aid, and support from the local Indonesian Consulate means that conditions are generally better than those available in Broome.

The period of time fishermen are detained in either Darwin or Broome depends on the judicial process. On average, this period extends for around 3–4 weeks, but in some cases fishermen have been held for much longer periods, even up to five months. In cases where fishermen have been given jail terms for repeat

---

[26] In the early 1990s the shore facilities included a small accommodation block and a partly finished recreation building (see Plate 5-1), but the fishermen generally slept on their boats.

offences they have been transferred to the Broome Regional Prison or to Berrimah Prison in Darwin. Fishermen are repatriated by plane, usually to Kupang or Denpasar (Bali), where they are sometimes met by officials from the Indonesian Social Department (Departemen Sosial) who may provide assistance for them to reach their home villages, but this service is erratic. Forfeited boats and equipment are normally burnt, but in some cases they have been sold or auctioned by AFMA.

Apprehensions in Darwin and Broome 1985–93

Although fishing outside the permitted areas in the expanded AFZ became illegal in 1979 it was six years before any vessels were apprehended. The apprehension of the first four *perahu* resulted from a surveillance program called 'Operation Roundup'.[27] On 27 February 1985, an RAAF Orion aircraft on a surveillance flight sighted 12 Type 2 Indonesian fishing vessels between 30 and 60 miles northwest of Cape Van Diemen off Melville Island in the Northern Territory. On 28 February, the HMAS Ipswich arrived in the area, and two of the boats, the Cari Damai and the Usaha Selamat, were boarded to the north of Melville Island and taken in tow to Darwin. At the time of boarding it was discovered that both vessels, each with a crew of nine, were from Wangi Wangi and had quantities of fresh and dried shark fin on board. The captain of the Usaha Selamat stated that there were up to 20 vessels from Wangi Wangi fishing in the area to the west and north. On 1 March, several Indonesian fishing vessels were spotted from the air northwest of Melville Island, and HMAS Cessnock was directed to the area. On this occasion the AFS in Darwin also chartered the MV Pacific Adventurer to assist in the search.[28] The Cessnock made visual contact with seven Indonesian vessels, one of which was boarded, but then left to pursue other vessels further north. On 2 March, the naval officers apprehended two more boats, the Tenaga Atom and the Tunas Muda, and took them in tow to rendezvous with the Pacific Adventurer.

The following is an extract from a record of the interview conducted on 6 March 1985 by a fisheries officer and an interpreter with the captain of the Usaha Selamat, Si Usman Basirang.

Q31. Do you have any knowledge of such a thing called the Australian Fishing Zone?

A31. No I don't know.

Questioning continued, and he replied:

---

[27] Information regarding the outcome of this exercise is taken from Northern Territory Apprehensions file 9005 in AFMA's Darwin office.

[28] The cost of chartering the Pacific Adventurer was A$ 1200 a day.

A39. I've been sailing from Masela Island for one night and one day. That we used to sail that length of time will still keep us in Indonesian waters therefore I don't think I have been in Australian waters.

Q40. At what speed would you think that your ship would do at the time you are talking about?

A40. I don't know the speed.

Q41. Was there a strong breeze at the time you are talking about?

A41. Yes. That's why we take some sail down.

Q42. Do you have anything else you wish to say?

A42. Therefore I don't feel guilty.

Si Usman also stated that he was from Mola and the vessel belonged to his parents. He and his crew had departed Mola on 31 January and had been catching shark over the previous seven days. They were intending to sell most of the catch back in Mola for Rp3 500 a kilogram and would eat the remainder.

The captains of the Usaha Selamat and the Cari Damai were charged with using a fishing boat for taking fish in the AFZ without a licence and appeared in Darwin Magistrates Court on 8 and 11 March 1985. The captains, represented by a solicitor from the NT Legal Aid Commission, pleaded guilty to the charges, despite Si Usman's earlier protestation of innocence. The defence gave evidence that the vessels were wooden sailing boats, had no charts or navigational gear, and only poor quality compasses. The prosecution sought an order for forfeiture of the catch and fishing gear on board the vessel, but this was opposed by the defence. Magistrate Sally Thomas ordered that the men be convicted but not fined, and since they had no means to pay, she said that she could not order forfeiture of the vessels. Instead she ordered that the fish and equipment be forfeited with the exception that the defendants be allowed to keep their canoes and enough fish and fishing equipment to provide for the sustenance of their crews on the journey back to Indonesia. [29]

The captains of the other two vessels were not charged at all, for reasons given in a telex from Coastwatch to the NT Fisheries Department dated 12 March 1985.

On information provided by Foreign Affairs, it appears that in 1981 an agreement was made with the Indonesian government that none of their boats be apprehended in a 'hot pursuit' situation. As a result of this there will be no prosecution of the second two boats Tenaga Atom and Tunas Muda that arrived in Darwin harbour on Sunday 3 March 1985.

[29] The details of this case are recorded in NT Apprehensions file 9005.

On 12 March the Pacific Adventurer towed all four vessels to the outer limit of the AFZ.[30]

In the late 1980s several waves of distinctly different groups of Indonesian vessels began operating illegally in the AFZ, leading to a dramatic increase in the number of apprehensions. This was to have a significant effect on the fishing operations of Bajo and other users of Type 2 vessels operating outside the permitted areas. Late 1987 and early 1988 saw the beginning of a wave of illegal activity by Type 3 motorised vessels (*perahu layar motor*) seeking access to trochus beds in the Kimberley region, especially at King Sound and further south at Rowley Shoals. The majority of the boats originated from islands in Southeast Sulawesi such as Maginti, Masaloka, Kadatua and Buton, with a few from Pepela, and their crews were drawn from Bajo, Butonese and Rotinese ethnic groups. Their activities were partly due to a rise in the price of trochus shell in the late 1980s coupled with the over-exploitation of the resource in Indonesian waters (Reid 1992: 4). With the exception of men from Pepela, the Butonese and Rotinese fishermen do not appear to have a long history of voyaging in the north Australian region, so this could be seen as a 'separate and discrete form of Indonesian fishing in the AFZ' (Campbell and Wilson 1993: 161).[31]

Between 1987 and 1990, 67 trochus boats were apprehended in Australian waters and taken to Broome.[32] In almost all cases, vessels, catch and equipment were confiscated and destroyed. The new policy of apprehension and forfeiture was adopted as a 'solution' to deter further incursions (JSCFADT 1993: 123). In addition, many of the captains and crew who were unable to pay fines after their convictions were jailed in Broome Regional Prison. This was also the time when the policy of burning boats at the detention site was introduced as a further deterrent (Reid 1992: 7; Campbell and Wilson 1993: 136). The sentiment at this time is expressed in a statement by the Minister for Defence, Senator Robert Ray, in a parliamentary debate on the cost of the surveillance operation.

> The boats themselves are deliberately of a very low quality so that when they are seized they cannot be sold. About the only fate for them is an annual burning and the sending of photos back to Indonesian fishing villages as a warning (Senate Weekly Hansard, 23 May 1990, p. 882).

---

[30] A fifth vessel, the Bunga Mawar, was also apprehended and towed to Darwin in the same month, but official files contain no information regarding the prosecution of the crew. The only reference is in a telex dated 19 March 1985, from the AFS in Canberra to the NT Fisheries Department, in which the latter is asked to arrange a charter vessel to escort the Bunga Mawar to the edge of the AFZ.

[31] In the mid to late 1970s, when Pepela and Bajo boats were illegally targeting trochus shell along the northwest coast, the majority were warned but not apprehended. The exception was two vessels apprehended in 1980.

[32] The first boat was apprehended in November 1987. Twenty vessels were apprehended in 1988, 16 in 1989, and 31 in 1990.

In 1991 only four trochus boats were apprehended, in 1992 none, and in 1993 another four. State fisheries officers argued that the decline was due to the newly improved surveillance and enforcement measures (JSCFADT 1993: 120), but others have suggested that it may have more to do with the declining price of trochus shell or other socio-economic factors (Campbell and Wilson 1993: 60).

In late 1988 another kind of illegal activity began in the northern Arafura Sea. Between October and November 1988, 25 large-scale, well-equipped, commercial Type 3 boats were apprehended in an area to the south of the Aru Islands. All but one originated from Dobo and all were targeting shark using large gill nets. Some of the captains and crews were wage labourers. In Darwin all captains were charged and found guilty under Sections 13AB(1a) and 13B(5) of the *Fisheries Act 1952*. Vessels, gear and catch were confiscated, two skippers were fined, and all captains were placed on good behaviour bonds (Campbell and Wilson 1993: 162–3). This group of vessels was the first of several waves of illegal activity by motorised *perahu* targeting shark fin and reef fish in the Arafura Sea (ibid.: 163).

Twenty of these industrial shark boats were apprehended in 1989 and 11 in 1990. The number fell after June 1990, and only two such boats were apprehended in 1991, but the number rose again to seven in the first half of 1992. All these boats were targeting shark except for one which was specifically targeting tuna (Campbell and Wilson 1993: 163–5). During the second half of 1992, AFMA's list of apprehensions records nine illegal incursions of 'ice boats' with similar technology targeting reef fish in an area known as the Timor Box which straddles the international border.

In November 1990, two motorised Type 3 *perahu* (*perahu motor layar*), similar in technology to the trochus boats, were apprehended for shark fishing a few miles inside the AFZ, and another 29 of this type were apprehended in March 1991. All captains were convicted, and their boats, catch and equipment were confiscated. The fishermen were either Butonese or Bajo and had come from a number of settlements and islands in South or Southeast Sulawesi, from East Nusa Tenggara, and from Dobo in the Aru Islands (Fox 1992; Stacey 1992; Campbell and Wilson 1993: 165–74). All had sailed to Dobo and then south into the AFZ where they fished for shark using longline gear. No more of these shark boats were apprehended in 1992. In the short term it appeared that the policy of forfeiture deterred further incursions (Campbell and Wilson 1993: 188), but boats like this were apprehended again in 1993 and subsequent years until 1997.

Around the same time as large numbers of trochus boats were being intercepted on the northwest coast, three Type 2 *perahu* were apprehended for violating the amended MOU in the permitted areas. On 19 May 1988, an unmotorised *perahu lambo*, the Karya Sama, with seven crew originating from the village of Suoi, opposite Pepela on Roti, was apprehended at Ashmore Reef

National Nature Reserve. The crew had been killing seabirds and collecting eggs on East Islet, which was now a protected area. In order to deter further infringements, the ANPWS recommended confiscation of the boat rather than confiscation of the catch or jail sentences. The captain and crew were placed on a good behaviour bond of A$ 50 for two years, the crew were repatriated, and the vessel was forfeited and later donated by the ANPWS to the Northern Territory Museum (Stacey 1997). [33]

In early July 1988 two *perahu*, the Cahaya Indah and the Alam Niaga, both from Pepela, were apprehended while fishing for trepang and trochus shell around Scott Reef and were escorted to Broome. Both Type 2 vessels had been equipped with auxiliary engines and therefore failed the new definition of a 'traditional' fishing boat. Both captains were convicted and their vessels, catch and equipment were confiscated. [34] Since that time, most Pepela and Bajo fishermen have largely complied with the 'no engine' rule in the MOU areas.

On 29 March 1990, two more Bajo *perahu*, the Kenangan Indah and the Rahmat Ilahi 2, were boarded some 20–30 nm north of Maret Island in the Bonaparte Archipelago off the Kimberley coast. [35] The local fisheries officer found that the crews had been shark fishing with handlines and shark rattles (**goro goro**). Both vessels had fresh and dried quantities of shark fin and shark flesh on board, along with reef fish for bait. The captain of the Kenangan Indah, Si Samading, had left Kaledupa with his seven crew members on 15 March, while the captain and owner of Rahmat Ilahi 2, Si La Ibu, had left Wanci with seven crew on 20 February. Both had sailed to Roti before departing to Ashmore Reef. The local official recommended a severe reprimand and warning, but AFS officials in Canberra were adamant that the vessels should be apprehended and transported to Broome. Both captains pleaded guilty to charges under Sections 13AB(1) and 13B(1A) of the Commonwealth *Fisheries Act 1952* and were placed on two-year good behaviour bonds of A$ 2000 each. The vessels, catch and equipment were forfeited and the fishermen repatriated to Indonesia. These were the first Bajo vessels to be confiscated for illegal fishing activity in the AFZ even though *perahu* had been operating outside the permitted areas for years. The forfeiture of the two *perahu* in 1990 represented a change in the treatment of Type 2 vessels found operating outside the permitted areas. By this time the policy of apprehension and confiscation of illegal motorised fishing boats was well established in both Broome and Darwin. The decision of the court in Broome to confiscate these two unmotorised vessels was influenced by the large number of apprehensions and

---

[33] The Karya Sama is held in the ethnographic watercraft collection of the Museum and is on display in the Boat Shed Gallery.
[34] The episode is recorded in WA Fisheries Department files 16/88 and 17/88 (see also Campbell and Wilson 1993: 132–3).
[35] This episode is recorded in WA Fisheries Department files 40/90 and 41/90.

confiscations of trochus boats and other *perahu* operating illegally in the AFZ over the previous three years (Campbell and Wilson 1993: 160).

From conversations with WA fisheries officers, Campbell and Wilson (1993: 179) state that *perahu* which had been engaged in shark fishing for many years in the Timor Sea did 'not constitute a serious problem' when Australia increased its AFZ to 200 nm since the vessels remained well out to sea. Fisheries officers generally tolerated shark boats operating between the coast and the MOU areas, and in most cases boats were only warned if found operating too far from the permitted areas. This point is supported by boarding reports which show a pattern of repeated visits by many of the same Bajo *perahu*, both inside and outside the permitted areas, in successive years between 1979 and 1989. [36] Regular contact with Australian authorities generally did not end in apprehension, and even if vessels were apprehended, they were not confiscated. However, this unofficial tolerance ended in 1990 when the AFS took a stricter approach to illegal fishing by Type 2 vessels.

On 5 October 1990 another *perahu* from Mola, the Wisma Jaya, was located approximately 20 nm northwest of Troughton Island off the Kimberley coast. Once again, at the time of apprehension, the crew were found to be engaged in shark fishing using handlines and shark rattles (see Plate 5-2). The captain, Si Kaboda, pleaded guilty to charges under Sections 13B(5) and 13AB(1A) of the *Fisheries Act 1952*, was convicted on both counts and placed on a 12-month good behaviour bond of A$ 500. On 13 October, the Usaha Selamat, previously apprehended in 1985, was boarded approximately 15 nm west of Bathurst Island and found to contain 200–300 kilograms of shark fin and shark flesh as well as handlines and shark rattles. The captain, Si Usman Basirang, pleaded guilty, was convicted and placed on a three-year good behaviour bond of A$ 200. In both cases, the vessels, catch and gear were forfeited and the shark fin was sold by public tender. The Wisma Jaya was deemed to be in poor condition, valued at A$ 800, and recommended for destruction, whereas the Usaha Selamat was deemed to be in fair condition, valued at A$ 1200, and recommended for use by the RAN to train naval boarding parties. [37]

---

[36] From 1981 the reports begin to use the labels 'shark fishermen' or 'shark boat' to refer to Bajo *perahu* from Mola and Mantigola.

[37] The details of these cases are recorded in NT Apprehensions files 9004 and 9005.

Plate 5-2: Navy officers inspecting the catch of the Wisma Jaya, 1990.

Source: Western Australian Fisheries Department.

One year later, in October 1991, five more *perahu* from Mola — the Sinar Jaya, Kota Alam, Asean, Toyota, and Suka Damai — were apprehended and taken to Darwin. All were targeting shark using handlines and shark rattles in an area north of Joseph Bonaparte Gulf and west of Bathurst Island, from about 38 nm to 97 nm inside the AFZ. This time the captains were each placed on a 12-month good behaviour bond of A$ 200 and all the boats were burnt except for the Toyota, which was sold to a Darwin restaurateur. [38]

On 20 March 1992, three more *perahu* from Mola — the Jaya Harapan, Usaha Baru (Green), and Usaha Baru (Blue) — were located approximately 2 nm inside the AFZ by a RAAF P3 Orion aircraft on a surveillance flight that was part of an Australian military exercise known as 'Kangaroo 92'. On 23 March, during a surveillance sweep as part of the same exercise, HMAS Cessnock and HMAS Derwent encountered the three boats about 22 nm inside the AFZ with lines set in the water. One *perahu* was boarded and the crew were warned, whereupon all three recovered their lines, hoisted sail and proceeded north. Later that day, the naval ships were ordered to relocate the vessels and carry out another investigation of the boats with a view to apprehension. The vessels were boarded at a position approximately 15 nm inside the AFZ, north of Bathurst and Melville islands. The Usaha Baru (Green) was found to have 10 kg of dried fish, 10 kg of

[38] The details of these cases are recorded in NT Apprehensions files 9131–9135.

shark fin and 5 kg of fresh whole shark, as well as a small longline with 37 hooks. The Usaha Baru (Blue) had 25 kg of shark flesh, 15 kg of fresh shark fin and a fresh whole shark, with three lines set. The Jaya Harapan had 2 kg of fresh fish on board and two lines set. The boats were apprehended and towed to Darwin.[39]

This time the captains were charged under Sections 100(2) and 101(2) of the *Fisheries Management Act 1991*, which had superceded the *Fisheries Act 1952*. Unlike the previous trials in 1990 and 1991, the fishermen pleaded not guilty to the charges and their case was strongly defended by a Legal Aid lawyer who argued that the boats had been becalmed and carried south into the AFZ by a strong current. [40] The longlines extending from the *perahu* at the time of boarding were said to be drag-anchors intended to stop the boats from drifting further inside the AFZ and the shark were said to have been caught while they were still in Indonesian waters. Based on the precedent from 1985, the defence also argued that the crew were only fishing for food to stay alive, the amount of catch was not significant enough to warrant forfeiture of the vessels, and forfeiture would result in severe economic hardships for the crews and their families. The captains were convicted and placed on two-year good behaviour bonds of A$ 1000 each, but the magistrate agreed that the offences were not serious enough to warrant forfeiture of the vessels. Instead, he ordered forfeiture of the longlines, hooks, floats, shark rattles and one canoe from each *perahu*, while allowing the fishermen keep their handlines so they could fish for subsistence on the journey back to their village (Fox 1998: 133).

The same consideration was not afforded the crews of nine Type 2 *perahu* apprehended and taken to Darwin between September and November 1993. [41] In September 1993, six *perahu* from Pepela — the Titian Muhibah, Bintang Selamat, Tegal Baru, Usaha Remaja, Sari Idaman I, and Sari Idaman II — were apprehended while fishing for shark fin with longline gear. Most had been warned previously. Five of the cases were heard together, and all five captains pleaded guilty to charges under Sections 100(2) and 101(2) of the *Fisheries Management Act 1991*. During the court hearing the prosecution valued the catch of shark fin in each boat at between US$ 2000 and US$ 4000. This was the first time such a high value had been placed on a shark fin catch and the prosecution did not state how the figure had been calculated. In the case of the Sari Idaman I, whose case was heard later that month, the same prosecutor then stated that shark fin was currently fetching US$ 50/kg dried weight. Since the Tegal Baru had a forfeited catch of only 19 kg of semi-dried shark fin, the sale price of its catch would have been US$ 950 — significantly less than the US$ 3000 value quoted in the earlier court case. However, the presiding magistrate was

[39] The details of these cases are recorded in NT Apprehensions files 9205–9207.
[40] The lawyer was briefed by a number of local Darwin sailors, some of whom had owned Indonesian built *perahu* or even visited Mola.
[41] The details of these cases are recorded in NT Apprehensions files 9302–9310.

moved to observe that Australia had to 'protect its fishing grounds from foreign exploitation since the fishing industry yields large profits' and that 'forfeiture is the only solution ... [for] if forfeiture was not imposed, others will follow'. All equipment, catch and vessels were confiscated, four of the captains were placed on five-year good behaviour bonds of A$ 5000; one on a 12-month bond of A$ 2000, and one on a bond of A$ 200. The vessels themselves were assigned values of between zero and A$ 500 and all of them were burnt (see Plates 5-3, 5-4, 5-5 and 5-6).

Three other *perahu* apprehended shortly afterwards received similar treatment. Two of them — the Kembang Sari and the Dasar Usaha — originated from Lasilimu in south Buton and Ereke in north Buton respectively, and both contained mixed Bajo and Butonese crews. The third one, the Alam Baru, was the first boat from Oelaba on Roti Island to be apprehended in the AFZ. Boats from Oelaba were known to have fished for sedentary species in the past, but some crews had now turned their hand to shark fishing. Mr Hannon, the magistrate presiding over this case, remarked: 'give them an inch and they take a mile — that's what they're doing'.

At no time during the court proceedings against the captains and crew of the Bajo and Pepela *perahu* was reference made to the fact that some of these fishermen were operating under the terms and conditions of the 1974 MOU and could be considered to be 'Indonesian traditional fishermen'. Although their vessels had no engines and the shark fin catch was relatively small, they were treated in the same fashion as the crew of a large industrial motorised fishing vessel using sophisticated navigation equipment with an ability to harvest significant catches. In the brief of evidence for the case of the Usaha Selamat in 1990, the only reference made to the MOU was in regard to the position of the *perahu* at the time of its apprehension. This was also the case with three Bajo *perahu* that were apprehended and allowed to sail home in 1992.

> At no time in the legal proceeding was any attention given to the Bajau as a specific population with the longest historically documented evidence of fishing in the Australian Fishing Zone. Nor were the Bajau distinguished from any other Indonesian fishermen. And even if this were to have been noted, it would have had no bearing on the case in terms of the Fisheries Act. A historical perception of the problem was irrelevant (Fox 1998: 134).

Plate 5-3: Bajo crew confined to their *perahu lambo* in Darwin Harbour.

Plate 5-4: Confiscated *perahu lambo* driven into the embankment in Darwin.

Plate 5-5: Boats dragged out of the water onto the land.

Plate 5-6: Boats destroyed by burning.

Policy Reviews in the Mid-1990s

In the short term, it appeared that the new policy regime had been effective in deterring further incursions by Type 3 vessels because there was an overall decline in the number of apprehensions by 1993. However, from 1993 onwards there was a steady increase in the number of Type 2 and Type 3 vessels apprehended in the AFZ each year, despite the fact that nearly all apprehensions resulted in the confiscation of vessels, catch and gear.

In 1993 the Joint Standing Committee on Foreign Affairs, Defence and Trade published the results of its inquiry into Australia's bilateral relationship with Indonesia, noting that 'the inquiry had its origins in concerns about illegal fishing off the north and north west coast of Australia' (JSCFADT 1993: xxvii). The committee found that illegal Indonesian fishing for shark or trochus in Australian waters was driven by two main factors — the 'monetary gain from a successful voyage which could amount to two or three months income for poor fishermen' and the 'resource depletion in Indonesian waters' — but it also noted that 'the general lack of development and a poor range of alternative occupations in Eastern Indonesia' was a further contributing factor (ibid.: 128). The committee observed that:

> illegal fishermen are Indonesian nationals and there are limits to the actions the Australian government can take. It is the Indonesian Government's responsibility to attempt to prevent nationals from fishing illegally in Australian waters (ibid.: 129).

Nevertheless:

> if there are deficiencies in some aspects of Australia's handling of the problem of illegal fishing they were probably caused in part by a lack of knowledge about complex social and economic situations in eastern Indonesia (ibid.).

In the committee's view, the 1974 MOU 'does not adequately deal with all categories of Indonesian fishermen' and it would be 'appropriate to reconsider all aspects of illegal fishing with the involvement of Indonesian authorities' (ibid.: 131). Following a submission by Bruce Campbell and Bu Wilson, the committee recommended a review of the MOU in light of the Torres Strait Treaty (between Australia and Papua New Guinea) which would pay special regard to:

> the definition of 'traditional' fishermen to provide broader categories which take account of a wider range of nautical, cultural and historical factors ... [and an] examination of the feasibility of a re-negotiation of the MOU to ensure the allowed areas coincide as far as practicable with historical fishing patterns (ibid.).

None of the committee's recommendations have been implemented since its report was published in November 1993. Instead, Australian policy has continued to focus on a high level of marine and air surveillance of the northern AFZ combined with costly apprehension and prosecution procedures.

In November 1994, the Fisheries Resources Branch of the Bureau of Rural Sciences, then part of the Commonwealth Department of Primary Industries and Energy, was commissioned by the department's Fisheries Policy Branch to undertake a review of Indonesian fishing activity in the AFZ. This was done in response to concerns raised by AFMA and the domestic fishing industry in northern Australia over the possibility that Indonesian fishing vessels may account for a substantial proportion of the recommended allowable catch for some target species. The review found that 'there are different ethnic groups [from Indonesia], fishing in different areas, using a number of methods and a range of technologies' (Wallner and McLoughlin 1995a: 13), and described a number of alternative strategies to deal with traditional Indonesian fishermen operating in the MOU area. Without making reference to any particular group of Indonesian fishermen, the authors concluded that current illegal Indonesian fishing activity has a minor impact on the marine environment and that 'it would appear surveillance, enforcement and prosecution efforts have been effective in minimising illegal fishing activity' in the AFZ (Wallner and McLoughlin 1995a: 32, 1995b: 121). However, they also suggested that the management of marine resources in the MOU area should be determined by granting 'priority access rights' in the form of licences to 'fishers who can demonstrate an historic interest in these waters' (Wallner and McLoughlin 1995a: 33).

The authors of this report may have overestimated the effectiveness of existing surveillance and prosecution efforts, because the number of illegal intrusions into the AFZ rose again in 1994. This prompted the formation of a joint government delegation to undertake an information and education campaign in a number of eastern Indonesian provinces in January 1995. [42] The purpose of this exercise was to explain the conditions under which traditional fishing was permitted in the AFZ and increase awareness of the consequences of illegal fishing (AFMA 1995: 63–4). During the visit several thousand information handouts and maps were distributed showing the maritime jurisdictions in the Timor and Arafura Seas. There were also preliminary discussions about Australian support for small-scale development assistance programs in fishing communities. [43]

In 1995, the Commonwealth Government established an inter-departmental committee to investigate the problem of illegal Indonesian fishing in the AFZ

---

[42] The delegation comprised senior government officials from the Australian Embassy in Jakarta, the Northern Territory branch of AFMA, and the Indonesian Directorate General of Fisheries (Direktorat Jenderal Perikanan).

[43] Two representatives from Mola attended meetings held in Kendari and Bau Bau in Southeast Sulawesi, and some representatives from Pepela attended a meeting was held at Ba'a on Roti Island.

and recommend solutions to it. Although this committee received one paper outlining a licensing arrangement for 'traditional fishermen' (see Fox 1998), there appears to have been no further consideration of current research by social scientists on issues previously raised by the Joint Standing Committee, despite calls by academics for ethnographic research into the social, economic and cultural organisation of fishing groups operating inside Australian waters (Campbell and Wilson 1993: 191).[44]

[44] At the World Fisheries Congress held in Brisbane in 1996, Bob Johannes remarked that 'social science is clearly still considered beyond the pale by many senior Australian fisheries researchers and managers despite the burgeoning literature on the subject and growing demonstration of its practical value' (Johannes 1996: 20).

Chapter 6: Bajo Responses to Australian Policy

During the period of developments in Australian responses to Indonesian fishing activity during the 1970s and 1980s, Bajo continued to operate both inside and outside the permitted zones. During that time surveillance patrols and repeated boardings of Indonesian *perahu* by Australian officials had little effect in deterring continued shark fishing operations in the prohibited offshore areas along the continental shelf. While shark was the main product sought after by the majority of Bajo *perahu*, at certain times they pursued other marine products including reef fish, trochus shell and turtle shell. However, the collection of valuable sedentary products such as trochus and turtle shell ceased with an increase in Australian surveillance and enforcement and eviction of fishermen from the northwest coast in the 1970s.

Bajo and Pepelan perceptions of the reasons for policy developments that resulted in their loss of access to certain fishing grounds during the 1970s show that Indonesian fishermen do not understand sophisticated Western principles concerning the need for border, customs and quarantine regimes, scientific notions of the need for resource management, or developments in international maritime law. The Bajo and other ethnic fisher groups in eastern Indonesia do not have a deliberate disregard for the law but, from their perspective, laws and regulations are meaningless if they restrict access to resources upon which their livelihood depends.

The recollections and personal experiences of men from Mola, Mantigola and Pepela who were part of the Bajo fishing fleets that accessed the Timor and Arafura seas in 1994 provide the evidence to support an argument that the official Australian perspective on the nature and extent of shark fishing is flawed. This group of 31 men, aged between 30 and 60 years, born in either Mantigola or Mola, were *perahu* owners and/or captains or senior crew members in 1994. The men were interviewed about when they first went sailing to the north Australian region, and particularly of their shark fishing activities during the 1970s. Many had first sailed to the Australian region in the late 1960s and early 1970s. A few of the older men had even sailed to offshore reefs and islands in the Timor Sea to catch reef fish in the 1950s and 1960s. For some of them, Australia has been the main destination for distant shore seasonal voyaging since they were old enough to sail. Bajo narratives also show that some of the Australian Government's attempts to educate and inform fishermen have been misguided.

The Growing Focus on Sharks

According to the Bajo, shark fin became the main product sought during the late 1960s and early 1970s when market prices in China and Southeast Asia rose in response to growing consumer demand. Twenty-eight men recall undertaking shark fishing voyages in the Timor and Arafura seas between 1969 and 1979, and for some, this was the first time they went sailing to Australia. Two of their accounts indicate the patterns and motivations for shark fishing at the time.

In 1970 we started fishing for shark because there was a price for it in Ujung Pandang. Between 1970 and 1975 we sold the fin to a trader in Ujung Pandang named Johnny Goh who had a shop near the harbour. Then in 1977, the boss started to buy the fin directly from Mola through Haji Djunaedy and some other *haji* in Mola. In those times we only needed a capital [*perongkosan*] of Rp 1–200 000 and the interest rate was only 2.5 per cent. In 1975, when the borders were still open, some Pepela people started to fish for shark and joined the Mola men. Before that Pepela people fished for trochus and trepang. We sold the fin in Mola until 1988–89 then we started to sell the fin in Pepela. It is better to sell the fin in Pepela because we can go out more times. If we have to sail to Ujung Pandang we can only go out once a season (Si Kaharra, Mola Selatan).

I first sailed to Australia in 1969. In the early 1970s we sold shark fin to traders in Ujung Pandang. This meant we could only sail once in a season. The price was Rp 1500 per kilogram for *potong biasa* [crude cut with some meat still attached]. When we arrived in Ujung Pandang, we dropped anchor and the traders would come to our *perahu*, ask what we had to sell, and give us coffee, sugar, and cigarettes. Later the boss would come out and buy the fin and pay us straight away. We still used shark rattles and handlines then. There were no borders and we caught a lot of shark, sometimes 400–600 kilograms, sometimes as much as 1 tonne. Usually, after selling the fin we obtained Rp 2–3 000 000 to share. The cost of the voyage was not much then, only about Rp 2–300 000 and each crew member only had to put in Rp 25 000 towards the cost of the voyage. In about 1974, Haji Djunaedy started providing the capital to cover the cost of the voyage, so we sold the shark to him in Mola, not in Ujung Pandang any more. This continued until the late 1980s and early 1990s. Then we started to sell the shark in Pepela. But during this time, some Bajo still sold the shark in Ujung Pandang or Bau Bau because the price of shark fin was always higher in Ujung Pandang (Si Nasir, Mola Selatan).

During the east monsoon (from April to November) Bajo departed from Mola and Mantigola in their *perahu lambo* and sailed to Pepela where they would take on extra supplies and wait for suitable wind conditions to sail south to fish around the reefs and islands in the Timor Sea and along the shallow waters of the continental shelf off the northwest coast of the Australian mainland. These shallow waters are known as *air putih* (white waters) and are considered to be very productive shark fishing grounds. They stretch from northwest of Cape Leveque and around Adele Island across to Holothuria Banks, and to the northeast and east of Ashmore Reef along the Sahul Banks (see Map 6-1). In order to reach fishing grounds along the Kimberley coast, *perahu* would navigate by means of beacons located on some of the islands in the Timor Sea or on the mainland along the Kimberley coast. At the end of a fishing expedition they sometimes travelled back through Pepela to replenish supplies or exchange dried strips of salted shark meat (**balur**) for lontar palm sugar (*gula air*) before sailing to Mola or Mantigola or to other towns or cities in eastern Indonesia to sell the catch.

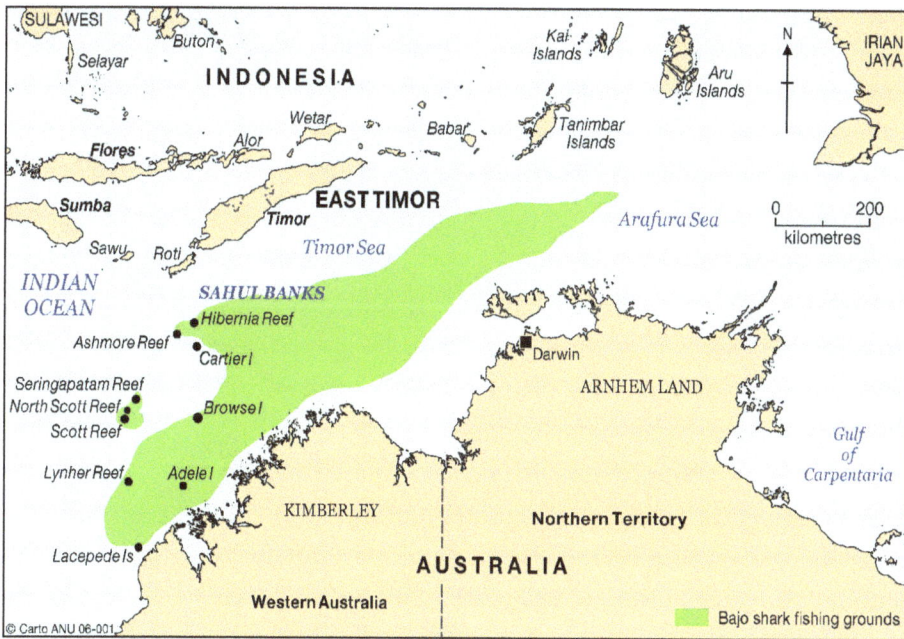

Map 6-1: Bajo shark fishing grounds.

During the west monsoon, especially during periods of light wind conditions in February and March, shark fishing expeditions focused on the eastern part of the Timor Sea and western part of the Arafura Sea. Although voyages at this time of year were never as regular or frequent as during the east monsoon, the end of the west monsoon is ideal for fishing. This period of light variable winds and smooth seas, known as the doldrums in English literature, is often interrupted by short intermittent squalls and possible cyclonic activity, and during these periods *perahu* would make for sheltered islands for protection.

During the west monsoon, vessels departing from Mola first sailed to one of the islands located off the eastern tip of Timor or to Selaru Island in the southern Tanimbar group. From here they would sail south, drifting and fishing along the Sahul Banks and shallow waters of the continental shelf lying to the north of Bathurst Island. Some also went from the Tukang Besi Islands to Dobo in the Aru Islands and from there sailed south to fish the waters north of the Gulf of Carpentaria (see Map 6-1). The boats would then travel back through the Banda Sea with the first of the southeast monsoon winds, usually in April. Bajo *perahu* apprehended and taken to Darwin in 1985 and 1992 were caught during shark fishing voyages in the Arafura Sea at the end of the west monsoon.

Occasionally some vessels also sailed to Pepela during the west monsoon and from there undertook short voyages, depending on the wind conditions, to fish around the reefs and islands in the Timor Sea. Three Bajo *perahu* apprehended off the Kimberley coast in 1975 and two apprehended and taken to Broome in March 1990 had followed this pattern. The distance between fishing grounds and trade centres, and the dependence on prevailing wind conditions, meant that until the late 1980s *perahu* would normally sail and fish just once during the east or west monsoon seasons. The duration of time spent fishing was variable and depended on both supplies and weather conditions. A trip could be between three to eight weeks, with longer periods spent fishing during the calmer months of the east monsoon.

Voyages were financed by complex credit arrangements. Financial capital, including the cost of provisioning vessels with firewood, water, rice and money for the families during the men's absence, was usually obtained in Mola or Mantigola. The capital came from the fishermen themselves, their extended family, moneylenders or village traders in marine products. The cost of a typical shark fishing expedition was around Rp 1–300 000, depending on the number of crew. Upon return, the shark fin was sold to traders in Mola, Ujung Pandang or Bau Bau, or sometimes to traders in Kupang, Ambon or Dobo, depending on the time of year. The cost of the voyage and provisions was taken out of the money made from the sale of the fin. The remainder was divided between the *perahu* owner and crew, with the owner of the *perahu* receiving three shares and each crew member one share.

It is difficult to ascertain specific prices for shark fin since they depended on the quality and type of fin and where it was sold. While Si Nasir stated that the price of shark fin was Rp 1500/kg in Ujung Pandang in the early 1970s, Si Goseng, a Bajo man living permanently in Pepela since the late 1980s, said that he received Rp 600/kg in 1971, but by 1974 the price had risen to Rp 1200/kg, and in 1987 he received Rp 15 000/kg. Si Sabaruddin stated that in 1979 he and his crew received Rp 25 000/kg in Mola. Si Acing, who went shark fishing for the first time in 1970, said that after a shark fishing trip in 1979, where he and his crew caught 400 kg of shark fin, they sold the catch in Ambon at Rp 6500/kg. Usman, the captain of the Usaha Selamat who was apprehended in 1985, stated in the Record of Interview that he expected to receive Rp 3500/kg for shark fin in Mola. These diverse responses, although dependent on a range of variables, indicate a gradual rise in the price of shark fin over time.

Between the 1960s and the 1980s, fishermen from Pepela also fished in the Timor Sea and off the northwest coast, but generally kept to the islands and reefs where they concentrated on collecting sedentary marine products and reef fish. Interaction between Bajo and Pepela fishermen meant that some Pepela fishermen adopted the Bajo shark fishing techniques using handlines and rattles. They also engaged in shark fishing around the reefs and islands in the permitted areas around Ashmore Reef (Russell and Vail 1988).

During the early 1970s, as well as shark fishing, some Bajo from Mola and Mantigola embarked on voyages to the Kimberley region along the northwest coast to harvest trochus shell and turtle shell. In the late 1960s the price of trochus began to rise due to a depletion of stocks in Indonesia and other parts of the world and to growing demand from button and paint manufacturers (Campbell and Wilson 1993: 43). During the years from 1971 to 1975, a number of *perahu* from Mola embarked on voyages to collect trochus shell at Yampi Sound, King Sound, Adele Island and Cape Leveque. [1] Their crews recall encounters with Australian naval patrol ships, having their *perahu* boarded and searched, being questioned, told to return to Indonesia, and even having their catch of trochus dumped overboard. For the Bajo, this period marked the beginning of increasing contact with Australian authorities.

> I met a patrol ship at Yampi, but they did not apprehend us, only ordered us to return home. There, I was looking for trochus. At that time, during the 1970s, there were hundreds of *perahu*, many of them went too close to the coast. They were spotted by aircraft. In 1975, there were lots of patrol boats. I remember one Bajo being hit on the shoulder by one of the officers (Si Badolla, Mola Selatan).

Si Ntole (from Mola Selatan) and his crew were fishing for shark fin in the Timor Sea in 1974 but during strong winds the unmotorised *perahu* was blown off course. The boat ended up at a reef further east near the Australian coast and there the crew discovered a large population of hawksbill turtles. Taking the opportunity over a few days, the crew captured a large number of turtles,

---

[1] Si Kaharra collected trochus in 1972 at Cape Leveque. Si Nasir visited Yampi Sound and Adele Island to collect trochus in 1971. Others, including Si Badolla, Si Usman, Si Kati, Si Hasim, Si Goseng and Si Nurdin, also speak of trochus collecting in the period 1972–76. Most men recall collecting trochus only once or twice during a trip while they continued to fish for shark as well. A *perahu* could undertake a voyage to King Sound to collect trochus shell and, on its return journey north, might fish for shark fin for a few days.

the shell was sold in Mola, and the crew made a large profit. Word of Si Ntole's success spread throughout the village. After obtaining directions on the location of the reef from the original crew, a number of boats left Mola in August that year. One was a *perahu lambo* owned by Si Usman from Mola Utara, and another was a motorised *perahu* owned by Haji Djunaedy from Mola Selatan. After calling in at Pepela, both *perahu* encountered strong winds while sailing south. Haji Djunaedy and his crew turned back. Si Usman and his crew, unperturbed by the weather, kept going but ended up at King Sound from where they slowly sailed east before finally locating the reef. Over one week they collected one tonne of turtle shell, then sailed to Ujung Pandang and sold it, making a small fortune. This enabled Si Usman to buy a motorised *perahu* and a few years later make the *haj* to Mecca. Haji Djunaedy, after waiting for the wind to die down, set off again from Pepela, located the reef and also collected a substantial amount of turtle shell.[2] The reef in question is Holothuria Reef, now known to the Bajo as **Sapa Ntole** (Ntole's Reef).

Another area where turtles were collected was a large reef located in Yampi Sound. According to Si Kariman, the reef was first 'discovered' by Si Darisa, from Mola Selatan, who named the reef Karang Bebek (Duck Reef) because the shape resembles that of a duck.

> When I visited Karang Bebek in the 1970s we caught a lot of turtle and filled the entire *perahu* with shell. We also met *orang* Marege [Aboriginal people] at the reef and we gave them some turtle meat. They were also catching turtles but not using the same method as us (Si Kariman, Mola Selatan).

With the increase in Australian surveillance and enforcement measures from 1974 onwards, including Operation Trochus in 1975 and 1976, trochus and turtle shell harvesting by Bajo along the Kimberley coast appears to have largely ceased. However, this only meant that shark fishing in the permitted areas and along the Sahul Shelf became more important.

---

[2] The Broome Historical Museum contains two interesting photographs taken from this period. One is in a file entitled 'Indonesian Illegal Fishing' and the other is framed and hanging in the front room of the museum. The first photograph is captioned 'Malcolm Douglas with Indonesian fishermen from four boats off our shores in 1974'. Malcolm Douglas is a local Broome resident who runs the crocodile farm at Cable Beach. The photograph shows Douglas in the foreground leaning on a dugout canoe with at least six other canoes in the background containing 14 fishermen. One of the fishermen is wearing a hat typically made and worn by Bajo people. The other photograph (Plate 6-1) is a close-up of a man sitting in a canoe. It was taken at a location off the top end of Montgomery Reef (east of Koolum Island) in the Kimberley region. The caption reads 'Indonesian fishermen located by Malcolm Douglas 1974'. The man in the photograph is easily recognised as La Toke, from Mola Selatan, who was a crew member on the *perahu* owned by Haji Djunaedy. La Toke was also a crew member on the Sumber Bahagia in 1994.

Plate 6-1: A Mola Bajo fisherman photographed in August 1974.

Source: Broome Historical Museum (photograph courtesy of Malcolm Douglas).

Bajo Perceptions of Australian Policy

When Bajo speak of the period between 1920 and the early 1970s, it is remembered as a time of relative freedom (*dulu bebas*) to fish in the Timor Sea. For example:

> In the past, it was open [*bebas*], we were not disturbed, in fact when we met with Australian navy or oil rig workers they gave us food and water but this is not the case now (Si Kariman, Mola Selatan).

But when Bajo speak about fishing in Australian waters since the 1974 Memorandum of Understanding, they commonly say '*nanti sekarang dilarang*' ('now it is forbidden').

The Mola Bajo understanding of the new restrictions on their fishing activities and landing rights differs from the official Australian point of view. They commonly say it is because other people — namely the Madurese and Pepelans — had broken into, vandalised and damaged buildings and store rooms on various islands in the past, and because of similar acts on the islets at Ashmore Reef, this area was also closed to fishing.

> After the time of the plane [1936], it was still all right for the Bajo to fish, even if we met with patrol boats we were still permitted to fish [*masih bebas*] at Ashmore Reef, Scott Reef, Adele Island and Rowley Shoals. But now the area is guarded and we were not allowed to fish there any more because of thieves. The Madurese people in *perahu lete lete* broke into the buildings, destroyed the inside and stole things, which ended in a serious result. If they hadn't done this we would have been allowed to continue fishing. At that time I encountered the patrol ship number 0090. On the ship was an interpreter, a Malaysian. He told me the reason we were not allowed to fish there any more. He said Indonesians are thieves. He said the buildings contained supplies, like water and food for people that are in trouble and had a shortage. He said 'don't break into the buildings and don't take anything'. Just imagine if they hadn't wrecked the buildings we would still be allowed to search for fish, trochus and shark (Si Badolla, Mola Selatan).

> The Pepela people broke into the buildings, took things, and Australia was angry (Si Idrus, Mola Utara).

> The Raas people destroyed storerooms on the islands, that's why we can't fish there any more (Si Hasmin, Pepela).

During the 1960s and 1970s, there were a number of reported acts of vandalism by Indonesian fishermen against Australian weather stations and store rooms on islands including West Islet at Ashmore Reef, Scott Reef, Browse

Island, Adele Island and Rowley Shoals. The following example is contained in the Ashmore Reef Plan of Management:

> An automatic weather station was erected on West Island in 1962. By 1970 all equipment had been stolen and the inner walls removed. The station was refurbished in 1971 but pilfering and vandalism again resulted in the destruction of the station. It was abandoned in 1973 (ANPWS 1989: 13).

On 17 August 1977, in reply to a question in the House of Representatives debate concerning the text of the sign erected at Ashmore Reef in 1975, the then Minister of Primary Industry, Mr Sinclair, read out the English-language version of the sign. Points 5 and 6 declared:

> You must not interfere with the automatic weather stations on Ashmore Island, Scott Reef, Browse Island, Rowley Shoals, Adele Island. Indonesian fishermen found anywhere in possession of material suspected of having been taken from those automatic weather stations are liable to be prosecuted in Australian courts. There is no food or water in any of the automatic weather stations. If you try to enter them they will send a radio message to Australia and the Royal Australian Navy will come to investigate.
>
> Unless you are shipwrecked, you must not take food from the food dumps left by Australia on the islands. If you are not shipwrecked and take the food, you could cause people who have truly been shipwrecked to die of starvation (DFAT 1988: 15).

In a House of Representatives debate on 19 November 1981, the Minister for Health, Mr MacKellar, replied to a question on illegal landings by Indonesian fishermen since July 1978. He stated that there had been 25 landings on Australian soil reported by surveillance air and sea patrols. One of these, dated 25 September 1979 reads:

> An Army Nomad aircraft sighted an Indonesian fishing vessel in the vicinity of Adele Island. The Transport vessel M.V. Cape Pillar responded and found that the food and water cache at Adele Island lighthouse had been stolen and there was Indonesian writing on the lighthouse walls. The fishing vessel was not relocated (DFAT 1988: 26).

It is easy for the Bajo to blame other groups of competing fishermen for acts of vandalism and destruction. By way of contrast, La Muru, a longtime Pepela resident who has fished for decades at the offshore reefs and islands, said: 'The Bajo wrecked the buildings and storerooms on the islands which is why it became forbidden to fish near the coast.' It is of little importance which group was ultimately responsible for the vandalism, but what is interesting is that the two competing groups of fishermen have the same ideas about why their fishing activity came to be restricted. Neither group thought the restrictions were the result of the heightened Australian immigration or quarantine concerns, the expansion of Australian maritime and fisheries zones under international maritime treaties and law, the impact of international agreements and obligations, concerns with over-fishing of certain marine resources, or the attempt to protect the conservation values of specific areas such as Ashmore Reef. Australian agencies have obviously failed in their campaign to educate the fishing communities of eastern Indonesia on the complex issues of border security, international law and environmental conservation. A more targeted, cross-cultural and socially informed communications campaign based on local perceptions would be more likely to achieve this educational goal.

Shark Fins and Longlines

Shark fins are one of the most expensive seafood commodities in the world. Shark fins consist largely of soft collagen and elastin fibres commonly referred to as fin needles. They are highly prized and sought after by the Chinese as a luxury culinary delicacy. When processed, they form the basis of a number of favourite Chinese dishes, most notably shark fin soup. Shark fin soup is associated with prestige, banquet dining and is used to honour or impress special guests on important occasions (Lai Ka-Keong 1983: 35).[3] The value of shark fins varies according to the species (black or white), the size, and the types of cut (Rose 1996: 49).

After World War II, the consumption of shark fin was discouraged by the Communist government in China as it was associated with élitism and bourgeois standards. However, in the mid 1980s, the relaxation of state market controls, increasing disposable incomes, and growing official acceptance of shark fin consumption led to a dramatic increase in domestic demand. The wider growth of Asian demand and the opening of China as a seemingly unlimited market for shark fin were accompanied by significant increases in world prices during the late 1980s and early 1990s (Rose 1996: 49–50).

A number of new developments occurred in the shark fin trade in Indonesia as a consequence. Centred largely in Ujung Pandang, new entrepreneurs entered the trade in the late 1980s, which led to increasing competition and a more directed shark fishery in places like Pepela.[4] Before 1989 there were no permanent traders living in Pepela. Visiting traders from Ba'a on Roti Island or

---

[3] Shark fin became established in formal banquets during the Ming Dynasty (1368–1644). During the Qing Dynasty (1644–1911), shark fin was listed as second among the 'eight culinary treasures' from the sea. By the end of the Qing Dynasty, shark fin banquet dishes were well established among wealthy consumers in both the southern Cantonese and Hong Kong cuisines (Rose 1996: 49).

[4] Similar developments took place in other parts of the world. For example, Chinese fin traders from Hong Kong established direct trade in West Africa, supplying outboard motors and gear to local fishermen in return for harvested shark fin (Rose 1996: 92).

Kupang in West Timor came across to Pepela during the fishing season to purchase various marine products. In addition, like the Bajo, the Pepela fishermen usually sold their catch directly to traders in Ba'a, Kupang, Ujung Pandang or Bau Bau. In 1989 the first of a number of wholesalers established a permanent direct trade in marine products in Pepela. This was a Hong Kong wholesaler who began a partnership with a member of one of the wealthier Pepelan families. He was followed by a trader from Ujung Pandang operating out of Kupang, who placed his own buyers in Pepela. The large-scale traders provided capital to their buyers in Pepela, who in turn supplied provisions and fishing materials for shark fishing trips, as well as cash to the fishermen on credit. The fishermen were then obliged to sell their shark fin catch to that buyer at the price offered and also to pay off the cost of provisioning. This was the commencement of the cycle of Bajo local indebtedness in Pepela. One of the traders also began to acquire his own fleet of *perahu lambo* which he loaned to fishermen in order to undertake shark fishing voyages. By 1994, the operation of at least four traders based permanently in Pepela reflected the rising demand for shark fin and its availability in the Timor Sea.

The migration of Bajo to Pepela also began around 1989. In the first wave of migration some Bajo men arrived in Pepela without their own vessels. After using boats owned by Pepelans, and sharing the profits with the owners, they embarked on a number of fishing trips on their own boats during the next fishing season. While some slept on their boats, others found temporary accommodation in the village. In the following year, more Bajo arrived, either with or without *perahu*, but they were accompanied by their families. Between 1990 and 1992 many of them lived in the main part of the village. They either rented or built small houses and shelters close to the *losmen* (guest house) or next to the coconut plantations in the east — an area which came to be known as Kampung Baru (New Village). During this period many Bajo families stayed on at the end of the east monsoon fishing season instead of returning to Mola or Mantigola.

In late 1992, with increasing numbers of Bajo families arriving in Pepela, the local district government agreed to set aside the sandy beach area to the east of the main settlement specifically for the Bajo. They were allowed to establish their own *kampong* there in an area called Tanjung Pasir. Overcrowding in the main part of Pepela had apparently caused some problems and friction between the Bajo, the local community and local government. The settlement of Bajo was welcomed by some of the local shop owners and traders because of the economic benefits to be gained by new residents engaged in fishing and trading. Some Bajo, who had built houses in the main part of the village and in Kampung Baru, continued to live there but upgraded their dwellings. Others moved to the Tanjung along with further new arrivals from Mola and Mantigola in 1993.

The first dwelling was built on the Tanjung in November 1992 (Plate 6-2), and by June 1993 some 36 houses were established on the beach. There are no reliable figures available on the actual number of people who migrated at this time, but it has been reported that some 113 Bajo families from Mola and a number from Oenggai had migrated to Pepela by June 1993 (Fox 1998: 128). By early September 1994 there were 42 houses on the Tanjung with approximately 50 Bajo houses in all of Pepela, inhabited by at least 65 families or approximately 300 people.

Plate 6-2: First Bajo house built on Tanjung Pasir, November 1992.

The migration of some Bajo from the Tukang Besi Islands to Pepela was evidently correlated with a rise in the price of shark fin, the establishment of permanent traders in Pepela, and the development of credit relations between fishermen and traders to support shark fishing expeditions and the families of absent fishermen. These conditions attracted more and more Bajo to settle in Pepela, and meant that larger numbers of Bajo and Pepelan *perahu* were separately targeting shark fin in the Timor Sea.

The presence of buyers who settled in Pepela also facilitated quicker financial returns for the fishermen. Since many Bajo were now located closer to their fishing grounds, they could fish between two and four times during an east monsoon season and more frequently during the west monsoon. Although large numbers of Bajo families relocated to Pepela, some vessels and crew continued their usual pattern of voyaging from the Tukang Besi Islands to Pepela and the Timor Sea and then returning to their villages again at the end of the east monsoon. With the establishment of traders in Pepela, these Bajo fishermen were also able to obtain materials, goods and cash on credit and later sell their catch in Pepela, so they too were able to embark on more fishing trips during a season.

With this system of trade in shark fin established, the number of boats operating out of Pepela increased. In the past, most of the *perahu* in Pepela were owned by individual families, and only a few of the wealthier residents owned more than one. However, with good profits for existing boat owners from a number of successful fishing trips over a short period of time, local residents, including some of the traders, purchased more *perahu lambo* in an attempt to further increase their returns. These *lambo* came from various places around eastern Indonesia, particularly Southeast Sulawesi. Some Bajo from Mola and Mantigola also saw this as an opportunity to sell their *perahu* in Pepela. In addition, there was no shortage of available crew, particularly with large numbers of Bajo living in Pepela eager to borrow a boat. This resulted in an increase in *perahu* available for Bajo shark fishing voyages as part of an overall increase in the number of boats operating out of Pepela. In 1988, 38 vessels, excluding those owned by Bajo, were reported to be based in Pepela (Darling 1994). By 1993, the office of the Harbour Master recorded approximately 82 Pepela-owned vessels excluding Bajo *perahu*. An examination of AFZ boarding reports between 1979 and 1991 shows that all *perahu* crewed by Bajo were owned by Bajo. However, by early 1992 some of the vessels boarded were owned by Pepelans but crewed by Bajo.

These changes also affected the fishing patterns of other groups of Indonesian fishermen operating in the Timor Sea. The fishermen of Pepela and Oelaba had previously targeted sedentary reef products and sometimes shark in the permitted reef areas. However, the ban on fishing at Ashmore Reef increased the pressure on existing sedentary stocks at other reefs (Campbell and Wilson 1993: 180). With higher prices offered for shark fin, more and more Pepela fishermen turned to shark fishing, as did fishermen from the village of Oelaba. The first *perahu* from Pepela and Oelaba were apprehended for illegal shark fishing in 1993. In addition, the higher prices motivated large numbers of motorised Type 3 vessels from other parts of Indonesia to target shark illegally in the northern Arafura Sea within the AFZ.

The dramatic rise in the value of shark fin during the late 1980s and early 1990s is shown in the prices paid to the fishermen. In a survey undertaken at Ashmore Reef in 1987, Russell and Vail (1988: 89) reported that fishermen from Pepela expected to receive Rp 3 000–20 000/kg for black fin species and Rp 6 000–50 000/kg for white (*lontar*) fin species. Most of the 13 crews of fishermen they interviewed stated that the price of shark fin had already doubled over the previous few years. But in 1994, fishermen in Pepela were receiving

Rp 10 000–150 000/kg for black fin species and Rp 60 000–175 000/kg for white fin species.

The increase in the price was not only a result of a general increase in the price of shark fin worldwide; it was also due to changes in the type of cut of black shark fin made by the fishermen. This occurred as a result of the closer relationship between fishermen and traders based in Pepela. According to the Bajo and the traders, shark fin was sold with a crude or straight cut (*potong biasa*) before 1993. This type of cut actually retains quite a lot of meat, is therefore heavier in weight, requires more processing, and commands a lower price. The more valuable cuts are the half moon cut (*potong semi*) and the full moon cut (*potong full*) which retain less meat and therefore weigh less (see Figure 6-1 and Table 6-1). In 1993, most of the Bajo continued to cut black fin with a crude cut as they had done for decades. However, later that year and during the 1994 season the Pepela traders instructed them how to measure fin and produce the higher quality cuts. By the height of the season in 1994 nearly all Bajo were producing either half moon cuts or full moon cuts.

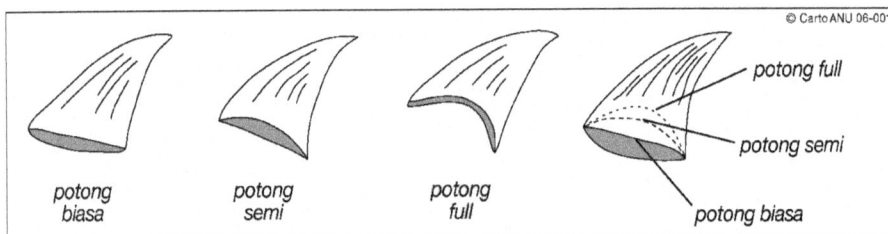

Figure 6-1: Types of cuts of black shark fin.

Table 6-1: Example of 1994 prices for types of cuts of black shark fin in Pepela.

Black fin cut	*potong biasa*	*potong semi*	*potong full*
Price per kilogram (Rp)	40 000	105 000	150 00

The 1989 amendments to the 1974 MOU came into force around the same time as these changes to the shark fin trade and Bajo voyaging patterns. This meant that a large part of the Bajo shark fishing grounds along the Sahul Shelf were now inside the 200 nm AFZ but still outside the area of the MOU box. These policy measures had their own impact on Bajo fishing technology.

Around 1991 the Bajo replaced handlines and shark rattles with a particular type of longline gear as the main gear used to catch shark. This example was quickly followed by the Pepela fishermen. The story behind the change to longline gear involves a Bajo captain and his crew from the village of Langara on Wowonii Island in the Kendari region who sailed into Pepela to sell shark fin after a successful fishing trip using longlines in the Timor Sea. A two-year period followed in which Pepela fishermen joined Bajo *perahu* to learn how to make and use the new type of longline gear, and this in turn contributed to the greater acceptance of Bajo people living in Pepela.

It should be noted that longline technology was not entirely new to the Bajo. Small set longlines had been used for decades (Russell and Vail 1988: 84). This type of gear, 100 m long with 5–7 large hooks, was usually set both inside and outside the reef. The difference between the two sets is that the smaller longlines were not deployed in the open ocean. The new form of longline was specifically designed to target shark found in deeper open waters.

AFS boarding reports also confirm the gradual adoption of longline gear and a gradual increase in its size. Reports from the 1980s indicate that all *perahu* were using handlines and shark rattles, and none of the Bajo *perahu* boarded in 1990 were reported to have longline gear on board. One of the Bajo *perahu* boarded in 1991, the Hasil Nelayan from Mola Selatan, was reported to have two sets of longlines on board, each 100 m long with 8–10 hooks, but seven of those boarded in 1992 had longlines ranging between 350 m and 1000 m in length with 50–60 hooks on each one. The six Pepelan *perahu* apprehended for illegal fishing in September 1993 all used longlines as the main gear.

In 1994 a standard design of longline (Figure 6-2) was in use by all Bajo shark fishermen. The dimensions of longlines differ between *perahu* and are dependent on personal preference, as well as the financial situation of the fishermen. A new set of longlines cost between 1 and 1.5 million rupiah in 1994, whereas shark rattles and handlines would only cost a few thousand rupiah.

The use of shark rattles and handlines was still viewed as a successful and quick method for catching sharks in shallow 'white water' along the northern Australian continental shelf. According to one Bajo captain:

> In white water there are many shark, [and] after two or three days fishing
> with shark rattles, we can catch enough and return home. If the water
> is too deep, the shark cannot hear the rattles (Si Kaharra, Mola Selatan).

So if the use of shark rattles and handlines was so productive why did the Bajo adopt longline gear as the main form of shark fishing gear?

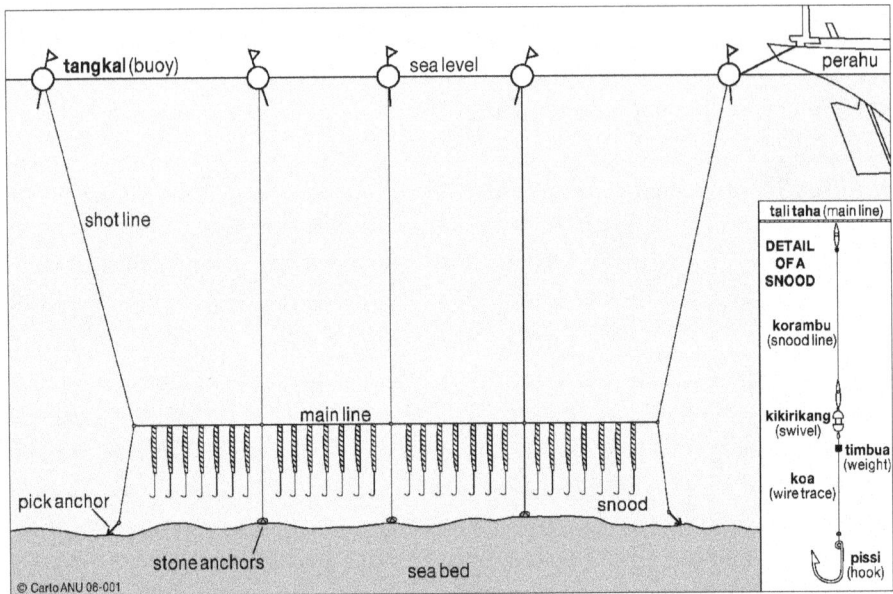

Figure 6-2: Diagram of a set longline and its components.

We do not use it [shark rattle] much now, since the place where the fish
are is forbidden to us so we can't use it. In the past, the place of the fish
was not forbidden and we still used shark rattles. In the past we could
sail to the shallow waters, but now we cannot — the water [where we
are permitted to fish] is deeper, and if we use shark rattles the shark do
not hear (Si Goseng, Pepela).

In former times, before it was prohibited by the Australian Government,
we fished here [shallow waters along the Sahul shelf]. We used shark
rattles. I myself, before it was forbidden, fished here. Within one day
we caught enough. But now it is prohibited. I am also afraid of them
taking my *perahu*, I would cry. So we do not use shark rattles anymore,
because in the deep water we already tried with shark rattles, but no
sharks emerged, no sharks ate the bait so that is why we changed
equipment (Si Idrus, Mola Utara).

The adoption of longlines was partly in response to the 1989 amendments to
the 1974 MOU. Under these arrangements fishermen lost access to much of the
shark fishing grounds along the shallow 'white waters' of the Sahul Shelf that
lie outside the box area and inside Australian waters. Having lost access to
shallow waters in the AFZ, the Bajo fishermen were forced into deeper waters
inside the MOU box and to the north, where handlines and shark rattles were
largely ineffective. They claim that longlines are used in waters at depths of 60
metres or more. Within the MOU box, there are only a few areas around Ashmore,

Cartier and Browse islands which they consider to be good shark grounds that are still suitable for fishing with handlines and rattles. The adoption of longline gear was facilitated by the availability of credit, but this also created a financial strain on the fishermen, contributing to the migration of Bajo to Pepela and further economic reliance on the Pepela traders.

Chapter 7: Sailing, Fishing and Trading in 1994

In this chapter I shall document the pattern of Bajo sailing, fishing and trade during the 1994 east monsoon fishing season in order to explore the social, cultural and economic motivations behind the perpetuation of these activities in the face of Australia's maritime expansion and the financial distress caused by boat apprehensions and confiscations.

Preparations in Mola began many months before the boats left their home villages for Pepela. Aside from the maintenance work to be done on each boat, it was also necessary to organise the social relations, roles and responsibilities of boat owners, captains and crew. Shark voyaging is a family enterprise. The majority of Mola owners join their boats either as the captain or as a member of the crew, and the crew are usually related to the owner or captain. Despite the availability of *perahu* in Pepela, only about 20 per cent of boats in the Bajo fleet of 1994 were owned by owned by Pepela bosses; the rest were owned by Mola Bajo, the majority from Mola Selatan. The boats undertook two or three fishing trips between September and November, each trip lasting 20–30 days. Relying on extensive local knowledge and navigation skills, the Bajo operated in an area covering hundreds of kilometers across the northern Timor and Arafura seas. By the end of the 1994 season the fleet had been reduced by 20 per cent, either through local sale or through apprehension by Australian authorities. Approximately 5 per cent of the Bajo fleet was apprehended for illegal fishing activity in the AFZ. At the end of the season, the majority of the fleet and members of Bajo families living in Pepela returned to the Tukang Besi Islands for a variety of social and economic reasons.

Preparations for Departure

Many of the *perahu lambo* in Mola had not been used during the previous west monsoon and had remained careened (**pangangsalaang**) close to the owners' houses for a number of months. Some had undergone substantial structural repairs during this period, but all required some repairs and maintenance during the weeks or months prior to departure.

Before a boat can go to sea the hull must be scraped, recaulked and covered in lime putty which is then painted over with anti-fouling paint. The entire boat is then repainted, often in a bright colour scheme, and it is common for related *perahu* owners to paint their vessels in a complementary style. The *perahu* is fitted out with equipment and the standing rigging is repaired, with ropes and wires replaced where necessary. Sails are repaired and new sets made if required. Most of this work is carried out by the owner with assistance from his extended family. The crew may also assist closer to the time of departure, but the owner is responsible for all maintenance and repair expenses. If funds are limited at this time, some of the maintenance work — especially making new sails or repairing older ones — is carried out once the boat arrives in Pepela where materials can be obtained on credit from a trader.

Owners, Captains and Crew

In Mola the majority of *perahu* owners (*pemilik perahu*) sail their own boats, usually as the owner-captain (**a'nakoda**) but sometimes as a crew member (**sawi**/*sawi*). If the owner does not accompany his boat, then his brother, son, or other close relative will usually become captain (**juragang**). Reference to the captain as **a'nakoda** or **juragang** therefore specifies his relationship with the boat. The owner of a boat may lend his own *perahu* to another person and join a different boat as a crew member. Alternatively, he may borrow another boat, for example a Pepela-owned boat, and act as captain to increase his returns. In this latter case, there is unlikely to be any familial connection between the *perahu* owner and captain.

One of the captain's tasks is to organise all the administrative letters and sailing passes for himself and the crew. He must obtain Identification Papers for Travel Permit (Surat Keterangan Izin Berpergian) from the office of the *kepala desa* and get them approved by the office of the *camat* (sub-district head), as well as the local police and military. Each *perahu* has a pass book (*buku pas*) that must be stamped by the *kepala desa* prior to departure and again on return. This contains details pertaining to the crew, cargo and destination. To comply with registration requirements, *perahu* are given their own names, but the owner may change the name from year to year. The Bajo themselves generally refer to a *perahu* by the name of its owner.

In addition to the captain, many of the Mola *perahu* also have a sea captain (**punggawa dilao'**/ *punggawa laut*), especially if the captain does not have much experience in shark fishing. The **punggawa** is usually an older man with considerable sailing experience and knowledge of fishing grounds (**lana**/*tempat mencari*). He is responsible for various aspects of navigation and fishing activity, including the catching of bait (*atur cari umpang*) and the setting of fishing gear (*atur pasang pancing*). This distinction between a land captain and a sea captain is less common amongst the younger generation, especially those Bajo living in Pepela, because many of the younger captains have considerable sailing skill as well as knowledge of sea and weather conditions.

All captains (and **punggawa**) are expected to have some esoteric knowledge (**pangatonang**/*ilmu*). This knowledge can be ritually powerful and involve a variety of skills or capacities: to determine auspicious days to travel; to perform prayers and ritual activity associated with sailing and fishing; to control the dangerous weather conditions that may result from failure to observe taboos; to repel evil spirits; to repair parts of a boat damaged at sea; or to cure sickness among the crew. A few Mola captains said they didn't know any *ilmu* and in this sense were no more than 'paper captains ... literate, and skilled in dealing with port authorities but lacking supernatural powers' (Southon 1995: 130). In such a situation, another crew member, usually the **punggawa**, is required to have *ilmu*.

During the weeks or months prior to departure the captain must find a crew. Depending on the size of the *perahu* the number of crew members will range between four and ten. The crew are usually related to the captain and/or owner of the *perahu*; some may come from other villages, but usually within the Bajo network. There are particular rules governing the composition of a crew. For example, it is considered taboo to have three brothers together on one *perahu*. Examples of Mola crew composition for the 1994 season are shown in Table 7-1.

Table 7-1: Examples of Mola *perahu* crew composition, 1994.

Perahu	Sumber Jaya	Cahaya Mola	Tunas Baru
Owner	father of captain	captain	crew member
Captain	eldest son of owner	owner	brother-in-law of owner
	Crew relationship to captain:	Crew relationship to captain:	Crew relationship to owner:
Crew 1	younger brother	younger brother	owner (sea captain)
Crew 2	first cousin	nephew	son
Crew 3	first cousin	nephew	uncle
Crew 4	second cousin	nephew	uncle
Crew 5	second cousin	uncle	first cousin
Crew 6	brother-in-law	second cousin (sea captain)	second cousin
Crew 7	brother-in-law	second cousin	second cousin
Crew 8	distant relative	son of Crew 6	father-in-law
Crew 9	no relation*		brother-in-law

* Married to Mola woman.

The success of a voyage is said to be dependent on harmonious relations between the captain and his crew. A captain who has a reputation for treating his crew harshly (*kejam*), expressing anger, or acting deceptively or dishonestly, has difficulty finding crew, but a captain who has a reputation for being successful each year will never have such trouble. Because a crew member's earnings depend on the success of the voyage there is a tendency for crew to seek out the most successful captains. If a *perahu* is not successful after a fishing trip undertaken midway through the fishing season, some crew may decide to shift to another *perahu*, making it difficult for the captain to embark on another voyage. Some crew only join a boat for one trip and then return to Mola. In some cases the crew may not change much from year to year, and that in turn may be due to the debts owed by the crew, captain and owner to a moneylender or trader. [1]

Once a crew has been assembled, the members meet with the owner and captain and crew to arrange the terms of the voyage. These may include the terms for borrowing the *perahu* and the value of the indemnity against its loss at sea; the source of capital and the distribution of cash to support families during the men's absence; the amount of provisions and equipment to be purchased; the choice between buying a new set of longlines or repairing an older set from the previous year's voyage; the dates for various pre-departure rituals; and the method of sharing the profits on the voyage. Most decisions are made by consensus. It is the captain's responsibility to keep records of all financial accounts.

Ritual Preparations

The next phase in preparations for departure takes place once the *perahu* is ready to go to sea. At this time, a ritual expert is consulted and a departure date is set. As the day of departure draws near, the *perahu* is moved from its dock inside the village (**pangangsalaang**) through a canal and placed at anchor in the outer boat harbour or the open sea. This action is accompanied by a prayer (**doa pamaloka'an**) that is usually performed by a ritual expert, although a few captains have the required knowledge to perform the ritual themselves.

On 21 July 1994, at six o'clock in the morning (high tide), a ritual expert named Si Gudang boarded the Cahaya Baru I — the first of three boats to be moved — while it was still docked. Holding a jug filled with water he recited a prayer into the jug. He then entered the cabin and descended into the hull of the *perahu*. At the navel in the keel he placed an offering of betel nut, leaves and tobacco and recited prayers for five minutes. Then he poured the water from the jug over the navel, emerged from the cabin, moved to the right along the deck and continued pouring water over parts of the *perahu* from the front to the back (see Plate 7-1). At the tiller he recited another short prayer. All the prayers were made to God (Papu) and to the three prophets of the *perahu* to inform them of the route the boat was about to take in order that they might offer physical protection to the front, stern and sides of the *perahu*. These prayers sought protection from misfortune and assurance that the spirits would protect the boat's good fortune (**jaga kami punya rezeki**). The *perahu* was then moved

---

[1] Boats returning to Mola at the end of the season appeared to have more stable crew membership than those returning to Mantigola.

through the canal into the harbour with the aid of long bamboo poles. Si Gudang accompanied the *perahu* until it was finally anchored and then returned to the village by canoe (see Plate 7-2).

Plate 7-1: Prayers performed before moving a *perahu lambo* from the village.

Plate 7-2: Moving the boat through the canal into the harbour.

Water is a significant feature of this ritual performance because a *perahu* is like a human being, and since a human always washes, so must a *perahu*. In the words of Si Gudang, it is so 'the *perahu* will be healthy, and not **maluntu** (hungry)'. Like a person, a *perahu* also has a vital force which requires regular strengthening. If it is lacking in this 'potency and effectiveness' (Errington 1989: 61), this will affect the sailing and fishing success of its owner and crew. The ritual navel of the *perahu* represents the source of the *perahu*'s good fortune and 'protect[s] their human occupants and ensure[s] prosperity' (Southon 1995: 136). The process of ritual strengthening (*kasih makan di perahu*) can take place once the *perahu* is anchored, but it is up to the owner to decide whether the *perahu* needs to be 'fed'. This ritual act can be undertaken before departure, during the course of a fishing season if the *perahu* has lacked success on any previous trips, every year or every few years. But it should be conducted at least once every three years. According to Si Gunda, another ritual expert who regularly conducts *perahu* rituals, it is possible to tell when a *perahu* is 'hungry' because it hasn't been successful for maybe one, two or three years.

> We give food to the *perahu* so we will have good fortune. Because a *perahu* searches for a share [of the catch] and because a *perahu* is like a human, the *perahu* must eat also. We can see if a *perahu* is hungry when it sails, one, two or three times and is not successful, then we must feed it. If the *perahu* is **maluntu**, it is lazy, and has no enthusiasm [**sumangaq**] for work and sleeps all the time. It's the same as not taking it sailing, because even if it sails, it won't be successful (Si Gunda, Mola Utara).

It is also possible that the *perahu* has been subject to sorcery (*guna-guna*) by a jealous enemy of the owner, someone seeking revenge on the owner, or even maybe a previous crew member who broke a taboo.

Ritual strengthening involves prayers performed by a ritual expert on the *perahu*, with the owner and crew gathered around the navel inside the hull. On a tray laid next to the navel are offerings such as rice, vegetables, cakes, cigarettes, betel nut, tobacco and bananas. Three lit candles are placed at the middle, front and back of the hull. The ritual expert then burns incense and begins a series of prayers. After waiting for the candles to burn out, more incense is burned, water is poured over the navel and everyone prays. The ritual expert then goes up into the cabin of the *perahu* and prays again before shaking hands with the owner.

After the ceremony, the male participants remain in the cabin and partake of the meal laid out on the deck, while the women and children sit out the back eating the portions they have saved for themselves. The owner pays for the cost of the meal, while his wife and other female kin will have prepared the food in the village and carried it to the *perahu*. A meal may also be organised by the owner of the *perahu* for the captain and crew to eat together in the house of the owner. The lavishness of this meal depends on the financial situation of the owner since he is required to pay for it. The ritual expert is usually invited and sometimes the local imam is called upon to deliver prayers for the safe passage of the crew. These meals also serve to reinforce the notion of a shared investment in the success of the coming voyage.

The final preparations and provisioning are then completed. In these last few days before departure, the crew may conduct a test sail in the vicinity of Mola to ensure that the *perahu* is in working order. Any necessary adjustments to rigging and sails are then made. The *perahu* is stocked with rice, coffee, tea, sugar, cooking oil, lamp oil, cigarettes and sometimes additional foods such as fresh coconuts, a sack of flour, chilli or tamarind. Wood is purchased for the stove and water is collected in jerry cans and transferred to large plastic drums stored in the hull. It is generally the wives, mothers and other female relatives of the captain or crew who undertake tasks of purchasing and transporting provisions to the boat. [2]

The Day of Departure

Departure is an important event since the crew will be away for many months. The crew and their belongings are taken to the boat by kin in canoes shortly before the time of departure. Usually the family members tie up their canoes to the stern of the *perahu* while waiting for it to hoist sails and depart. Male or female relatives of the captain or crew may accompany a boat to Pepela. A ritual expert is summoned to perform the ritual prayer of departure (**doa palamakang**/*doa perahu berlayar*).

The Tunas Muda was the first boat to depart Mola for Pepela during the 1994 fishing season. The captain had built a house on the Tanjung in Pepela in April 1993 and lived there with his wife and five children. He left for Mola in late April and was anxious to return — hence the early departure. The following is an extract from my field notes recording the moment of departure:

> 28 June 1994: At 2.30 pm I paddled out to Tunas Muda which was anchored off Mola Selatan to watch the departure. Many people, family of the captain, owner and crew came out by canoe to deliver the crew members to the *perahu*. The owner of the boat also came out. The captain was the first on board. One by one the crew arrived and stowed their few belongings — one bag and a plate and glass. Some brought a few coconuts, a spear gun or handlines. A few carried bottles of water which they hung inside the cabin. I saw only one sleeping mat and pillow. Maybe they were on the other side of the cabin out of my sight. The

---

[2] In some cases, provisions are only sufficient for the trip to Pepela, and additional provisions are acquired on arrival there — usually on credit from a trader. The credit arrangements can also include the transfer of cash back to Mola.

fishing gear was already stowed below. They also had a cargo of ready-made thatched palm leaf sections for the walls of a house on the Tanjung. By the time all the crew and family were on board the boat was full of people (around 40).

The last person to arrive was the *orang tua* — Gunda from Mola Utara, a ritual expert and boat builder, to perform the prayers. Gunda built Tunas Baru, the owner's other *perahu,* and has carried out repairs on Tunas Muda in the past. He boarded the *perahu* from the side and first placed the tiller into the rudder stock. He then sat down facing the tiller with his back to the cabin and prayed [see Plate 7-3]. Next he poured water from a glass which someone gave him onto the rudder stock and put his right hand over the wetted area — and his left hand over his lower stomach. He prayed again for about 3 minutes. After this he went to the front of the boat and prayed to the main sail rope and then began to hoist the main sail. The crew then took over and continued to hoist the sail. At this point, I left Tunas Muda and paddled over to Penasehat Baru anchored nearby and sat on the deck, watching and taking photos. Gunda then prayed again to the anchor rope and then all the crew helped to pull up the anchor. Gunda left the *perahu* by the side and got into a canoe tied to the rear of the *perahu.* Some family also left Tunas Muda at this point and paddled back to the village, while some remained in their canoes being towed along behind the *perahu.* Some family were still on the *perahu* as it slowly started under sail. They hoisted the jib sail and sailed towards Otouwe Island and then tacked in front of Mola Selatan for a short distance and south towards Kaledupa Reef. One by the one the people in the canoes behind the *perahu* let go and returned to the village. As the *perahu* disappeared from sight, I paddled back.

According to Si Gunda, the moment of departure is the time when the Bajo enter the domain of the ancestors (**mbo madilao**) and thus prayer must be directed at them as well as the older twin sibling of the Bajo (**Kaka**):

> I pray to **mbo madilao**, who ask Kaka, Kaka answers to **mbo madilao** who answer to me; I receive a reply usually later when I am sleeping or dreaming. We must do this so we don't get into danger at sea. We ask Kaka to accompany us, so Kaka must know our destination. If we don't let **mbo madilao** and Kaka know, then Kaka will become our enemy and we will get into danger at sea or get sick (Si Gunda, Mola Utara).

Two other ritual experts suggested prayers are directed to God and the prophets at this time. Si Mbaga told me that for this prayer:

I pray to the prophets and God for the crew to be spared from danger at sea; to avoid big waves, strong wind, and so as not to collide into a reef. We must mention the name of God to protect us from danger at sea.

Success in fishing is conceived of as being the result of good fortune deriving from the navel of the *perahu*. All rituals surrounding the boat prior to departure 'are aimed at increasing good fortune' (Southon 1995: 7).

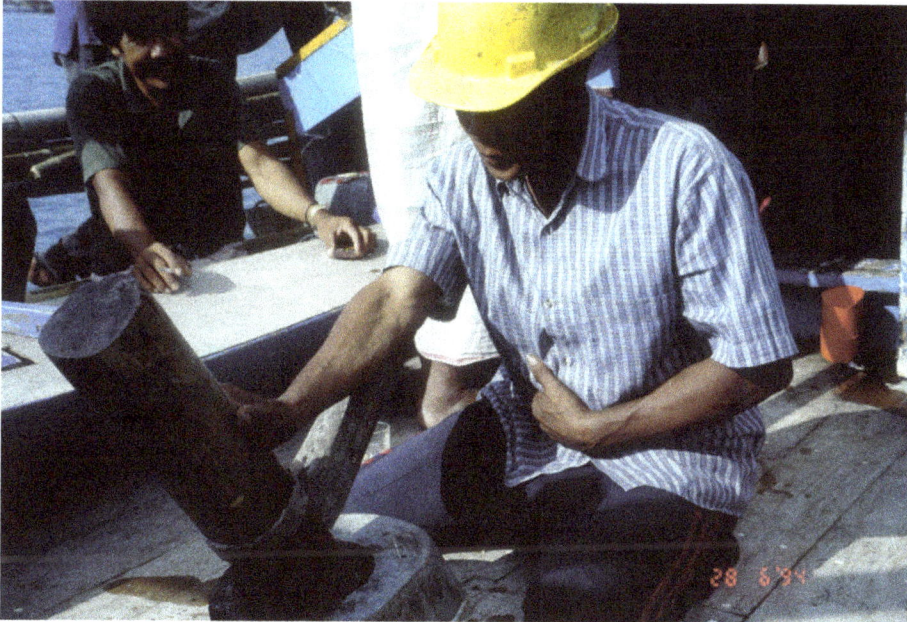

Plate 7-3: A prayer at the rudder stock and tiller of the Tunas Muda.

The Bajo Fleet in Pepela

The majority of *perahu* from Mola departed for Pepela during the months of July and August. The journey typically takes around one week depending on the wind conditions and number of stops along the way. [3] Another phase of preparations takes place in Pepela, which includes restocking the *perahu* with food, water and cut timber, and maybe obtaining extra supplies or equipment. A sailing clearance also has to be obtained from the local harbour master.

In late August 1994, Pepela was bustling with activity. The harbour was a picturesque sight rarely seen in any other port in eastern Indonesia, with dozens

---

[3] From Mola, the *perahu* sail south through the Flores Sea, often stopping at the southern end of the Tukang Besi coral reef complex, west of Tomia, to fish for a day or two. The route takes the boats through the Maco Strai, passing the islands of Adonara and Lomblem. Some vessels stop briefly at the village of Wywuring, on the southern end of Adonara, to sell fish previously caught at the reef. The route continues through the Savu Sea towards Kupang, with a possible stop at the villages of Sulamu or Tablolong south of Kupang, before they reach Pepela.

of brightly painted sailing boats at anchor. All of the Mola *perahu* and most of the Mantigola *perahu* had already arrived. Bajo *perahu* were anchored off Tanjung Pasir and to the east side of the pier while the locally owned *perahu* were generally anchored to the north and west of the pier. The combined Bajo and Pepelan fleet operating out of Pepela during 1994 numbered around 140–150 *perahu*.

Pepela's harbour also acts as a stopping off point and base for *perahu* from other villages like Oelaba (on Roti), for Madurese *perahu lete lete*, and for motorised *perahu* from other parts of eastern Indonesia. In 1994, a number of motor boats from Sinjai in South Sulawesi, with Bugis crews, also used Pepela as a base to process trepang and restock supplies between each fishing trip.

From August to December 1994, records were kept of the activities of all 74 Bajo *perahu lambo* operating out of Pepela. Table 7-2 shows the distribution of this fleet between six categories of ownership and origin.[4] Table 7-3 shows the total number of trips taken by these 74 boats over this period.

Table 7-2: Number of Bajo *perahu* operating for each category of the Bajo fleet, August to December 1994.

Mola boats based in Mola	Mola boats based in Pepela	Mantigola boats based in Mantigola	Mantigola boats based in Pepela	Pepela boats with Bajo crew	Bajo from other areas	Total
26	22	6	3	13	4	**74**

Table 7-3: Number of boat trips made by 74 Bajo *perahu*, August to December 1994.

No. of trips	1	2	3	4	Total
No. of *perahu*	6*	26	32	10	**194**

* This number includes three *perahu* recorded as making the minimum number of one voyage each because it is not known exactly how many voyages each of these *perahu* made during the season.

The usual duration of voyages is between 20 and 30 days. As the length of a fishing voyage can depend on the prevailing wind conditions and the amount of supplies, this does not equal the number of fishing days. The majority of voyages were undertaken during September, October and November. The

---

[4] A small number of Bajo men crewed on boats owned a partially crewed by Pepelans. Men from a number of ethnic groups can come together to form a crew and borrow a *perahu* from a Pepelan boss. Aside from *perahu lambo*, there were approximately ten motor boats of various sizes owned by Bajo from Mola and Mantigola who were living in Pepela. These were used to fish for shark using longlines in the northern Timor and Arafura seas.

majority of *perahu* departed Pepela for the first fishing trip in the first week of September and returned to Pepela in the first two weeks of October. The majority of Mola *perahu* departed for their second trip during the third week of October, returning during the second and third week of November. At any one time, the harbour can be full of boats, numbering a 100 or more. In contrast, within a matter of days it can be almost deserted and remain quiet for a few weeks. In early September there were only 20 *perahu lambo* in the harbour but one month later, in the first week of October, the harbour was bursting with activity after dozens of boats had returned from fishing trips (see Plate 7-4).

A mass exodus of boats within a period of a few days is due to the association of favourable wind conditions with the lunar cycle. According to the Bajo, the end of a lunar cycle when there is no moon (*bulan mati*) is usually a period of strong winds and not considered a safe time to depart, but the winds die down with the appearance of a new moon. By departing at that time, the crews also have the advantage of fishing during a full moon (see Plate 7-5).[5]

Plate 7-4: Bajo *perahu lambo* anchored off Tanjung Pasir, October 1994.

---

[5] Motorised vessels are much faster and can therefore make round trips of seven days or less, with a much higher proportion of the time spent fishing. For this reason they are also smaller and have limited storage capacity.

Plate 7-5: Setting sail from Pepela.

There is no set period for the amount of time a boat remains in Pepela in between voyages. Generally, the crew spend one or two weeks there, which is time enough to sell the catch, carry out maintenance, clean the *perahu*, repair fishing gear, buy more supplies and wait for suitable wind conditions to depart again. After returning from their second trip in 1994, some *perahu* returned to Mola in late November. For other captains and crews the decision go out to sea again was influenced by factors such as the financial success of the season and their observation of the current weather conditions. Towards the end of the year, prior to the onset of the west monsoon, the weather becomes increasingly unpredictable. Some *perahu* departed a third time only to return to Pepela later the same day because of strong wind conditions. [6]

At the end of the 1994 fishing season, the size of the Bajo fleet had decreased: some had been sold in Pepela, Wanci or Kaledupa, while others had been apprehended for illegal fishing activity in the AFZ (see Table 7-4).

---

[6] Although some fishing trips may be hampered by strong winds, between August and November another problem may be the lack of wind: *perahu* may be becalmed during the doldrums. In such conditions, the crew may be required to row the *perahu* using a set of long oars kept on every boat. This is also necessary in order to prevent them from drifting into forbidden areas within the AFZ.

Table 7-4: Number of *perahu* sold or apprehended, and number remaining at the end of the season, December 1994.

	Mola boats based in Mola	Mola boats based in Pepela	Mantigola boats based in Mantigola	Mantigola boats based in Pepela	Pepela boats with Bajo crew	Bajo from other areas	Total
Sold	4	0	2	1	0	0	7
Apprehended	2*	3	0	0	2	0	7
Remaining	21	19	4	2	11	4	61

* The *perahu* Tunas Baru was apprehended in November 1996, but the crew were able to pay a security bond and return with the boat, so it is not included in the total numbers lost.

At the end of the fishing season approximately two thirds of the Bajo *perahu* fleet returned to Mola, Mantigola or other villages from which they had originally departed. Most *perahu* returning to Mola or Mantigola took on extra passengers, including women and children, or crew from boats that had been sold or apprehended (see Plates 7-6 and 7-7). The Sumber Jaya, for example, had a total of 17 people on board for the return journey of seven days duration. As well as the original crew, this included one other female, the sister of the captain; some crew from the Nurjaya that had been apprehended and confiscated in November; and the captain of the Sinar Jaya II who had returned early to Mola in October but then come back to Pepela by motor boat to collect his two sons.

Plate 7-6: Bajo sailing to Mola in early December 1994.

Plate 7-7: Squally west monsoon conditions on the return voyage to Mola.

During the west monsoon period from December 1994 to March 1995, most of the remaining Bajo families in Pepela also returned to Mola and Mantigola. Many of the Bajo women living on the Tanjung during the 1994 fishing season had stayed on during the 1993–94 west monsoon and found living conditions difficult, many having to evacuate their houses during strong winds and wet conditions. Families returned home to visit relatives, attend religious feasts and celebrations, and check on houses. This time also provided an opportunity for men to work in the live fish trade that operated in Southeast Sulawesi and the Tukang Besi Islands during early 1995.

The Fishing Grounds

After sailing south from Pepela and into the Timor Sea, the captain decides the destination for fishing. This depends on the prevailing wind conditions. Fishing activity takes place in a number of different areas along the continental shelf both within and outside the MOU box area. The areas fished by the Bajo include the area known as *bagian perusahan* (oil rig area) to the east of Cartier Island. [7] In the MOU box area, fishermen operate in the vicinity of Ashmore Reef and Cartier Island, to the east and northeast around Scott Reef, in waters between Cartier Island and Browse Island, and along the edge of the continental shelf around Browse Island (see Map 5-1). Outside the MOU box, fishing is conducted along the Sahul Shelf in waters to the east of the eastern boundary and to the south of the southern boundary of the MOU box. Bajo boats also operate along the area called *bagian timu* (the eastern region), which refers to the northeastern part of the Timor Sea south of the Tanimbar Islands. [8] This is the area between the Provisional Fisheries Surveillance and Enforcement Line (PFSEL) and the deep waters south of Timor. Since the best fishing grounds are located outside of the permitted areas, some fishermen often deliberately access these parts of the AFZ, thereby risking the possibility of apprehension. In other cases, fishermen are not knowingly aware that they are outside the permitted areas. This is particularly the case when they may only be a few nautical miles outside the MOU box or south of the PFSEL.

Navigation Techniques

Bajo navigate by a system of dead reckoning with reference to familiar landmarks, navigation lights, and oil rigs. Sea features such as reefs, shoals and channels, the directions of currents, waves and swells, tide patterns, prevailing wind directions and the stars are all essential directional markers. Wind directions are named after a system of compass directions called mata sangai, the 'points

---

[7] This is near to the Skua rig, known as *perusahan merah* (oil rig with red flame) and the Jabiru and Challis rigs, known as *perusahan putih dua buah di atas* (two oil rigs with white flames above).
[8] Generally speaking, Pepela fishermen do not sail as far east as the Bajo but confine their fishing activities to the MOU box, the area around the southern and eastern boundaries of the box, and around the oil rigs.

of origin of the winds' (Ammarell 1995: 202). An example of a Bajo directional system is shown in Figure 7-1. The naming of wind directions corresponds to the main points on a magnetic compass (**pedoman**) which is now often used as an additional navigational aid. [9]

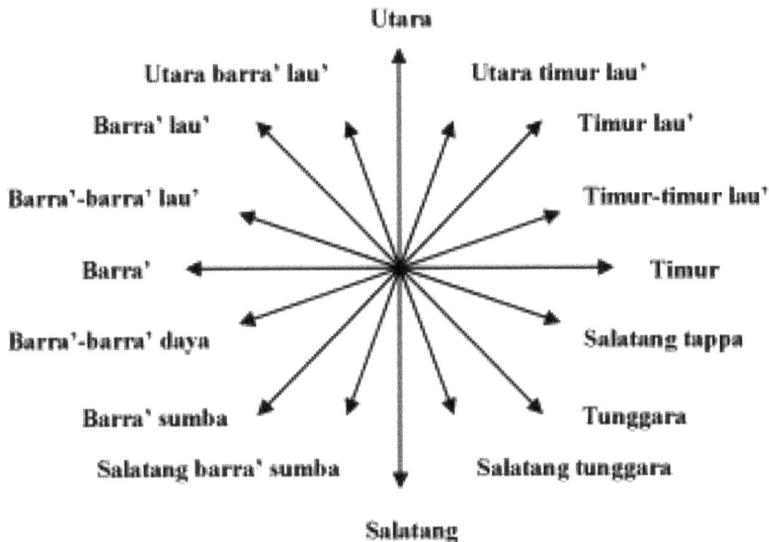

Figure 7-1: Sixteen-point Bajo wind compass.

The Bajo sailors have an extensive knowledge of the navigational techniques required to reach destinations all over eastern Indonesia, as well as specific islands, reefs and fishing grounds in the northern Australian region. Since they are rarely out of sight of an island for more than a few days, positions can be checked by reference to landforms. For example, if fishing along the northern Sahul Shelf, a short sail in a northeasterly direction will bring a boat within sight of specific features along the southern coast of the island of Timor, and a crew member will then climb the mast to gain a better vantage point. The time taken to travel between a set of reference points is counted in days and nights.

As well as dead reckoning, the Bajo employ extensive sounding of the seabed to determine their position in relation to permitted areas and find a depth of water suitable for fishing. Fishermen have an extensive knowledge of the seabed in the MOU box area and the Timor Sea. Depth is regularly monitored with a lead line (**nduga**) made from a prism-shaped lead weight of 1–2 kg attached to

---

[9] It is not known how long the Bajo have carried magnetic compasses aboard their boats, but Ammarell (1995: 202) says that the Bugis have been familiar with this device since European contact.

a long length of nylon fishing line. Fishermen can also determine if they are in permitted or forbidden waters by checking the colour of the water. Men frequently said that if they find themselves in 'white waters' they know they are outside the permitted areas. However, despite this range of navigational aids and skills a *perahu* may sometimes get lost (*jatuh haluan*). Some carry charts or maps on board, but these are almost impossible to use with any reliability without modern navigational instruments. That is why the use of the magnetic compass is becoming more common on frequently sailed routes.

Fishing Methods

Before shark fishing commences the crew must first catch bait (**umpang**). The most efficient way to do this is to locate a suitable fishing ground (lana/*tempat mencari*) which is usually a reef. Bait is also caught using troll lines with lures while the *perahu* is under sail, or from a canoe in the open sea, either under paddle or sail. In this case, canoes are launched from the *perahu* and the crew may travel a few hundred metres or more away from the *perahu* trolling for fish. Bait can also be caught using handlines from the deck of the *perahu*, particularly if it is too rough to sail canoes. [10] The amount of bait required depends on the number of longline hooks to be baited and the size of baitfish caught, but is often around 70–200 fish. Bait can be kept longer by salting it.

Once sufficient fish are caught to bait the hooks the *perahu* will sail to a suitable place to set the longlines by sounding the sea bottom. All hooks and snoods are lined up along a plank or along the top of a hatch and baited. Usually the lines and snoods with baited hooks are fed out while the *perahu* is under sail, but if there is no wind the boat has to be rowed. The setting of longlines takes up to an hour and is usually done in the afternoon. The lines are marked by buoys andattached to the *perahu* while it is anchored overnight. Once the lines are set the evening meal is prepared and the crew entertain themselves, sleep, and take turns on watch.

Just before dawn, the crew begin the arduous process of hauling in the longlines. This can take hours since no mechanical devices are used, and is even more difficult if there are strong winds or adverse currents. If the wind conditions are right a *perahu* can sail under a half-set jib sail while pulling in the longlines. It is not uncommon to lose a section of the longlines, or occasionally the entire set, during a fishing expedition if they get eaten by the fish. It is often difficult to recover the gear, particularly if it has been damaged some hours before the crew become aware of it, or if there is little or no wind by which to sail after the lines. That is why most *perahu* carry some extra fishing equipment with them.

---

[10] The staple diet at sea is rice and fish so Bajo are nearly always handlining. When good eating fish are absent crew may eat left over bait or shark meat.

Sharks caught using longlines are usually dead by the time the lines are hauled in. They are landed onto the deck of the *perahu* with the aid of gaffs or harpoons (**iddi**) and their fins are then cut off. The body is trimmed of excess meat and laid or hung out in the sun to dry. It takes about three days for the fins to dry and longer for the tails. The flesh from the body is either cut up into strips, salted, and hung up to dry, or else the carcass is dumped overboard. The catch may be highly variable: a crew might set longlines on ten occasions in the course of a month at sea but only make a total catch of six or seven sharks.

Many *perahu* still carry a few handlines and shark rattles. If the crew find themselves in shallow waters at any time during the expedition, or when there is little or no wind, handlines and shark rattles may be deployed for a few hours or a day or two, and sometimes at night. Usually the main sail is hoisted and the *perahu* drifts slowly when fishing with hand lines or while crew members shake the rattles over the side of the boat. This method of fishing is more dangerous than longlines since the sharks are alive when caught and must either be clubbed to death or killed with harpoons (with detachable iron heads) before the fins are removed.

The established use of longlines as the main gear has resulted in a preference for smaller *perahu*. Because longlines are anchored to the bottom of the sea with stones, the crew must pull the *perahu* towards the lines to pull them up. A bigger *perahu* is heavier and therefore more difficult to pull whereas a smaller *perahu* is lighter and faster. The use of motorised vessels is also advantageous since it is possible to motor slowly towards the lines while hauling them in. The speed with which longlines can be hauled in is itself an important factor in determining whether a boat is apprehended, because the time taken over this task could be the time between a reported sighting of illegal fishing activity by Coastwatch and the arrival of a patrol vessel to investigate the activity. Some Bajo remarked that the advantage of fishing with handlines while the *perahu* is slowly under sail is that they can immediately sail away if a surveillance aircraft flies overhead.

Fishing Rituals

Once the Bajo sailors are at sea, they regard sailing and fishing as sacred activities. This is because they have crossed into the domain of their ancestors and their fortunes depend on appropriate behaviour towards these beings. At this cosmological level, Australian ownership of marine resources in the AFZ is not recognised at all. Continued activity in waters now claimed by Australia is partly driven by a belief that the Bajo have a legitimate right to fish in the AFZ in waters controlled by their ancestors.

Shark fishing is complemented by the observance of taboos (**pamali**) and performance of prayers (usually accompanied by offerings.[11] It is taboo to throw anything such as food or ashes from the fire box directly into the water; the refuse material must be thrown over the deck of the *perahu* and later washed off with water. The Bajo also prohibit crew and passengers from spitting or cleaning their teeth directly into the sea, from urinating or defecating anywhere from the *perahu* but via the toilet box, and from combing their hair or using soap to wash the body or clothes while at sea. If these rules are not observed, strong winds or storms may arise. The results can be big waves, strong currents or no wind at all, and people may succumb to sickness or have no fishing success. When a crew member died after he returned from a fishing voyage with a sickness, it was thought he had failed to observe one of these taboos.

Shark fishing is a 'social interaction' (Zerner 1994: 27) between people and spirits. The practice of propitiating the spirits prior to fishing activity has persisted through the substitution of longlines for rattles and handlines. Before the crew begin shark fishing operations, the captain or the punggawa recites a prayer and makes a simple offering of betel nut and leaves, lime and tobacco, to the mbo madilao. This only has to be done once during a shark fishing expedition at the first fishing location. The prayer is intended to praise the ancestors and 'to show respect' to those who live in the sea. In the words of Si Mudir, it is 'to ask permission from **mbo madilao** if we can take fish and to give us good fortune' and 'to be kept away from danger, like big waves, or strong wind'.

> In the past our ancestors gave offerings to the sea. This is the custom [*adat*]. We also do this. We still do this now. We lower offerings first and ask the ancestors for this and that, to give us fish and good fortune. Then we can start fishing. We must. Whatever region we go to we have to inform the ancestors because they are not fixed at any one place. Because it is not us who have possession of the sea. It's the same if we want to ask for water or rice or wood, we have to ask the person who owns it before we can take it. It's the same with our ancestors that live in the sea (Si Mudir, Mola Selatan).

> If we do not ask for permission from the guardians in the sea to take products usually they will hide the sea products, sometimes under a rock, or under the sand, under seaweed or sometimes the sea will become hazy or clouded or strong winds and big waves will come. But if we politely ask the sea guardians, we can have everything and also we will not have difficulties harvesting products from the sea because we have already asked permission (Si Kariman, Mola Selatan).

---

[11] The villagers of Pepela also recognise the strength of Bajo adherence to *adat* prohibitions and rules.

Additional consequences of failure to seek this form of approval are explained as follows:

> If Bajo have an accident at sea or misfortune or sickness [sore stomach or vomiting] they must ask forgiveness from the people who live in the sea who have taboo. If you want to ask for forgiveness we must say 'we ask for forgiveness because we already took your riches [marine products] and especially because we did not have permission to do so first because we are only stupid people and don't know anything' (Si Kariman, Mola Selatan).

> If we get the consequences of taboo, we must apologise to **mbo madilao** in order that we are safe from danger, from the consequences of taboo. When we have given them food, **mbo madilao** will go away, and the condition of the sea will be safe and the consequences of the taboo gone (Si Dudda, Mola Selatan).

Fishing success is said to be also dependent on the correct construction and use of fishing gear.

> Before we begin fishing with a shark rattle we must say a prayer first to the ancestors, and ask to be given good fortune so we can aim to return home quickly. Then we dip the end of the shark rattle in the water three times. Once this is done then we can begin fishing (Si Mudir, Mola Selatan).

Each person operating a shark rattle must also wear a hat. If there are no hats available they must tie a sarong or shirt around their head. In the words of Si Mudir, 'it is taboo to not wear a hat, if we don't wear a hat, the fish will not appear, or if they appear, the fish will not eat the bait'.

The Economics of Shark Fishing

Bajo shark fishing voyages in 1994 were financed by a system of credit between fishermen and traders or money lenders that served to strengthen and maintain the regional trade in shark fin. The practice of obtaining credit to fund fishing voyages was not something new to the Bajo, but credit relationships have become the mechanism through which changes in market prices affect the practice of shark fishing. If the price of shark fin were to fall to the level prevailing in the mid-1980s, the entire fishery would undergo considerable change.

An examination of credit and profit-sharing arrangements reveals the economic incentive for Bajo to base themselves in Pepela. There are also clear economic reasons why Bajo continue to fish in the AFZ. First, while shark fishing does not guarantee good returns, or any returns, it can provide higher returns for the owner and crew of an unmotorised *perahu lambo* than any other long distance voyaging activity. Second, the debts that fishermen owe to bosses, traders or money lenders as a result of a poor fishing trip or season, or because of the apprehension and confiscation of their boats, equipment and catch, force them to return to Pepela and embark on further shark fishing ventures in the Timor and Arafura seas. In other words, they are caught in a cycle of indebtedness and poverty from which further voyages offer a means of escape. This means that the Australian policy of apprehension and confiscation does not appear to be effective as a deterrent to further fishing incursions.

The Trader-Bosses of Pepela

The Pepela traders are only interested in the fishermen as suppliers of marine commodities in exchange for credit to fund the search for them. The relationships between fishermen and traders are of a type that Acciaioli (1987: 10) describes as 'transitional ties of dependence' rather than 'traditional ties of patronage'. This type of indebtedness has replaced traditional patron–client relations throughout the maritime societies of eastern Indonesia (Pelras 1996: 332).

In Pepela in 1994 there were four main traders, each with his own network. These men are often called buyers (pembeli) by the fishermen, but the most common term is **bos** (after the English word 'boss'). Some of these traders operated in conjunction with other members of the local community (also called bos) who supplied the fishermen with boats, capital and provisions.

The largest and wealthiest trader (Bos A) [12] was born in Pepela and was of part-Saudi descent. He worked for a husband-and-wife team based in Hong Kong who provided him with capital to purchase sun-dried fin for export to that destination. **Bos** A provided interest-free financial capital to fishermen or bought fin from fishermen who were financially independent. He also worked in conjunction with his uncle (**Bos** B), who operated from his own premises and offered capital and provisions to fishermen on credit with the condition that their product be sold to Bos A. **Bos** A owned 18 *perahu* and would lend these to Bajo and Pepela fishermen. It is difficult to know for certain but Bos A probably controlled 40–50 per cent of the shark fin trade in Pepela.

Bos C was of Chinese descent and lived in Ba'a on Roti. Of all the traders, he had the longest established relationship with fishermen in Pepela, being the first local trader to buy marine products from them although he had never lived in the village or directly supplied goods on credit to its residents. **Bos** A worked for Bos C for a time before he started working with his current Hong Kong partners. **Bos** C co-operated with another trader (**Bos** D), who was himself a relative of **Bos** A and **Bos** B. Bos D owned six *perahu lambo* which he would lend to Bajo fishermen, and would also provide supplies and money if needed. But Bos D did not buy shark fin himself; the fishermen indebted to him would

---

[12] In the following discussion, the personal names of bosses have been replaced with letters in order to conceal their identity.

sell their fin to Bos C who would forward it to his partner in Ujung Pandang (Makassar).

A Kupang-based Bugis trader (Bos E) started operating in Pepela in 1992, with finance supplied by another trader from Surabaya. His three Bugis collectors would buy provisions in Kupang, transport them to Pepela, supply the fishermen on credit, and purchase catch in return. Another Kupang-based trader provided capital for at least one Mola *perahu* in 1994 and would buy fin directly from some of the Bajo fishermen who were financially independent of the Pepela traders.

As a result of the good profits from shark fishing in the early 1990s, some of the wealthier residents and boat owners in Pepela purchased more *perahu lambo* and eventually branched out to become entrepreneurs in their own right. One of these newer entrepreneurs (**Bos** F) was selling fin to **Bos** E in Kupang, or sometimes to other traders. He also owned a fleet of 11 *perahu lambo* which he would lend out, and in 1994 he provisioned a total of 40 Bajo and Pepelan *perahu* operating out of Pepela. [13] Other wealthy Pepela residents were also buying fin from the crew of vessels that they owned and selling it to traders in Pepela or Kupang. Local shop owners were making a profit on the higher price charged to fishermen for goods obtained on credit, and they too would sometimes buy fin and sell it to local or Kupang-based traders.

Grading and Marketing Shark Fin

The prices commanded by fins from different shark species vary in accordance with the quality and quantity of the fin needles used to make shark fin soup. The highest commercial value is attached to white-finned sharks and shark-like rays such as the white-spotted guitarfish (*Rhynchobatus djiddensis*), both of which are known to the Bajo as **kareo nunang** or *lontar*(white shark). Then come the five types of black-finned shark (*Carcharhinus* spp) know to the Bajo as **kareo simburoh, kareo tarang tikkolo, kareo lapis gigi, kareo pote'**, and **kareo angtugan**. Least valuable are the tiger sharks (*Galeocerdo cuvier*) known as **kareo mangali**)and the hammerhead sharks (*Eusphyra blochii* and *Sphyrna* spp) known as **kareo bingkoh**.

In the traditional grading system, fins are classified either according to the species or the colour of the skin, and then distinguished by their size, dryness, and the type of cut. The best quality fins from one shark are normally sold as a set comprising two pectoral fins, the first dorsal fin and one caudal fin (see Figure 7-2). The second dorsal, ventral and anal fins and the fins from small sharks are

---

[13] After a financially successful year in 1994, he and his wife made the *haj* to Mecca in early 1995.

not sold as a set but as mixed dried fins (Lai Ka-Keong 1983: 38). The upper lobe of the tail has little or no commercial value. [14]

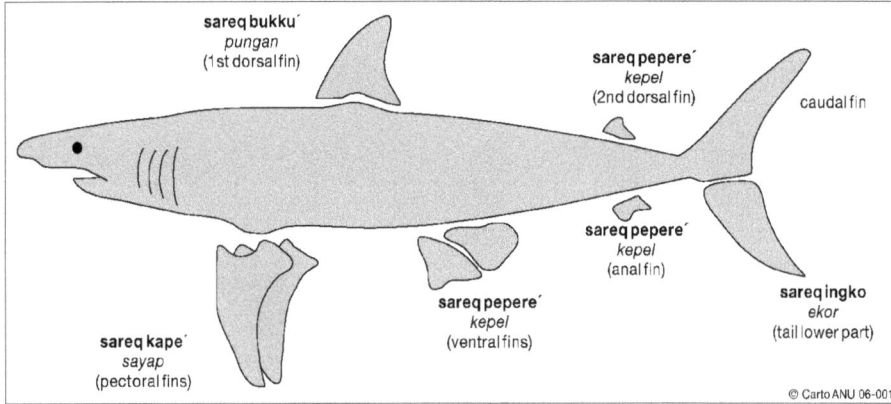

Figure 7-2: Location and names of shark fins.

Shark fins are now simply graded by size, colour and type of cut because each exporting country had its own grading practices and species are often hard to identify (Lai Ka-Keong 1983: 38). Most of the black fin sold in Pepela in 1994 had a half moon cut (*potong semi*), with only a few fishermen attempting the full moon cut (*potong full*), and only In some instances, the fins from the larger black species were sometimes sold in sets of four (see Plate 7-8). The fins from white species were sold in sets of three and were always crude cut (*potong biasa*) (see Plate 7-9).

Tables 7-5 and 7-6 show examples of the grading and pricing systems used by traders in Pepela in 1994. The range of prices depended in part on the quality of the fin. There were small variations between traders but competition between them meant that the average price of a given colour, size and cut of fin was relatively stable. However, fishermen might be offered lower prices or might lose a percentage of the total price if their fins were not completely dry.

---

[14] In Pepela some fishermen retained this portion of the tail and sold it for Rp 1000/kg. According to one trader, it was used to make pig feed.

Plate 7-8: A set of black shark fins.

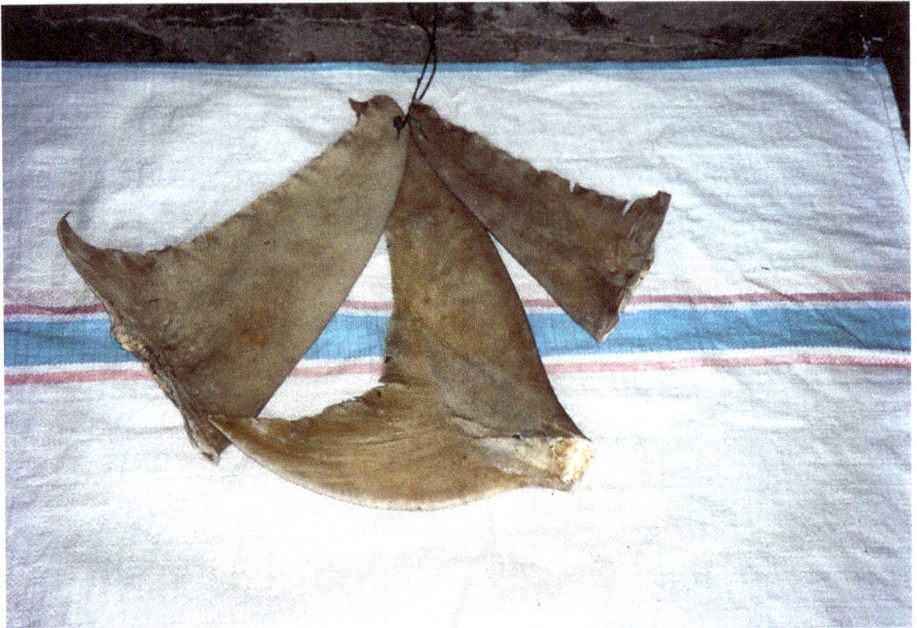

Plate 7-9: A set of white shark fins.

Table 7-5: An example of grading and prices of black shark fin at Pepela, September 1994 (prices shown are in rupiah per kilogram).

	Crude cut	Half moon	Full moon
Large (30 cm and above)	40 000–45 000	105 000	150 000
Medium (25–29 cm)	22 000–22 500	55 000	75 000
Small (15–24 cm)	10 000–12 500	27 500	40 000
Miscellaneous (*kepel*)*	5000	17 500	

* The term *kepel* refers to ventral fins, anal fins, and second dorsal fin.

Table 7-6: An example of grading and pricing for white shark fin from two traders in Pepela, 1994 (prices shown are in rupiah per kilogram).

Trader 1		Trader 2	
Super (38 cm and above)	175 000	Super (38 cm and above)	170 000–175.000
Large (30–37 cm)	150 000	Large (34–37 cm)	140 000
Medium-large (29–36 cm)	125 000	Medium-large (25–33 cm)	120 000
Small (28–35 cm)	100 000	Medium (22–30 cm)	100 000
		Small (16–22 cm)	60 000

Traders made a profit on the resale value of the fin at each level. For example, the largest black fins (*hitam besar*) with the most common half moon cut would be purchased from fishermen at Rp 105 000/kg and then sold to another trader — say in Surabaya — for Rp 110 000/kg if the cut remained the same. However, if the first trader re-cut the fin to a full moon, he would sell it to the next trader for a higher price and make a bigger profit. The profit margin must be high enough for traders to cover local tax and transportation costs. A local fisheries officer from the *camat*'s office in Eahun would visit Pepela daily to collect tax at the rate of Rp 500/kg of shark fin from each trader, but traders would often make false declarations to avoid this tax. From Pepela the shark fin was transported to Kupang and thence by air to Surabaya in Java or Ujung Pandang in Sulawesi at a freight cost of Rp 2500/kg. From there it was either sold to the local domestic Chinese market or exported to Hong Kong, mainland China, Singapore, Taiwan or Korea. It is impossible to know precisely how much shark fin actually passed through Pepela in 1994, but the local fisheries officer reckoned that 29 tonnes had been exported from Pepela in 1993.

To give some idea of the cost of shark fin soup in Indonesia, in April 1995 the manager of the Surya Super Crab restaurant in Ujung Pandang said that he purchased 5 kg of partly processed shark fin from a local trader for Rp 210 000/kg. From that amount he could make approximately 50 bowls of shark fin soup, each of which would sell for Rp 35 000 in his restaurant, which meant a final mark-up of more than 300 per cent over the purchase price. One of the reasons why shark fin soup is so expensive is because of the complex processing required to extract the fin needles. This involves the removal of the skin and any meat attached to the fin and base of the cartilaginous platelets, followed by a process of soaking, washing and bleaching to remove any blood in the cartilaginous base. Before the fins can be cooked they are soaked to make them soft, then bleached and boiled before the base is kneaded by hand to separate the fin needles from the membrane. The needles from one fin may be cooked in their original shape or converted into a fin net before cooking (Lai Ka-Keong 1983: 35–7). The fins and fin needles may be sold in either wet or dry state at different stages in the process.

Hong Kong has long been the main hub of the global trade in shark fin (Rose 1996: 57). In the mid-1990s, retail prices for shark fin in Hong Kong ranged from US$ 40/kg to US$ 564/kg, while a bowl of shark fin soup ranged in price from US$ 4.50 to US$ 90.00 (ibid.: 50). As well as local consumption, a percentage is exported to other overseas Chinese markets from Hong Kong. At that time, more than 80 per cent of shark fins sold in Hong Kong were consumed in local restaurants, and strong ties were established between processors and restaurants to ensure a steady supply of prepared fin. [15] The remaining product was re-exported to other Chinese markets or sold through retail outlets in packages or cans.

Credit and Profits

Bajo departing from either Mola or Pepela usually finance their shark fishing voyages through credit arrangements. Dependence on credit is commonplace in the artisanal fishing communities of Southeast Asia and is 'closely bound up with the nature of fishing' (Sather 1997: 132), where 'the peaks are sharper and the valleys deeper' (Alexander 1982: 58). The highly variable and fluctuating returns from fishing mean that at certain times of the year income is not sufficient to cover daily household expenses or the costs of education, life cycle rituals, religious feasts, fishing equipment or boat maintenance. Most households dependent on this economic activity do not have any significant cash savings nor do they own the assets required to guarantee a conventional bank loan.

In Mola, credit is generally secured from relatives, from wealthy local residents, or from specialised money lenders based in Wanci. Money lenders either charge interest of 10–15 per cent per month or else charge a higher rate (normally 50 per cent) for a loan without a fixed repayment date. In both cases,

---

[15] The market demand lasts all year round but reaches a peak from October until Chinese New Year at the end of February because these are the preferred months for weddings and other feasts (Lai Ka-Keong 1983: 37).

the standard form of security is gold jewellery. Another type of credit is the profit-sharing arrangement known as saduh, or sometimes as *bagi dua* (two parts). In this case, the interest on a loan consists of a share in the proceeds from the sale of the catch that is equivalent to the share normally allotted to each crew member. The agreement normally covers two fishing trips within a single season. There is no security for the money lender, but if the trips are successful, the profit may be substantial.

Many Mola and Mantigola Bajo were attracted to Pepela in the 1990s because of the opportunity to obtain credit from local bosses on better terms than those available in their own villages. In 1994, most of the Mola fishermen would still raised the operating capital needed to cover the cost of food, equipment and supplies for the voyage to Pepela and the first fishing trip before setting out from their home villages. Crew members would also borrow enough money (Rp 50–250 000 each) to cover the household expenditures of their families during their absence. On arrival in Pepela, these fishermen would then obtain extra supplies or equipment, and sometimes cash, from a **bos** on credit. Some Mola-based crews would initially buy just enough provisions to sail to Pepela, and then obtain the rest of their supplies on credit from a **bos**, along withcash to send back to their families in Mola. The disadvantage of this strategy was that the traders charged a higher price for goods supplied on credit than the normal shop or market prices, [16] but since there was no interest charged on this type of credit, there was a lower risk of higher debts in the long term if the fishing trip were to be unsuccessful, especially when cash loans would cost 10 per cent interest per month. In 1994 a few Bajo managed to finance their own fishing voyages, and since they were independent of the bosses in Pepela, they were able to sell their shark fin to any trader offering the highest price in either Pepela or in Kupang.

The distribution of the earnings or profits from shark fishing is based on the allocation of shares to the providers of capital, the boat owners, and the crew. The share system 'effectively increases the motivation of the crew by making them partners in the enterprise, and reduces the risk for boat owners by ensuring that they will not have to pay fixed wages if catches are poor' (Acheson 1981: 278). The Bajo have two systems for dividing the profits from a fishing voyage, which they call the Mola system (*bagi* Mola) and the Pepela system (*bagi* Pepela). Both are contemporary versions of systems that have been in use for a long time in the maritime societies of Indonesia. [17] The choice of system depends on the way the capital was obtained.

---

[16] The market price for provisioning a vessel in Pepela was Rp 4–700 000 — significantly less than the equivalent cost in Mola or Mantigola.

[17] This would include the fishing and trading voyages made by Macassans to northern Australia in the 18th and 19th centuries (Macknight 1976: 19–23; Hughes 1984: 128, 175; Southon 1995: 67–9).

The following examples illustrate the differences between the two systems following the sale of shark fin to a trader in Pepela. The first case study examines the arrangements for the financing of a Mola *perahu* under the saduh system, while the second details arrangements for a Pepela-based Bajo *perahu* financed by a local trader. In both cases, the longlines were not new but had been repaired, and the cost of repairs was included in the total expenses. [18] The Mola-based *perahu* had a crew of nine, while the Pepela-based *perahu* had a crew of seven.[19]

The nine crew and owner of one Mola-based *perahu* obtained a total capital of Rp 3 600 000 in Mola under the saduh system. This was calculated as follows: at a rate of Rp 300 000 for one share, the crew of nine (including the captain) held one share each, while the *perahu* (or its owner) held three shares, thus making a total of 12 shares in all. The capital covered the cost of the voyage from Mola to Pepela and the first shark fishing trip, including the purchase of fishing gear and food supplies, and also the allocation of Rp 150 000 in cash for each of the families of the owner and each crew member. On arrival in Pepela the crew obtained Rp 100 000 worth of extra supplies on credit from a local trader. The fishing trip lasted four weeks and Rp 6 000 000 was made from the sale of shark fin back in Pepela.

The net profit on the sale (Rp 2 300 000) was then divided into shares as follows. The owner of the *perahu* got three shares, while the captain and crew got one share each. One share was allocated to the owner of the longline gear, which in this case was the crew as a whole. The owner of the two canoes, in this case the captain, was allocated a quarter share for each canoe. And finally, for each of the 12 shares in the original capital, the borrower had to repay the lender one share in the net proceeds. The proceeds were thus divided into 25.5 shares with a value of Rp 90 200 each, and each crew member received a total of Rp 100 200 (then worth about 62 Australian dollars) for six weeks of sailing and fishing.

Since the arrangement under the saduh system was for two fishing trips, the original capital would still attract an equal share of any profits from the second trip. However, provisioning expenses for the second voyage would not be as much as for the first — maybe Rp 4–700 000 altogether. Under this system, the owner and crew would not be free to split the whole profit between themselves unless or until they undertook a third trip.

If the original capital had been obtained from a money lender in Wanci at prevailing interest rates, then each crew member would have ended up with a smaller net income from the first fishing trip. However, the advantage of a cash

[18] The owner of a set of longlines, usually the *perahu* captain or owner, will normally value the longlines at an agreed price — say Rp 500 000 — and each crew member, including the captain, will then carry an equal share of this cost which is added to the total cost of the voyage.
[19] Mola-based *perahu* generally have larger crews.

loan over the saduh system is that the loan would then be paid off and the income obtained from a successful second trip would be much higher.

The crew of a *perahu* based in Pepela secured their original capital, including provisions and cash to be left for their families, on credit from a local **bos**. The total value of the debt was Rp 700 000. The longlines belonged to the boat owner and he was responsible for any expenses associated with them. The canoes were rented from the owner for a fixed price. As in the first case, the fishing trip lasted four weeks and the crew obtained Rp 6 000 000 from the sale of shark fin on their return.

Under the Pepela system, the proceeds were divided as follows. One third of the total was taken by the owner of the boat. From the balance of Rp 4 000 000, the bos then collected his Rp 700 000 while the owner collected another Rp 50 000 as rent for his two canoes. The remainder was then divided into eight shares, one for each crew member (including the captain), and one for the owner of the longlines (who was also the owner of the boat). [20] This meant that each crewmember received a net income of Rp 406 250 from four weeks at sea. The income was much higher than in the previous example because the amount of capital required at the outset was much lower, and so was the effective rate of interest.

The owner of the boat obtains a significantly greater share of the profits under the Pepela system than under the Mola system (Rp 2 000 000 as against Rp 270 600 or Rp 111 120) because his share is taken out of the gross amount of the sale price while the cost of the voyage is deducted from the shares allocated to the crew. This means that the boat owner always receives a share, even if the voyage makes a net loss. Under the Mola system, the cost and risk of the voyage is shared more equally between the owner and the crew. Under the **saduh** system, the return to the boat owner on the capital invested in his boat is relatively low compared with the return on other forms of capital.[21] The owner receives the same number of shares irrespective of the boat's seaworthiness or value. A *lambo* worth Rp 4 000 000 receives the same number of shares as a *lambo* worth Rp 9 000 000. Likewise, the share allocated to the owner of a longline worth Rp 750 000 is the same as for one valued at Rp 1 500 000. According to Acheson (1981: 278), the effect of this kind of share system, which seems to be a widespread feature of indigenous fishing societies, is that:

> it inhibits capital investment, because boat owners ... do not receive full
> returns on the investment they make. That is the owner pays all the costs

[20] According to one Bajo informant, the *perahu* owner sometimes gives the captain 10–20 per cent of his own share as a reward for the safe return of the boat.
[21] Southon (1995: 69) found the same feature in his analysis of returns to boat owners from trading voyages in Lande on Buton.

of investment, but the crew receives part of the increases in catch that result.

Even though the *perahu* represents a significant financial investment for the Bajo under the Mola share system, its value as a capital asset cannot be depreciated over time due to usage or damage, nor can it be used as collateral for raising investment finance. The *perahu* participates in the voyage as three persons rather than as capital (Southon 1995: 120). The practical advantages of boat ownership therefore depend on the success of the voyage, and a Mola or Mantigola boat owner has an incentive to increase his returns by participating as a crew member. In 1994 approximately half of the Mola *perahu* owners participated in the voyage as captains or crew members.

Since no security was required to obtain credit in Pepela, it is unclear why more men and their families had not migrated from Mola to Pepela to take advantage of the credit arrangements there. Some Bajo told me that they preferred their families to remain in Mola so that their children's schooling was not interrupted. However, it was also apparent that there were fewer opportunities in Pepela for women and children to obtain food for subsistence through fishing and collecting, and there were also difficulties associated with housing and living conditions.

Financial Independence and Indebtedness

The earnings from shark fishing are variable since there is a 'large element of unpredictability' (Sather 1997: 131). One trip may provide good returns while the next may see the crew suffer a loss. Similarly, one boat crew may be successful throughout the entire season while another may not have been able to clear their debts. The success of a shark fishing expedition and the crew's earnings over a season depend on a number of variables. A boat may be forced to return to Pepela after a few days because of adverse weather conditions or because a crew member has fallen ill. Fishing gear may be lost or fouled on the seabed at some point during the voyage, and the crew must then return to Pepela and make a further investment to repair or replace their equipment. Sails may be torn in bad weather, or the boat may otherwise become unseaworthy. Such occurrences were relatively common during the 1994 season among, even the most skilled of the Bajo fishermen.

Only six Bajo *perahu* made catches worth more than Rp 10 000 000 on one trip during the 1994 season, and the highest return from one trip was reported to be Rp 20 000 000. For the boat owners these trips were very profitable, especially for those based in Pepela and for Mola *perahu* on their second trip. Some Mola *perahu* owners reinvested their profits in repairs to their vessels during the west monsoon. The owner of the Suka Bakti used his profits to finance the *haj* to Mecca in 1995, while another owner made a special trip to purchase a cow from Buton for an extravagant feast to celebrate a rite of passage for his infant daughter.

The size of the Bajo fleet meant that it was not possible to collect information about the earnings of all the boats over the entire season, but Table 7-7 shows the variation in earnings between a sample of the boats in the fleet. At the end of the season the net earnings for each crew member ranged between Rp 100 000 and Rp 500 000 after 4–5 months of fishing.

Table 7-7: Amount received from sale of shark fin for 11 Bajo *perahu*, August to December 1994 (prices shown are in rupiah).

Mola-based *perahu*	Trip No. 1	Trip No. 2	Trip No. 3
Harapan Jaya	6 000 000	4 500 000	
Karya Satu	1 200 000	6 000 000	
Purnama	1 500 000	520 000	900 000
Sejati 02	3 176 000	15 504 000	
Sumber Bahagia	10 000 000	3 000 000	
Sumber Jaya	7 000 000	6 083 000	
Tunas Muda	[captain sick]	600 000	900 000
Pepela-based *perahu**	Trip No. 1	Trip No. 2	Trip No. 3
Madelina II	5 000 000	4 400 000	
Suka Bakti II	4 000 000	400 000	1 000 000
Kembang Harapan	2 700 000	2 300 000	
Mekar Indah	7 940 200	3 000 000	4 000 000

* The Madelina II was owned by a Mola Bajo man living in Pepela, and the Suka Bakti II was owned by a Mantigola Bajo living in Pepela. The other two Pepela-based *perahu* were borrowed by Mola Bajo from their Pepelan owners.

In one case, the crew of the Sumber Jaya who financed their voyage under the **saduh** system, sold their catch for Rp 7 000 000 after the first trip and received a net income of Rp 100 000 each. After the second trip they sold their catch for Rp 6 083 000 and received a net income of Rp 185 000 each. On the third trip the *perahu* was forced back to Pepela because of strong winds and the crew decided to return to Mola rather than risk fishing in early December. However, since the *perahu* had been provided with goods on credit from a trader to the value of Rp 250 000, the crew still had this amount of debt. Since the overall returns for each crew member for the entire season were fairly modest, the captain was obliged to leave his longline gear with the trader as security until the amount could be paid off at a later date.

For some Pepela-based Bajo, moderate returns for the season still enabled them to invest in a new vessel. The captain of the Mekar Indah, who had lived in Pepela for a few years, was successful enough to return to Mola with his family at the end of the season and finance the construction of his own boat. The owner of the Bintang Nusantara purchased a second hand *perahu* at the end of the season, while the owner of the Usaha Marni purchased a newly built boat in late November. In contrast with these successful fishermen, none of the owners, captains or crew from Mola or Mantigola purchased new *perahu* or began construction of a new boat at the end of the season.

Some crews made poor catches throughout the season. An unsuccessful trip means that fishermen are placed further in debt and have to borrow more goods on credit for the next trip. They are then under further pressure to obtain a good catch on the following voyage in order to repay these debts. At the end of the season a few *perahu* had not been successful enough to break even and clear themselves completely of all debts. After three trips for the season the crew of the Purnama had gross earnings of less than Rp 3 000 000, which did not even cover the costs of their voyages. This meant that the owner and crew made a net loss on the season, because each had accumulated an additional debt of Rp 70 000. A crew that has been repeatedly unsuccessful is forced to resume a relationship with their creditors in the following season, and that is how the cycle of indebtedness begins.

If a boat's owner and crew are in debt to a **bos** in Pepela and want to return to Mola, then the trader may demand that they leave some form of indemnity behind. This might be their longlines or, in the worst case, the *perahu* itself. To pay off debts the owner may even be forced to sell the *perahu* to the trader if credit is refused to cover the following season's fishing. This is what became of the Mola *perahu*, the Penasehat Bar, and the Mantigola *perahu*, the Suka Bakti II. Such cases partly explain the increase in ownership of *perahu* among the traders in the mid-1990s. After an unsuccessful season, a *perahu* may also be sold at the end of a season to repay debts to a money lender in Wanci. This is what became of the Karya Satu.

Fishermen deciding to remain in Pepela during the west monsoon may survive for a few months on any profits they made during the season. When this source of income runs out they can obtain cash and basic supplies on credit from a bos. If the men have not made any additional income from fishing by the end of the west monsoon or during the earlier months of the east monsoon, they may owe a considerable debt by the time the main fishing season begins in addition to the costs required to equip a *perahu* for its next voyage.

The subsistence needs of most Bajo households are normally met by harvesting local marine resources or by other small-scale economic activities undertaken by the female members. The returns from shark fishing and other forms of long distance voyaging provide the means to pay for such things as housing and furniture, fishing equipment, canoes and small boats, religious feasts and ceremonies, or the children's education. This type of income is also used to pay off prior debts, sustain the family during the west monsoon and periods of bad weather, and purchase the gold that embodies the household savings. However, even if the net earnings from sailing are negligible and therefore make little contribution to the household economy, the subsistence needs of the men who are absent from their villages for months at a time on fishing voyages have at least been covered in the process.

The Risk and Cost of Apprehension

Long-term indebtedness can also arise from the apprehension and forfeiture of a *perahu*, its catch and equipment. In the case of a Mola-financed *perahu* apprehended on its first voyage, where an indemnity is placed on the boat by the owner, the debt acquired by the crew could run into millions of rupiah. In 1994, Pepela-based *perahu* did not carry such indemnity, which was a further incentive for Bajo to borrow boats from Pepela owners.

Between August and December 1994, seven Bajo-crewed *perahu* were apprehended for suspected illegal fishing in Australian waters. Two of these (Nurjaya and Tunas Baru) were Mola-based *perahu*, three (Harapan Bersama, Teluk Pepela and Usaha Bersama) were owned by Bajo living in Pepela, and two (Putra Bahari II and Usaha Nelayan) were owned by Pepela traders. All the crews were convicted and only one boat, the Tunas Baru, escaped forfeiture. This case was unusual because the crew had sold the catch from their first voyage for Rp 11 865 000 and still had the cash on board, so they were able to pay a security bond of Rp 3 000 080 (the estimated value of the *perahu*) and return to Indonesia.

The seven crew of the Nurjaya were apprehended on their second trip after just clearing most of their debts in Mola with Rp 3 000 000 obtained from the sale of their first trip's catch, but they still had debts amounting to Rp 450,000 from provisioning the vessel with credit from a Pepela boss. It was not clear whether the crew would be required to pay back the indemnity to the owner since the crew had no means to do so in the foreseeable future. In the case of the Putra Bahari II, there was no indemnity for the *perahu* and the crew had paid the costs of the their second voyage (Rp 800 000) out of the returns from their first one (Rp 3 000 000 in total).

Apprehension nearly always results in some level of additional debt for the crew. As well as the costs of the voyage which have to be repaid, they also have to replace or pay for the fishing equipment which has been confiscated. The biggest loss is faced by the owner of the *perahu* itself — a substantial capital investment which has provided a livelihood for several families. In addition, the fishermen suffer a loss of earnings while in detention in Australia, and this may be extended by the imposition of jail sentences for repeat offenders in breach of good behaviour bonds. While the men are absent, their families may have to borrow money or supply their basic needs on credit.

A *perahu* captain or owner may be fearful of being apprehended for a second time, only to be burdened with more debt and the likely prospect of a jail sentence, so may stay well clear of profitable fishing grounds outside the permitted MOU box area. In doing so, however, he has less chance of obtaining a good catch. One Mola *perahu* owner and captain apprehended in 1992 had a reputation for never being successful and was continually in debt because he was reportedly frightened of fishing too close to the AFZ and MOU borders and being apprehended for a second time. At the end of 1994 he was so deep in debt that he was forced to sell his boat to his boss. On the other hand, the captain of the Sinar Jaya II, who had been apprehended in 1991, said he was not scared to go fishing in the Timor Sea because he would otherwise not earn enough money to support his family.

For a small minority of Bajo captains, the deterrence strategy appears to be effective. A few are discouraged from entering the AFZ and from fishing illegally outside the MOU box. However, even for the minority who are deterred — people who are poor to begin with — they are faced with the prospect of bad fishing and poor returns. This is turn creates a situation where people are unable to extract themselves from the cycle of further debt and poverty. The majority of captains and crew are not deterred, however, and they continue to embark on voyages. The economic pressure is far too great for them to have any trepidation about return forays in the AFZ.

There is little ethnographic evidence that apprehension and forfeiture of vessels has, in fact, deterred continued illegal fishing activity over recent years. The situation is infinitely more complex. The philosophy that 'removing the boat removes the threat' does not actually work since there is no shortage of *perahu lambo* in Pepela or in eastern Indonesia. Most of the captains and crew from Mola and Mantigola apprehended in 1990, 1991 and 1992 were still embarking on shark fishing voyages during the 1994 season. This does not suggest a deterrent result. In fact, it appears that apprehension and forfeiture of vessels may have the opposite effect. Indebtedness as a result of apprehension compels the fishermen to go shark fishing again in an attempt to clear their debts. And since the best fishing grounds are located outside the permitted areas, illegal fishing may be well worth the risk. [22] For the bosses of Pepela who own large fleets of *lambo*, the apprehension of a few boats each year does not act as a

[22] Campbell and Wilson (1993: 156) make a similar observation about the high rates of apprehension of illegal trochus collecting voyages between 1987 and 1992: 'crew members continue to participate in voyaging out of desperate attempts to service their debts, encouraged also by genuine reports of successful voyages'.

deterrent since the possible gains from the remaining boats are more than enough to compensate for the loss.

Chapter 8: An Evaluation of Australian Policy

There are a number of reasons why Australian policy is not effective in deterring illegal activity. A key feature of Australian policy has been the definition of 'traditional' fishing encapsulated in the 1974 Memorandum of Understanding (MOU) that regulates access for Indonesian fishermen in the AFZ. This concept of the 'traditional' reflects a simplistic but popular evolutionist view that emphasises the static, timeless, and non-commercial aspects of culture and ignores any process of cultural change and adaptation. While contemporary anthropological and legal opinions in Australia depict tradition and culture as dynamic in the face of changing circumstances, government policy towards Indonesian fishermen and indigenous Australians still tends to oppose the 'traditional' to the 'commercial'. This adherence to a notion of the 'traditional' as something culturally inert is at odds with the understanding and behaviour of Bajo fishermen, and regulation of access to the MOU area by reference to 'traditional' technology has resulted in all sorts of misunderstandings and inconsistencies.

In practice the Bajo have lost their 'traditional' access rights to areas of the AFZ where they previously fished, while the Australian definition of 'traditional' fishing provides the Australian Government with a justification for continuing the policy of apprehension, confiscation and forfeiture of *perahu*. Moreover, it appears that such views have contributed to a lack of will on the part of the Australian Government to consider alternative approaches to managing a traditional Indonesian fishery in the AFZ. The extent to which the MOU has been effective in providing recognition of fishing rights and curbing illegal fishing activity is debatable. Under the terms of the MOU, no specific rights exist for groups who operated in the region prior to Australian maritime expansion. Bajo fishermen are denied normal cultural dynamism in pursuit of their livelihood. There are double standards being applied here: Australians can change, but Bajo cannot — Bajo must operate 'traditionally'.

Over-exploitation of marine resources has occurred within the MOU box area because there are no restrictions on access to it, so it is now regarded as a poor shark fishing ground. Fishermen therefore fish illegally in order to access more abundant shark populations to secure reasonable profits. The basic nature of Bajo navigational methods also means that it is often difficult for the fishermen to determine the location of marine boundaries. Educational campaigns and the policy of deterrence have been largely ineffective. Large numbers of fishing boats continue to be apprehended for illegal incursions in the AFZ. The burning of boats that provide a livelihood for some of the poorest people in eastern

Indonesia while Australia continues to fund aid projects to alleviate poverty in the region represents a seriously inconsistent and counterproductive foreign policy.

A range of complex and competing political, territorial, commercial, environmental and legal factors continue to influence government inaction on the complex problem of illegal fishing in the AFZ. A more inclusive, culturally informed approach should now be taken to devise new agreements for specific groups with a historic interest in the area prior to Australian maritime expansion. The challenge for Australian and Indonesian policy makers is to find a flexible arrangement that incorporates the cultural dynamics of a traditional Indonesian fishery while at the same time maintaining the legal, territorial, commercial and environmental principles and objectives of the nation state.

What is 'Traditional' Activity?

The Eurocentric worldview has been criticised for the 'distorted way that it constructs and presents alien societies' (Carrier 1992a: 195). Debate on this subject was stimulated by anthropological reflections on the 'colonial encounter' (Asad 1973), and then by Said's (1979) study of 'Orientalism', which focused on the way that Oriental or Asian societies have been portrayed in essentialist terms as static and simple, isolated from Western influence (Carrier 1992b: 3). Fabian (1983: 31) calls this the 'denial of coevalness' which positions the 'Other' in another time, or out of time, from the West — a process that developed out of nineteenth century evolutionary schemes which placed all societies in a developmental sequence of progress, 'a temporal slope ... a stream of Time — some upstream and some downstream' (ibid.: 16). This discourse holds that societies passed through stages of development from the 'savage' to the 'civilised'. Terms used in 'temporal distancing' (ibid.: 71), like 'primitive' or 'traditional', came to refer to less technologically developed societies that were untouched, static survivals of the past. From these discourses arose a tendency to discuss 'Other' societies in terms of dichotomies such as progress versus stagnation, development versus underdevelopment, and modernity versus tradition (ibid.: 144). These dichotomies obstructed the realisation that 'Other' societies also have histories (Wolf 1982) and exist in the same time and space as ourselves.

Much early anthropological writing about so-called 'traditional', 'native' or 'indigenous' societies focused on 'traditionalism' (Fabian 1983; Marcus and Fischer 1986; Carrier 1992b; Miller 1994: 59; Merlan 1998: 3). This 'traditionalism' is the process of 'the reproduction of idealized representations of native societies as they allegedly are, in the terms of how they supposedly were' (Merlan 1998: 231). These 'traditionalist' accounts of indigenous peoples 'support a vision of the world in which at least some portions of it, some peoples of it, remain customary, unchanged, and therefore different from 'us', inherent and unreflective in their relation to their "culture"' (ibid.: 4).

Anthropology has since 'involved itself in a thorough-going critique and rejection of static models of culture' (Scott 1993: 322). Studies concerning 'the invention of culture' (Wagner 1975), the 'invention of tradition' (Hobsbawm and Ranger 1983), or the 'reinvention of traditional culture' (Keesing and Tonkinson 1982) point to processes whereby people actively formulate and codify their traditions. Anthropologists now generally agree that 'there is no traditional baseline of unchanging homeostasis' from which to measure tradition, 'nor is there any one-sided change caused by colonialism and modernisation', but 'in encounters with colonial and other "modern" powers, so called traditional systems tend to generate creative responses to the challenges from afar' (Hviding 1996: 29). Or as Marcus and Fischer would have it:

> Most local cultures worldwide are products of a history of appropriation, resistances, and accommodations. The [present] task ... is ... to revise ethnographic description away from [a] self-contained, homogenous, and largely ahistorical framing of the cultural unit toward a view of cultural situations as always in flux, in a perpetual historically sensitive state of resistance and accommodation to broader processes of influence that are as much inside as outside the local context (Marcus and Fischer 1986: 78).

In an overview of developments in the 'invention of tradition' literature since 1982, specifically in regard to Oceania, Tonkinson (1993: 598) explored aspects of tradition 'that continue to offer useful avenues for further research ... in light of what we know about it as a complex and ramifying domain of meaning, discourse and action'. He concluded that 'tradition is most effectively conceptualised as a *resource* employed (or not employed) strategically by certain (but not all) of a community's members' (ibid.: 599). This approach is particularly useful in places like Australia and North America, where the nation state demands that indigenous minorities 'present their claims to rights and resources largely in terms of "traditional" validatory criteria, such as kin group affiliation, land tenure principles, religion and language' (ibid.: 603).

Following the 1992 Australian High Court decision known as the Mabo decision, the Commonwealth Government passed the *Native Title Act 1993*. Despite the fundamental changes thus made to the recognition of native title, claimants are required to demonstrate their possession of 'traditional law and custom', so the concept of traditionalism is still embedded in Australian law. In a subsequent paper dealing with native title controversies, Tonkinson made the following observation:

> Adopting a perspective on tradition that conceptualises it as a resource, strategically deployed by groups of people in the defence or furtherance of their interests, raises larger political issues, particularly in societies like Australia where indigenous cultures coexist with a dominant nation

state. For example, it poses a considerable challenge to law-makers: how to frame and implement heritage and similar legislation so as to take account of the dynamism inherent in indigenous constructions of tradition and the variety of pressures that influence the nature and trajectory of these constructions. The difficulty here is the tension that exists between the need to ensure some degree of flexibility — to allow for the dynamism inherent in these constructions of tradition — and legal requirements for sufficient boundedness or closure to allow legislators to formulate widely applicable criteria for assessing 'significance' (Tonkinson 1997: 12).

He then went on to describe the way in which emergent traditions were labelled as 'suspect' and 'inauthentic', and to note that they are especially vulnerable to attack when they 'threaten in any significant way the interests of governments or the private sector, and potentially large financial returns are seen as endangered by successful invocation of Aboriginal heritage legislation (ibid.: 18). In Australia, there remains a 'lack of public awareness' of the dynamism inherent in Aboriginal culture and a failure to recognise that 'the inevitable transformations through time are due partly to powerful external forces' (ibid.: 19). This is also a problem that needs to be addressed in the way that Australian laws and policies have dealt with Indonesian fishermen.

'Traditional' Activities in the MOU

The idea that Indonesians were engaged in subsistence fishing influenced the 1968 decision to permit 'traditional' Indonesian fishing to continue within the 12 nm territorial sea adjacent to Ashmore Reef, Cartier Island, Seringapatam Reef, Scott Reef, Browse Island, and Adele Island, provided their operations 'were confined to a subsistence level' (DFAT 1988: 1). The 1974 Memorandum of Understanding made no direct reference to the mode of production; 'Indonesian traditional fishermen' were instead defined as 'fishermen who have traditionally taken fish and sedentary organisms in Australian waters by methods which have been the tradition over decades of time' (see Appendix B).

Under the 1989 amendments to the MOU, further qualifications were introduced when access to Australian waters was limited to 'Indonesian traditional fishermen using traditional methods and traditional vessels consistent with the tradition over decades of time, which does not include fishing methods or vessels utilising motors or engines' (see Appendix C). Since 'decades' had to refer to a minimum period of two decades,[1] 'traditional vessels' were defined as *perahu* without motors. The direct reference to Indonesian fishermen with a history of activity in the AFZ was dropped, is indirectly present in the inference that 'traditional fishermen' have been fishing 'over decades'. Implicit in the

---

[1] It is not clear whether the point of reference for this minimum period is 1974 or 1989.

MOU is the notion of traditional societies operating in a static and unchanging fashion over a long period of time. Traditional rights of access are thus determined by continuing use of 'traditional' — that is, unchanging — technology.

The notion of the 'traditional' in the 1974 MOU reflects the essential elements of a popular and prevailing view of indigenous tradition, common both in Australia and elsewhere, as ancient and unchanging (Handler and Linnekin 1984; Merlan 1991; Hovelsrud-Broda 1997; Ewins 1998; Ritchie 1999). An everyday definition of tradition used in relation to the Pacific is 'those beliefs and practices that have been handed down from generation to generation' (Ewins 1998: 3). This view assumes that 'an unchanging core of ideas and customs is always handed down from the past' (Handler and Linnekin 1984: 273) — in the case of the MOU 'over decades of time'. The prevailing view of 'traditionalism' (Merlan 1998) is that changes in tradition, such as the adoption of new technologies as a result of adaptation to changing circumstances, are considered to be 'inauthentic' and therefore not 'traditional'. Since 'modern' often means 'commercial', 'traditional' is equated with 'subsistence', and this 'underpins the belief that "traditional" is, and should continue to be associated with primitive technology' (Campbell and Wilson 1993: 75–6).

While such notions and dichotomies are now rejected in social theory, they still inform the Australian Government's understanding of Indonesian fishing activity in the AFZ. Australia's version of the Orientalist discourse is based on a fictionalised cultural inertia ascribed to Indonesian fishermen. The irony is that Australia makes allowance for its own cultural dynamism by expanding its territorial waters, appropriating Indonesian fishing grounds, and continually upgrading and modernising its maritime technology to patrol these waters. Indonesian fishermen, on the other hand, are forced to use simple fishing gear and unmotorised vessels in order to remain traditional, primitive, stagnant, underdeveloped and technologically unsophisticated. And the Bajo suffer a double jeopardy, because they are also subject to pressure from Indonesian authorities who have 'traditionally' viewed minority cultural groups in much the same light.

The regulations in the 1974 MOU effectively lock Indonesians and their material culture of fishing into a time-bound past. They are forced to operate outside of their own time (Fabian 1983: 2), in a state of 'reified timelessness' (Carrier 1992b: 11), resulting in a technological freeze (Campbell and Wilson 1993: 185). The modernisation of Bajo fishing vessels means that Australian authorities consider they are no longer operating 'traditionally', but are commercial operators whose activities fall outside the regulations of the MOU. The following court case illustrates the shifting status of Indonesian fishermen caught in this traditional/commercial dichotomy.

The Case of the Karya Abadi

On 18 May 1997, a Mola Bajo captain, Si Nasir, and four crew of the Karya Abadi were apprehended for illegally fishing outside the MOU box area, exactly 10.7 nm south of the southern MOU boundary, south of Browse Island, and taken to Broome. The crew and captain were charged under Section 100 of the Commonwealth *Fisheries Management Act 1991* with using a foreign fishing vessel in the AFZ without a licence. The captain was also charged under Section 101 with being in charge of a foreign fishing vessel equipped for fishing. The captain and the crew pleaded not guilty to the charges. Although legal aid was not provided, a lawyer from Perth decided to defend the fishermen on a *pro bono* basis. The crew were held at Willie Creek until their case was finally heard five months later in the Broome Court of Petty Sessions on 16 and 17 October.

The case received an unprecedented level of print and television media coverage before and during the trial because the defence lawyer presented a Mabo-style sea claim and asserted that the fishermen had a native title right to fish in areas of the AFZ outside the MOU box area. If the defendants were all traditional fishermen exercising traditional fishing rights recognised under Australian law, then Sections 100 and 101 of the *Fisheries Management Act 1991* would not apply to them (Vincent 1997).

Legal precedents set in previous cases in Australia had outlined the evidence required to prove native title rights for land or sea, and these formed the basis of the defence case. The first traditional fishing rights case in Australia was heard in the New South Wales Supreme Court in March 1993.[2] It dealt with a man called Mason who was arrested for having more than the allowed limit of abalone in his possession. Mason's defence was that he was 'exercising his native title right to fish and therefore outside the scope of the fisheries regulations' (Peterson and Rigsby 1998: 11). The court 'recognised the existence of a traditional right to fish but questioned whether the defendant was actually practising that right at the time of his arrest', so Mason lost his case (Cane 1998: 66).

Justice Kirby's judgement on appeal found that the right to fish based upon traditional laws and customs is a recognisable form of native title under common law. Justice Kirby also set out the type of evidence required to establish a successful common law claim for native title. The criteria adopted by Nasir's defence to demonstrate the validity of the Bajo claim were informed by this judgement. These were that: (1) the traditional laws and customs covering the right to fish were observed by the communities from which the defendants originated immediately before Australia exercised its sovereignty over the waters in question; (2) the defendants were indigenous people and descendants ('or

---

[2] The case is documented as *Mason v Tritton* in 34 *New South Wales Law Reports* 572 (1994).

within the permitted group') of the relevant communities; (3) they had continued, uninterrupted, to observe the relevant traditional laws and customs; and (4) their activities in fishing for shark fin were an exercise of those traditional laws and customs. [3]

In submissions to the magistrate the defence highlighted two contentious questions about the definition of 'traditional' activities. The first was whether fishing for shark fin for sale or barter could be regarded as a traditional practice and the second was whether the use of longline gear could be regarded as a traditional fishing method. Not only did the defence argue that sale of shark fin is in keeping with the traditional practices of the Bajo; it was also argued that there is in law no requirement for customary practices to be immutable or fixed in time. The second argument was based on judgements by Justice Brennan in the Mabo case and by Justice Kirby in the Mason case.

The magistrate handed down his decision on 11 November 1997. He ruled that the *Fisheries Management Act 1991* was plainly intended to extinguish foreign traditional fishing rights in Australian waters. Since the MOU set aside areas within the AFZ where traditional fishermen could operate, he said that this indicated a legislative intention to abrogate any such rights that may have existed in other parts of the AFZ (Roberts 1997: 15). He also found that the defendants could establish points (1) and (2) in their main argument, but could not establish points (3) and (4), and could not therefore be properly regarded as 'traditionally fishing' (ibid.: 19). One of his reasons was that evidence presented by a Western Australian fisheries officer showed that longlines cannot be considered as a traditional fishing method because of their recent adoption and size.

> Previously shark boats used only handlines and the fishermen kept all of the shark. Now they only keep the fins or a small proportion of the body.... Further, the price of shark fin has increased dramatically whereby Indonesian fishermen may receive up to $80A per kilo for No 1 grade product.... Even allowing for cultural dynamics, the recent development of relatively sophisticated longlining appears to be as a direct result of the high price paid to Indonesian fishermen for shark fin and the desire to maximise profits. In my view this method of fishing cannot be said to be a traditional fishing practise [sic] — even making allowances for changing fishing equipment technology (ibid.: 21).

---

[3] The International Commission of Jurists, as well as various philanthropists, anthropologists, historians, and members of the Broome based Kimberley–Indonesia Friendship Society provided funding and evidence to support the defence case. Because of my research into the activities of the Mola Bajo in the AFZ, I was asked to submit a report on evidence in defence of Nasir and the crew addressing the four criteria outlined above. I also appeared as an expert witness during the trial.

The magistrate also noted that the *Torres Strait Fisheries Act 1984* 'excludes traditional fishing from the definition of commercial fishing', but no such exclusion is made in the *Fisheries Management Act 1991*, so he concluded that the defendants were engaged in commercial fishing (ibid.: 6).

> I have reservations in accepting the proposition that a defence based upon a traditional fishing right extends to fishing for commercial purposes ... the formal written contract entered into by Nasir with the money lender, the sale and/or exchange of shark fin for goods or money and the use of the longline demonstrate that his venture was of a commercial rather than traditional nature (ibid.: 21–2).

The magistrate convicted the fishermen on all charges and placed them on good behaviour bonds of A$ 3000 for five years. He ordered forfeiture of the fishing gear but not the vessel. His reasons for this decision were that six months in detention awaiting the trial and judgement amounted to fair punishment for the crew, and that the vessel was only 10.7 nm outside the MOU box. However, he added that by using what he called 'imprecise' and 'primitive' navigational equipment (compass and depth lead line), the captain was reckless to be fishing so close to the MOU box boundary. A few days later, the vessel was stocked with food and towed for three days to the outer edge of the AFZ from where the captain and crew returned to Indonesia.

The Broome decision is strangely contradictory. Fishermen using longline gear operating inside the MOU box area are not apprehended for being non-traditional and therefore engaged in illegal activity. The Karya Abadi had been boarded by a senior WA fisheries officer inside the MOU box area northeast of Ashmore Reef ten days before its apprehension. According to the evidence presented in court, the officer stated that he informed the captain where he could and could not fish and also inspected his fishing gear. In doing so, he acknowledged that the men were 'traditional fishermen' since they were carrying out 'traditional fishing' within the terms of the MOU regulations. No Indonesian *perahu* has ever been apprehended and convicted for charges of being 'non-traditional' in the MOU box. However, if the same vessel is found operating outside the MOU box area using the same longline gear, the activities of the crew become 'non-traditional', 'commercial' and 'illegal'.

Commerce and Tradition

There is now widespread academic awareness of the paradoxical fluidity of tradition (Ewins 1998: 12). Culture is shaped by changes in social, economic and historical circumstances although 'it has taken some time for anthropology to come to terms with a humanity that is equal, that is universally dynamic and changing, possibly in different ways within different cultural projects, but which could not simply be sundered into the progressive and the traditional'

(Miller 1994: 59). Legal precedents in Australia, in some instances informed by contemporary anthropological opinion, have come some way towards acknowledging cultural dynamism, and rejecting a definition of 'traditional' activities based on technology, but this is in stark contrast to the approach written into the 1974 MOU and its amendments.

In 1986, the Australian Law Reform Commission rejected such a definition of 'traditional' Aboriginal hunting and fishing activity:

> In determining whether an activity is 'traditional' attention should focus on the purpose of the activity rather than the method (LRC 1986: 181).

The Commission also acknowledged the changing nature of Aboriginal traditions:

> Aboriginals have had to adapt to change and outside influence ... [and] in many cases hunting and fishing practices have incorporated new materials. Nylon fishing nets may have replaced those made of bush fibre ... guns may very often have replaced spears, aluminium dinghies are used instead of dugouts (ibid.: 121).

The Commission's findings related to Aboriginal subsistence activities, broadly including 'consumption within local family or clan groups ... even though elements of barter or exchange may be present' (ibid.: 181). They do not directly apply to Indonesian fishermen since the latter are not fishing for subsistence and are not Australian citizens. However, as Campbell and Wilson (1993: 78–9) have previously argued, a definition of 'traditional' activity based on the purpose rather than the method has already been applied to foreign fishermen in the *Torres Strait Treaty 1978* between Australia and Papua New Guinea.

According to Article 10(3), the principal aim of this treaty is 'to acknowledge and protect the traditional way of life and livelihood of the traditional inhabitants including their traditional fishing and free movement'. In Article 1(l), the treaty defines traditional fishing as 'the taking, by traditional inhabitants for their own or their dependants' consumption, or for use in the course of other traditional activities, of the living resources of the sea, seabed, estuaries and coastal tidal areas, including dugong and turtle'. In Article 1(k), it defines 'traditional activities' as:

> Activities performed by the traditional inhabitants in accordance with local tradition, and includes, when so performed —
>
> (i) activities on land, including gardening, collection of food and hunting;
>
> (ii) activities on water, including traditional fishing;
>
> (iii) religious and secular ceremonies or gatherings for social purposes, for example, marriage celebrations and settlements of disputes; and
>
> (iv) barter and market trade.

In the application of this definition, except in relation to activities of a
commercial nature, 'traditional' shall be interpreted liberally and in light
of prevailing custom.

There is no reference to the methods of traditional fishing, only to the purpose,
and there is a recognition that customs can change. This last point has been
recognised more recently in the Australian High Court's second Mabo decision,
where Justice Brennan stated that the 'laws and customs of any people will
change'. [4] The Broome decision contradicted these important findings.

There is still contention in Australia about whether a traditional fishing
activity or right can have a commercial purpose. The *Torres Strait Treaty* denies
this possibility.

[A]fter a century of commercial fishing by the Strait's indigenous
inhabitants it was uncertain what fishing activities could be legitimately
regarded as 'traditional'. By adopting a narrow definition of traditional
which excludes commercial activities, the Treaty failed to acknowledge
the fluidity of tradition as well as the dynamic quality of economic
decision making in the face of changing social conditions (Schug 1996:
219).

In Nasir's case the magistrate relied on Section 3 of the *Torres Strait Fisheries
Act 1984*, which defines 'commercial fishing' as 'fishing for commercial purposes,
but does not include traditional fishing'.

In Australian courts there have been no clear legal determinations on whether
Aboriginal native title rights include commercial activities (Sutherland 1996:
28; Peterson and Rigsby 1998: 12). There are indications that the right to native
title and traditional practice extends to commercial use (Kilduff and Lofgren
1996) but this has yet to be successfully tested. It would appear that in Australia
official perceptions of Indonesian fishermen are consistent with representations
of indigenous Australians. The 'traditional' is still largely represented as an
inversion of the 'commercial'. But for as long as Indonesian fishermen are known
to have been fishing in the north Australian region, this has primarily been for
commercial rather than subsistence purposes (Campbell and Wilson 1993).
Drawing a distinction between traditional and commercial fishing activity is
untenable in the case of the Bajo fishery.

There is, as the Broome case illustrates, a generally held belief on the part of
the Australian authorities that fishermen have switched from 'traditional' to
'commercial' fishing because of increases in the price of shark fin in recent years
and are now catching more sharks with the adoption of more 'modern' fishing
gear (Wallner and McLoughlin 1995b: 120). Campbell and Wilson (1993: 75)

[4] The quotation is from *Mabo No 2* 1992-175 *Commonwealth Law Reports* 1 at 61.

provide an alternative account of this perception: 'shark fishermen take shark fin "traditionally" provided the profit is small; once they begin to make significant commercial returns their activities cease to be traditional'. This understanding was reflected in the Broome case, and parallels the point made by Tonkinson (1997: 18) about Aboriginal traditions ceasing to be 'traditional' if they change in ways that threaten government or private sector interests. The Australian Government focuses on the high returns Indonesians are making on successful shark fishing trips and the perceived loss of Australian revenues as a result of this activity. As one Darwin magistrate stated in his decision to convict the Mola Bajo captain of the Bintang Nusantara for illegal fishing in the AFZ in March 1999: 'Clearly fish in the AFZ is an asset which the court jealously guards, and an asset if not properly controlled will be plundered by a people with no legal right'.

This sort of thinking provides a justification for continuing the policy of apprehension and prosecution. The Australian authorities apprehend Bajo and other groups of fishermen operating in sail-powered boats outside the MOU box area using longline gear to fish for shark fin because they are seen to have betrayed their earlier authentic 'traditional' status and thus forfeited any 'traditional' rights they may have previously had.

How Effective is Australian Policy?

The 1974 MOU recognises some form of traditional fishing rights and attempts to regulate access for traditional Indonesian fishermen in an area now under Australian control. However, in the words of Fox (1998: 114), 'numerous problems have arisen as a result of this seemingly well-intended endeavour' and led to a succession of 'unintended consequences'.

The MOU does not specifically identify who is allowed access into the MOU area. Rather, access is open to any Indonesian 'traditional' fishermen as long as they comply with the regulations which narrowly define 'traditional' methods and vessels. Access is not determined by historically recognised use rights for specific groups who operated in the region prior to Australian maritime expansion; any group of fishermen using a sail-powered boat is allowed to fish in the region. By failing to identify the specific groups who historically accessed the AFZ, the effectiveness and original intention of the MOU has been undermined and its outcomes severely attenuated.

The original purpose of excluding the use of motorised vessels and methods in the face of increasing motorisation in the small-scale *perahu* sector in Indonesia was to limit the number of boats entering the area. This policy was designed to control the level of resource exploitation and therefore function as a form of resource management. The idea was that if the technology was unsophisticated or 'primitive' it could offer some protection for marine resources. But this technological freeze has failed to achieve the desired outcome. By not restricting the numbers of vessels or the amount of product taken, it opened the area up to an unlimited number of fishermen in sail-powered vessels, of which there is no shortage in eastern Indonesia, and this has resulted in over-exploitation of resources in the MOU box area, particularly sedentary species on reefs and inshore waters.

By not permitting the use of motorised vessels in times of bad weather, the Government has also been accused of enforcing a policy that subjects the fishermen to unnecessary risks (Campbell and Wilson 1993; Fox 1998: 121). Over the last decade, a number of sailing boats and their crews have been lost during cyclones in the MOU area. For example, in April 1994, four Pepela-owned boats and their mostly Bajo crews drowned during a cyclone in the Timor Sea. On the other hand, in periods of little or no wind, or strong currents, when it is impossible to make any headway in a sail-powered vessel, strong currents can easily drag a sail-powered vessel beyond the permitted areas.

Legal fishing in the MOU box area can also be seen as a gateway to illegal fishing (Fox 1998). The 1989 amendments that created this area did not incorporate the most productive Bajo shark fishing grounds. Apart from a few areas around reefs and islands and along the edges of the MOU box, it is a relatively poor shark fishing ground (Wallner and McLoughlin 1995a: 34). No motorised Type 3 *perahu* have been apprehended for illegal shark fishing activity in this area. Butonese and Bajo fishermen from across eastern Indonesia who use motorised boats to target shark prefer to concentrate their activities in the more productive waters to the north and east of the MOU box (ibid.). Bajo fishermen often seek access to these waters by passing through the MOU box, but in doing so they run the risk of apprehension. Fishermen are forced to fish illegally outside the MOU box area in an attempt to secure adequate returns. Illegal fishing and boat apprehensions thus occur in direct response to the ineffectiveness of the MOU itself.

Naturally, the borders of the MOU box area cannot be marked or signposted. They only exist as lines on maps, unconnected to any geographical features. Bajo navigation is based on reference to familiar landmarks and sea features. Their sailing and fishing activities have, until recently, never been confined to areas bounded by lines on maps. Even for the most experienced navigators, it is difficult to determine exactly where the boundaries of the MOU box are. The MOU restricts access to fishermen using 'traditional methods' but expects the accuracy of modern navigation. Accurate determination of latitude and longitude requires the use of marine charts and sophisticated navigational equipment such as a Global Positioning System. Prior to the early 1990s, fishermen found within an unspecified reasonable distance of the permitted areas were generally warned but not apprehended. The tougher approach adopted by AFMA in recent years has seen Bajo and other fishermen apprehended as little as 5–8 nm outside the MOU box. Fishermen who are denied the use of motors and sophisticated equipment under the MOU are treated in the same fashion as an industrial foreign fishing vessel worth millions of dollars caught illegally fishing in the AFZ.

Neither the 1974 MOU nor the Plan of Management for Ashmore Reef National Nature Reserve (ANPWS 1989) makes any mention of this reef's cultural heritage value. At least eight Indonesian graves have been identified on West Island and others on East and Middle islets (ANPWS n.d.), and fishermen are officially prohibited from landing on the islands to visit these sites. [5] However, formal requests by fishermen are made to the caretaker to obtain permission to visit and maintain the graves, perform ceremonies and present offerings, and the caretaker often accompanies the fishermen on these visits (personal communication, Paul Clark, 1999).

Indonesian fishermen have played no role in shaping the MOU itself. The agreement makes some attempt at recognising their rights but they have not been invited or allowed to participate in its formulation or implementation. They are not alone, for the interests of maritime peoples are often 'ignored, dismissed or marginalised' (Schug 1996: 210) in the formulation of international maritime boundaries and agreements designed to protect *their* livelihood. The case of the indigenous people of the Torres Strait is one example: the boundaries between Papua New Guinea and Australia established under the *Torres Strait Treaty* were developed 'without sufficient consultation with the people who would be affected most directly by the political division', and this has 'created an unstable situation which threatens to undermine intention the Treaty's efforts to provide for the protection of the Strait's marine environment' (ibid.: 222). In the case of the MOU, dialogue may be effective at a government-to-government level but other stakeholders, such as Indonesian fishermen, are unable to participate.

The Australian Aid Program

Included in the minutes of the meeting between Australian and Indonesian government officials in April 1989 is a provision which states that:

> Indonesian and Australian officials agreed to make arrangements for cooperation in developing alternative income projects in Eastern Indonesia for traditional fishermen traditionally engaged in fishing under the MOU. The Indonesian side indicated they might include mariculture and nucleus fishing enterprise scheme (Perikanan Inti Rakyat or P.I.R.). Both sides mutually decided to discuss the possibility of channelling Australian aid funds to such projects with appropriate authorities in their respective countries.

---

[5] At least one of these graves is that of a Bajo man from Mola Selatan.

The 'nucleus fishing enterprise scheme' is a transmigration program in the fisheries sector which is used to shift the rural and/or fishing population from densely populated areas to those islands where population density is low. No Australian aid was subsequently directed to the Bajo fishermen who operate in the AFZ, and it was not until the late 1990s that any official Australian delegations visited the villages of Mola, Mantigola or Pepela. The idea of direct engagement with fishermen and an understanding of the issues from their point of view appeared to be completely alien to the Australian authorities.

The educational and information tours undertaken by Australian officials to eastern Indonesia in 1995 were in response to high levels of incursion into the AFZ in 1994. During the visits, maps were distributed in an effort to explain the complex maritime jurisdictions existing between Australia and Indonesia in the Timor and Arafura seas and the MOU area. These were accompanied by two handouts in Indonesian entitled *Pesan Permerintah Australia untuk Nelayan* ('Message for Fishermen from the Australian Government') and *Pesan Pemerintah Australia untuk Pemilik Perahu /Kapal dan Otorita Pelabuhan* ('Message for *Perahu* /Boat Owners and Harbour Authorities from the Australian Government'). [6] The Australian authorities seem to think that their maps are readily understood by Indonesian fishermen and that they can help them to determine where they can and cannot fish. Fishermen with maps certainly have no excuse if found outside of the permitted areas. However, some Bajo captains, especially those who were illiterate, found the maps highly confusing and difficult, if not impossible, to comprehend.

During the course of their awareness-raising tours, officials from the Australian Agency for International Development (AusAID) did explore the opportunities for delivery of aid to poor isolated fishing communities. As a result AusAID has implemented some small projects, but these have not been directed to fishermen whose activities are covered by the MOU, but to people from Sinjai in South Sulawesi who were apprehended in large numbers in 1994–95 following a wave of illegal trepang fishing activity in the northern part of the AFZ. Some support from the Direct Assistance Program of the Australian Ambassador to Indonesia was given to other fishing communities, including Pepela, but the outcome was somewhat ironic. In one instance the money was used to purchase a *perahu lambo* on the understanding that the proceeds from fishing would be distributed among the community, but the *perahu* (the Bintang Pagi) was subsequently apprehended, confiscated and destroyed in Darwin.

---

[6] The first maps produced in late 1994 were A4 black-and-white photocopies. These were replaced a few months later with larger A3 plastic colour-coded maps. A second edition was produced in August 1997 and reprinted in February 2000. The third edition was produced in December 2004 and is now available on the AFMA website in both English and Bahasa Indonesian (www.afma.gov.au/management/compliance/illegal/default.htm).

There is a serious inconsistency here. Australia has a policy commitment to deliver aid to eastern Indonesian fishermen operating under the terms of the MOU, yet retains a policy of confiscating and destroying the sources of livelihood of these very same people. In February 1995, an ABC journalist interviewed a representative from the Australian Embassy in Jakarta and a senior officer from the WA Fisheries Department who had just returned from the first educational tour of eastern Indonesia. The embassy representative explained that the Australian Government was exploring opportunities for the delivery of aid for 'isolated poor fishing communities in eastern Indonesia ... who need, for their livelihood, to gain income to support their families and are ready and willing ... to often engage in some risky fishing activities south of the border' (ABC Radio National 1995: 2). In the same interview, the fisheries officer discussed the effectiveness of the deterrence policy:

> From our experience ... we've found the only real deterrent is to continue prosecuting them and to take their boats off them and just fly them home.... I think this is the only real way we can deter them is to continually confiscate and burn their boats, so they lose all their boats and *all* their fishing equipment, and fly them home back to Indonesia. And just continually do that (ibid.: 5).

As Fox (1998: 131) noted, it is an 'outright contradiction' for the Australian Government to fund aid projects to alleviate poverty in eastern Indonesia while burning vessels belonging to some of the poorest inhabitants of the region.

The Record of Apprehensions

For over a decade, the policy of apprehension and confiscation of boats, catch and equipment as a form of deterrent to further illegal activity has been in place. Between 1988 and 1993, there was an overall decline in the number of boat apprehensions, which gave the impression that the policy of apprehension and confiscation was working. However, there was a dramatic increase over the course of the next four years, and this included an increase in the apprehension of Type 2 *perahu* using longline gear (see Figure 8-1). Of the total number of Indonesian boats apprehended between 1975 and 1997, approximately 22 per cent or 134 boats were Type 2 vessels.

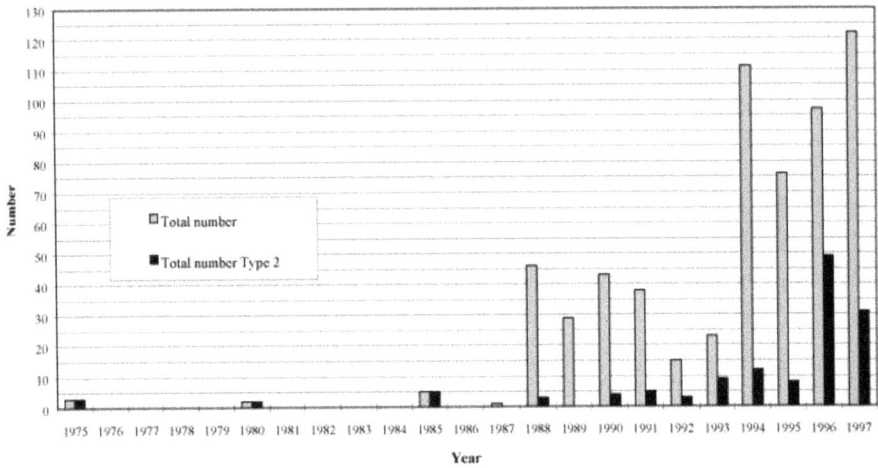

Figure 8-1: Total number of boat apprehensions and total number of Type 2 boat apprehensions, 1975–97.

The educational and information campaigns of the 1990s seem to have introduced the AFZ to coastal peoples who may not have previously been aware of the existence of the MOU and the permitted areas. The campaigns themselves may therefore have contributed to larger numbers of boats from eastern Indonesia beginning to engage in illegal activity. If we look at the proportion of Bajo Type 2 *perahu* among the total number of Type 2 *perahu* apprehended in those years when there were any apprehensions of such vessels, we can see that the proportion declined in those years when the total number of apprehensions suddenly began to increase (Table 8-1). In 1996, when 49 Type 2 *perahu* were apprehended, only 18 of them were Bajo *perahu*.

The present enforcement and prosecution approach costs the Australian taxpayer millions of dollars each year. Expenses include the costs of towing the vessels to Darwin or Broome, carrying out immigration, quarantine and customs checks, maintaining crews and vessels until the completion of court hearings, repatriation of fishermen and destruction of forfeited boats. The costs incurred for each apprehension boat crew depend on the length of time the fishermen are detained, and this in turn depends on the prosecution process.[7] It is difficult to obtain official government figures on these expenses because there is a reluctance to place such information in the public domain and many different government departments and agencies are involved in the process.

---

[7] The average stay for fishermen has been reported to be 27 days (Commonwealth Ombudsman 1998: 30), but some fishermen spend months awaiting court hearings.

Table 8-1: Total number of Type 2 apprehensions and Bajo Type 2 apprehensions, 1975–97.

Year	Total Type 2	Bajo Type 2
1975	3	3
1980	2	0
1985	5	5
1988	3	0
1990	4	4
1991	5	5
1992	3	3
1993	9	0
1994	12	8
1995	8	1
1996	49	18
1997	31	15
Total	134	62

Source: AFMA Apprehension lists, Northern Territory and Western Australia.

In its submission to the Joint Standing Committee on Foreign Affairs, Defence and Trade (JSCFDAT) in 1991, AFMA reported that the costs associated with the apprehension of Indonesian vessels in 1989–90 was A$ 750 499 (Fox 1998: 132). A senior AFMA official has stated that his organisation spent around A$ 3 500 000 on 124 foreign fishing apprehensions, of which 113 were Indonesian, in the financial year 1997/98. This amount included the salaries of 15–20 fisheries officers on AFZ patrolling duties and other fisheries support functions and the costs of caretaking and security operations while fishermen are in detention. In Darwin the contracting caretakers receive about A$ 1000 a day from AFMA for each vessel and crew in their care. This amount covers staff salaries and the cost of providing food, medical treatment, and transport for the fishermen who have been detained. Legal Aid lawyers say that the cost of legal representation for the fishermen is also around A$ 1000 a day. From Darwin, fishermen are normally repatriated to Kupang on a Merpati flight. A one-way ticket costs A$ 244–319 depending on the time of year. Repatriation from Broome is more expensive. For those few fishermen who are able to pay security bonds and return to Indonesia in their boats, the Australian authorities incur several thousand dollars in additional costs by towing the vessels to the international border.

The effectiveness of the policy of apprehension in deterring illegal activity was questioned by the JSCFDAT in 1993. The committee concluded that was a drop in the price of trochus shell, and not surveillance and enforcement, that had caused a decline in illegal trochus harvesting in the AFZ in the early 1990s. The committee also considered that similar enforcement and prosecution approaches were 'unlikely to be effective' against illegal shark fishing while the price of shark fin remained high (JSCFDAT 1993: 129).

New Policy Approaches

Current Australian policies toward Indonesian fishermen are clearly inappropriate and ineffective. Apprehension and confiscation of Bajo *perahu* should cease. New approaches and new agreements are needed to regulate Indonesian fishing in the AFZ. The MOU is a simple document designed to deal with a complex situation. Despite its failings, it does grant some form of fishing rights to small-scale fishermen from Indonesia. However, an open access fishery system, which determines the right of entry by reference to technology rather than specific user rights, and which then confines fishermen to inappropriate fishing grounds, cannot achieve an equitable allocation of resources or prevent illegal activity. A new agreement should be negotiated in line with the 'spirit of cooperation and good neighbourliness' of the original MOU.

A number of alternative approaches and regulations have been suggested (Russell and Vail 1988: 139–42; Reid 1992: 8; Campbell and Wilson 1993: 186; JSCFDAT 1993: 132–3; Wallner and McLoughlin 1995a: 34, 1995b: 121; Fox 1992, 1996: 174, 1998: 130). Taken in combination, they indicate that Australia should move to: (1) abandon the current definition of traditional fishing that defines access in terms of technology and assumes that traditions cannot change; (2) identify specific groups of fishermen who have historically fished in the AFZ and guarantee specific rights of access for them; (3) introduce some form of management intervention in the form of a quota or licensing system to avoid over-exploitation of existing stocks; and (4) provide access to an area that more closely resembles traditional fishing grounds and takes account of resource availability.

A Licensing System

Some suggestions have already been made about how a licensing system could operate and what benefits it would deliver to Indonesia and Australia once groups with a historical interest in the AFZ have been identified (Reid 1992; Campbell and Wilson 1993; Wallner and McLoughlin 1995a; Fox 1998). [8] An arrangement of this kind could be operated through the harbour master in Pepela who currently keeps records of arrivals and departures and issues sailing clearances. In one version of the system, the harbour master would be responsible

---

[8] Fox (1998: 129–30, 138) notes that the details of any such system would need to be negotiated with the Indonesian authorities.

for issuing seasonal non-transferable licences to *perahu* captains in line with conditions set down by the Australian Government. Decisions about who obtained the licences would be made by local community members and carefully monitored. The Australian authorities would be informed at the beginning of each season of the details of all licensed *perahu*. Any violations would result in the suspension of the licence for three years.

The licensing of boats to fish for shark only inside the existing MOU box area (Fox 1998) would not actually deter illegal fishing outside the box since there are not sufficient stocks available in the box area. Bajo fishermen are prepared to pay relatively large amounts of money for licences as long as they are assured of access to fishing grounds that have reasonable fish stocks. Many fishermen would then have no further incentive to engage in illegal fishing activities and this in turn would save Australia millions of dollars in apprehension and prosecution costs. Fishermen with specific access rights

> would be reluctant to commit offences which risked their privileged access; they would have an interest in helping Australian authorities protect "their" resources from illegal voyaging ... [and their new rights] would deliver aid to certain communities in the form of guaranteed access to resources (Campbell and Wilson 1993: 194).

Through direct engagement with fishermen in the implementation of new policies and procedures, there could also be education in the appropriate forms of resource management and conservation (ibid.: 195).

Reasons for Inaction

New policy approaches have not been tried because there is a lack of political will on the part of the Australian and Indonesian governments to instigate or support research on the groups that would qualify for specific user rights. Only when this information is known can consideration be given to developing appropriate conditions under which a traditional fishery could operate in the AFZ. [9] The Bajo are one group of Indonesian fishermen who historically fished in the AFZ prior to Australian maritime expansion and have continued to do so. However, we need to know much more. A detailed analysis of the other groups operating in the MOU still needs to be undertaken. Groups of fishermen from the villages of Pepela and Oelaba, as well as the Madurese, can also claim to have legitimate rights of access to Australian waters.

There is also lingering uncertainty over seabed and water column boundaries between Indonesia, Australia and Timor Leste. In 1973, a bilateral agreement between Australia and Indonesia established seabed boundaries extending from

---

[9] There has also been a lack of reliable data on the actual status of marine resources in the northern AFZ and MOU box area that could be used to assist in designing future levels of access for Indonesian fishermen.

the Papua New Guinea border in the east to waters between Ashmore Reef and Roti Island in the west, but left a gap in the boundary south of the then Portuguese colony of East Timor which became known as the Timor Gap (Kaye 1995: 45). The western extension of the seabed boundary between the two countries from a point north of Ashmore Reef was also undecided. Once the two countries had extended their exclusive economic zones, the Timor Gap Treaty established a Zone of Cooperation between Australia and Indonesia that provided for the sharing of oil revenues under the seabed south of East Timor (ibid.: 53). This was re-negotiated in 2002 as the Timor Sea Treaty between the Government of Australia and the newly independent state of Timor Leste during a period when that state was both politically and economically fragile, so it remains a bone of contention in the area. Map 8-1 shows the current maritime boundaries between the three countries, with the letter 'A' designating the Joint Petroleum Development Area defined by the Timor Sea Treaty between Australia and Timor Leste.

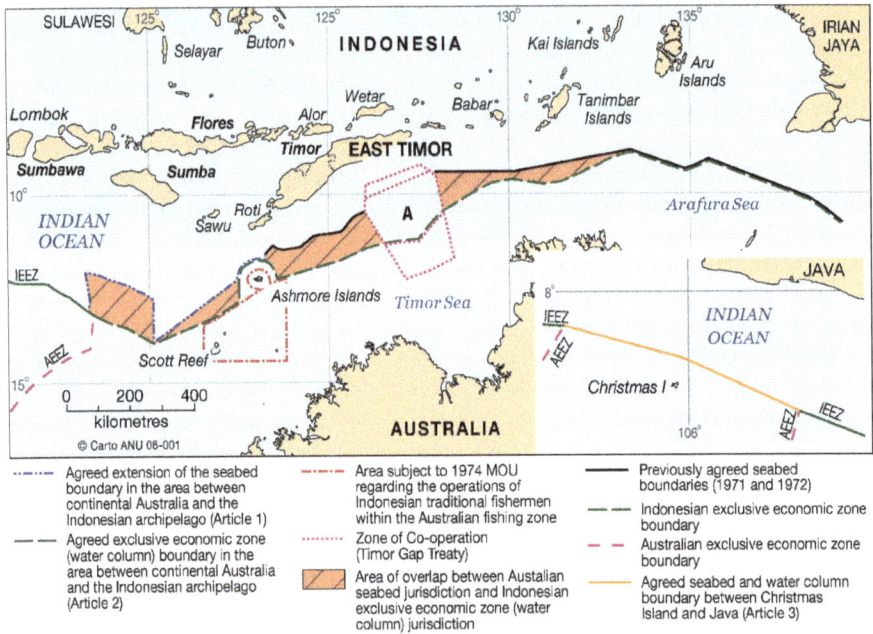

Map 8-1: International maritime boundaries in the Timor and Arafura seas.

The maritime boundaries between Australia and Indonesia should have been further clarified by the Australia–Indonesia Maritime Delimitation Treaty signed in 1997 (DFAT 1997), but a number of problems arose in the process of ratification, and these became the subject of an inquiry by the Commonwealth Joint Standing Committee on Treaties. Under the provisions of this treaty, Ashmore Reef would generate a 24 nm exclusive economic zone in place of the

12 nm zone recognised in the 1974 MOU, and this would place an additional restriction on the rights of Indonesian fishermen as well as raising more enforcement problems. The committee therefore recommended that

> the Australian Government in consultation with the relevant State and Territory governments, review the 1974 traditional fisher Memorandum of Understanding with Indonesia in light of the changes to the Exclusive Economic Zone boundary in the vicinity of Ashmore Islands, and ... review the issue of ongoing Indonesian traditional fisher access to Australian waters and its impact on the sustained management of Australian fish resources (JSCT 1997: ix).

Political developments in East Timor since 1999 have entailed a further reassessment of the 1997 treaty which could still have significant implications for Bajo fishing activity in the Timor Sea.

There appears to be a perception by the Australian government that the education, enforcement and prosecution approach is a workable solution to illegal fishing activity. The approach may work for certain groups operating in the AFZ at certain times, but it has been ineffective against other groups by virtue of the ongoing access afforded under the MOU. As one commentator observes:

> without serious reconsideration ... [the policy] is difficult to comprehend. One can only speculate on why Australia persists with a policy that is so evidently inappropriate to the problem that it is intended to solve (Fox 1998: 134).

One possible explanation is the belief generated in Australian government circles that the Government of Indonesia is responsible for the activities of its many small-scale fishermen and has the capacity to control the thousands of boats used by villagers (Fox 1998: 134–5; see also JSCFDAT 1993: 129; JSCT 1997: 36). There is also a belief that the situation could be remedied by regulating the activities of those entrepreneurs in Indonesia who control the trade in marine products and the middlemen who are thought to control the activities of the fishermen (Fox 1998: 134).

The antiquated definition of 'tradition' also enters into the equation. According to Fox:

> Other, perhaps deeper, attitudes are involved in maintaining present policy — a determination on the part of some Australians to uphold, at whatever cost, the integrity of territorial boundaries and an equal determination to preserve a strict interpretation of the law. Perhaps more pertinent is a perceived difficulty in dealing with what has been defined as 'traditional', as if tradition was something frozen in time and not

amenable to processes of reasonable discussion and negotiation (ibid.: 135).

Another commentator has suggested that the Australian Government's refusal to change its understanding of tradition

> is nothing else but a rhetorical device serving the legitimation and execution of its policies. There is obviously no political will to adopt any other definition, as the present one serves the stated objectives of territorial, commercial, and environmental protection quite adequately. It is, therefore, in Australian policy makers' interests to continue to view Indonesian fishing in the AFZ as a largely homogenous phenomenon, with virtually no differentiation made between fisheries and fishermen … without considerations of time-depth, or a clear understanding of the social complexity which underwrites small-scale commercial fishing (Van der Spek 1995: 21–2).

This logic provides the necessary justification to continue the policy of apprehensions, potentially cancel the MOU with Indonesia, and close access to the AFZ for Indonesian traditional fishermen.

There is also an antiquated but powerful form of conservation thinking that has informed Australian policies; one that considers indigenous peoples as 'enemies' and 'threats' to natural resources, rather than as the key to their sustainability (Stevens 1997: 4). The exclusionary management regime of the Ashmore Reef National Nature Reserve exemplified this kind of consciousness.

The Way Forward

Australia does in fact have some legal obligation to recognise prior activity in the AFZ by people from Indonesia. Under Article 62(2) of UNCLOS III, the nationals of foreign states are technically entitled to the surplus of the total allowable catch in an Exclusive Economic Zone. In allocating this surplus to foreigners, a coastal state is required by Article 62(3) to take account of several factors, including the significance of the living resources of the area to its own economy and the need to minimise economic dislocation in states whose nationals have habitually (that is, traditionally) fished in the zone. However, Article 77(2) says that foreign states and their citizens do not have any direct legal rights to the resources on the continental shelf, which relieves Australia of any obligation to grant Indonesian fishermen access to sedentary species around offshore reefs and islands in the MOU area. Furthermore, UNCLOS III does not specifically protect the rights and interests of indigenous peoples, and the way forward for Australia and Indonesia will depend less on their legal obligations under this convention than on bilateral relations and commitments between the two countries (Campbell and Wilson 1993: 194; Tsamenyi 1995: 10).

Australia has other international obligations with regard to indigenous peoples' rights of access to resources. Multilateral environmental and human rights treaties, to which Australia is a signatory, have recognised that indigenous people retain traditional ecological knowledge and methods of natural and cultural resource management which can contribute to sustainable development.[10] International human rights standards require that governments recognise indigenous people's rights to 'customary use of resources, even in protected areas, rights to participate in decision-making and be included in management regimes which recognise customary resource use, and rights to benefit equitably in the returns generated by resource use' (Sutherland 1996: 5).

The MOU needs to be renegotiated on the basis of contemporary circumstances and fishery management principles and practices, not those of the early 1970s. Future strategies need to excise outdated assumptions and be brought into line with national and international standards. Contemporary approaches to fisheries management are now moving away from biological management, scientific modelling and centralised government responses. They are moving towards partnerships between people, administrative decentralisation, and co-management between government and local communities. It is now clear that fisheries management will not succeed without the involvement of the fishermen themselves (Pomeroy 1994: 2; White et al. 1994; Hviding and Baines 1996: 80; Mace 1997: 2). More specifically, fishermen must have a recognised 'stake' in resource management in the form of rights if they are also to have incentives for resource protection (Bailey and Zerner 1992: 11; White et al. 1994: 14).

Fisheries management also needs to take into account the social, cultural, and economic dimensions of resource use and exploitation (White et al. 1994: 9). These issues were reiterated in a number of presentations at the Second World Fisheries Congress held in Brisbane in 1997 (Hancock et al. 1997). Guidelines developed by the UN Food and Agriculture Organisation on precautionary approaches to fisheries management also emphasise the necessity for cooperation between stakeholders in the development of management plans (Mace 1997: 13). One of the guiding principles of AFMA's management philosophy is to ensure active participation of user groups in the 'development and implementation of fisheries management measures' (McColl and Stevens 1997). It is now an appropriate time for the Australian Government to apply its stated philosophy to Indonesian fishing activity in the AFZ.

---

[10] The most notable examples are the *International Covenant on Civil and Political Rights* (1991) and the *Convention on Biological Diversity* (1993).

Appendix A: Sources on Indonesian Fishing in Australian Waters

The history of Indonesian voyages to northern Australia, from the early seventeenth century to the early twentieth century, has been the subject of detailed archaeological research. The major work on the Macassan trepang industry is Macknight (1976). More recent archaeological research on Macassan visits to the Northern Territory was undertaken by Mitchell (1994) and on Macassan activity in Western Australia by Morwood and Hobbs (1997).

The main bodies of literature on the diverse groups of fishermen from Indonesia who have fished in the northwest Australian waters from the early twentieth century until the late 1960s are reports from various newspapers and government archives, an unpublished compilation of material by Bottrill (1993), and publications by Bach (1955) and Bain (1982). Both Bach and Bain devote some attention to foreign fishing and poaching activities in their studies of the northwest Australian pearling industry. Other sources on Indonesian fishing activity include: the records of a 1949 Commonwealth Scientific and Industrial Research Organisation fisheries survey in the Timor Sea (CSIRO 1949), including one publication by the senior scientist in the survey team (Serventy 1952); an account by Lind (1994) who was a resident in the Kimberley region in Western Australia; the Australian Customs Service file on the apprehension of an Indonesian *perahu* in 1957; and sections of the doctoral thesis by Crawford (1969) which was subsequently published in 2001.

There is also a range of material stemming from research on Indonesian fishing vessels held in museum collections around Australia (see Stacey 1997). The Australian National Maritime Museum in Sydney has the Madurese *perahu lete lete* Sekar Aman and associated fishing equipment in its collection. Articles and reports from research on the voyage of the Sekar Aman and other Madurese voyages to the Timor Sea region can be found in Mellefont (1988, 1991a, 1991b, 1997) and Scott (1988). The Western Australian Maritime Museum in Fremantle has a *perahu lambo*,theSama Biasa, which originated in Pepela and was later confiscated and donated to the museum in 1980 along with other collections of fishing equipment. This has vessel has been the subject of research on *perahu lambo* boat building traditions (Burningham 1989). The Museum and Art Gallery of the Northern Territory (MAGNT) in Darwin has the largest ethnographic collection of Indonesian watercraft and fishing material culture in Australia. Some of the boats in the collection (such as the Karya Sama and the Tujuan) were donated to the museum after being confiscated for illegal fishing activity, and one has been the subject of detailed research (Stacey 1992).

From the early 1970s, the major sources on Indonesian fishing activity in Australian waters are reports and records from various government departments. These include both files and databases on boat apprehensions and prosecutions from the Western Australian Fisheries Department in Broome (cited in literature as the AFS Indonesian Database and the Western Australian Fisheries Files), and the records of the Foreign Fishing Operations Branch of the Australian Fisheries Management Authority held either in Canberra or at the Northern Territory Department of Primary Industries and Fisheries in Darwin (cited in literature as the Northern Territory Fisheries Files). Parks Australia boarding and patrol reports from Ashmore Reef are located at the Commonwealth Department of Environment and Water Resources offices in Canberra. A variety of published and unpublished material is held by the Commonwealth Department of Foreign Affairs and Trade, including a compendium of information compiled in 1988 (DFAT 1988).

MAGNT staff were engaged as consultants to investigate the impact of Indonesian fishing activities on the Ashmore Reef National Nature Reserve for the Australian National Parks and Wildlife Service (Russell and Vail 1988). Their report summarises historical data on traditional Indonesian fishing activities at Ashmore Reef, provides an analysis of the various groups of Indonesians visiting the region during the years 1986–1988, presents data on the status of marine resources targeted by these fisherment, and includes information collected from interviews with 13 *perahu* crews and captains present at Ashmore Reef during their fieldwork. There is also a separate consultancy report on Indonesian fishing at Cartier Island (McCarthy 1989).

A comprehensive, but as yet unpublished, report by the Fisheries Resources Branch of the Bureau of Rural Sciences, now part of the Department of Agriculture, Fisheries and Forestry, assesses the nature and extent of Indonesian fishing activity in the AFZ based on an analysis of information from various government departments gathered in 1994 (Wallner and McLoughlin 1995a). The report assesses the impact of Indonesian fishing on marine resources in the AFZ and makes recommendations for future management of these resources, ways of improving the information base, and alternative strategies to deal with traditional Indonesian fishermen operating in the MOU area.

Appendix B: Memorandum of Understanding Between the Government of Australia and the Government of the Republic of Indonesia Regarding the Operations of Indonesian Traditional Fishermen in Areas of the Australian Exclusive Fishing Zone and Continental Shelf (7 November 1974)

Following discussions held in Jakarta on 6 and 7 November, 1974, the representatives of the Government of Australia and of the Government of the Republic of Indonesia have agreed to record the following understandings.

1. These understandings shall apply to operations by Indonesian traditional fishermen in the exclusive fishing zone and over the continental shelf adjacent to the Australian mainland and offshore islands.

By "traditional fishermen" is meant the fishermen who have traditionally taken fish and sedentary organisms in Australian waters by methods which have been the tradition over decades of time.

By "exclusive fishing zone" is meant the zone of waters extending twelve miles seaward off the baseline from which the territorial sea of Australia is measured.

2. The Government of the Republic of Indonesia understands that in relation to fishing in the exclusive Australian fishing zone and the exploration for and exploitation of the living natural resources of the Australian continental shelf, in each case adjacent to:

Ashmore Reef (Pulau Pasir) (Latitude 12° 15' South, Longitude 123° 03' East), Cartier Islet (Latitude 12° 32' South, Longitude 123° 33' East), Scott Reef (Latitude 14° 03' South, Longitude 121° 47' East), Seringapatam Reef (Pulau Datu) (Latitude 11° 37' South, Longitude 122° 03' East), Browse Islet (Latitude 14° 06' South, Longitude 123° 32' East).

The Government of Australia will, subject to paragraph 8 of these understandings, refrain from applying its laws regarding fisheries to Indonesian traditional fishermen who conduct their operations in accordance with these understandings.

3. The Government of the Republic of Indonesia understands that, in the part of the areas described in paragraph 2 of these understandings where the Government of Australia is authorised by international law to regulate fishing or exploitation for or exploitation of the living natural resources of the Australian continental shelf by foreign nationals, the Government of Australia will permit operations by Indonesian nationals subject to the following conditions:

a) Indonesian operations in the areas mentioned in paragraph 2 of the understandings shall be confined to traditional fishermen.

b) Landings by Indonesian traditional fishermen shall be confined to East Islet (Latitude 12° 15′ South, Longitude 123° 07′ East), and Middle Islet (Latitude 12° 15′ South, Longitude 123° 03′ East) of Ashmore Reef for the purposes of obtaining supplies of fresh water.

c) Traditional Indonesian fishing vessels may take shelter within the island groups described in paragraph 2 of these understandings but the persons on board shall not go ashore except as allowed in (b) above.

4. The Government of the Republic of Indonesia understands that the Indonesian will not be permitted to take turtles in the Australian exclusive fishing zone. Trochus, beche de mer, abalone, green snail, sponges and all molluscs will not be taken from the seabed from high water marks to the edge of the continental shelf, except the seabed adjacent to Ashmore and Cartier Islands, Browse Islet and the Scott and Seringapatam Reef.

5. The Government of the Republic of Indonesia understands that the persons on board Indonesian fishing vessels engaging in fishing in the exclusive Australian fishing zone or exploring for or exploiting the living natural resources of the Australian continental shelf, in either case in areas other than those specified in paragraph 2 of these understandings, shall be subject to the provisions of Australian law.

6. The Government of Australia understands that the Government of the Republic of Indonesia will use its best endeavours to notify all Indonesian fishermen likely to operate in areas adjacent to Australia of the contents of these understandings.

7. Both Governments will facilitate the exchange of information concerning the activities of the traditional Indonesian fishing boats operating in the area west of the Timor Sea.

8. The Government of the Republic of Indonesia understands that the Government of Australia will, until the twenty-eighth day of February 1975, refrain from applying its laws relating to fisheries to Indonesian traditional fishermen in areas of the Australian exclusive fishing zone and continental shelf other than those specified in paragraph 2 of these understandings.

Appendix C: Agreed Minutes of Meeting Between Officials of Australia and Indonesia on Fisheries (29 April 1989)

1. In accordance with the agreement reached by Mr. Ali Alatas, the Foreign Minister of Indonesia and Senator Gareth Evans, the Foreign Minister of Australia in Canberra on 2 March, 1989, Officials from Indonesia and Australia met in Jakarta on 28 and 29 April 1989 to discuss activities of Indonesian fishing vessels under the Memorandum of Understanding between the Government of the Republic of Indonesia and the Government of Australia regarding the operation of Indonesian traditional fishermen in an Area of the Australian Fishing Zone and Continental Shelf, concluded in Jakarta on 7 November 1974. They also discussed activities of Indonesian fishing vessels in the Australian Fishing Zone off the coast of North West Australia and in the Arafura Sea, and fishing in the waters between Christmas Island and Java.

Memorandum of Understanding of 1974

2. Officials reviewed the operation of the MOU. Both sides stressed their desire to address the issues in a spirit of cooperation and good neighbourliness. They noted that there had been a number of developments since 1974 which had affected the MOU. In 1974 Australia and Indonesia exercised jurisdiction over fisheries on 12 nautical miles from their respective territorial sea baselines. In 1979 and 1980, Australia and Indonesia respectively extended their fisheries jurisdiction to 200 nautical miles from their respective territorial sea baselines, and in 1981 a provisional fishing line was agreed. Since the areas referred to in the MOU are south of this line, new arrangements are necessary for the access by Indonesian traditional fishermen to these areas under the MOU.

3. The Australian side informed the Indonesian side that there were also changes in the status of Ashmore Reef and Cartier Islet as a separate territory of the Commonwealth of Australia and the establishment of the Ashmore Reef National Nature Reserve. The Australian side further informed that there had been a considerable increase in the number of Indonesian fishermen visiting the Australian Fishing Zone and a depletion of fishery stocks around the Ashmore Reef, that wells on Middle Islet and East Islet where Indonesian traditional fishermen were permitted under the MOU to land for taking fresh water had been contaminated; that Australia had also incurred international obligations to protect wildlife, including that in the territory of Ashmore and Cartier Islands. The Indonesian side took note of this information.

4. Since the conclusion of the MOU, both Indonesia and Australia had become parties to the Convention on International Trade in Endangered Species of Wild Fauna and Flora (CITES).

5. The Indonesian and Australian Officials discussed the implications of the developments mentioned in the preceding paragraphs. They affirmed the

continued operation of the MOU for Indonesian traditional fishermen operating by traditional methods and using traditional fishing vessels. An Australian proposal that Indonesian traditional fishermen could conduct fishing not only in the areas adjacent to Ashmore Reef, Cartier Islet, Scott Reef, Seringapatam Reef and Browse Islet as designated in the MOU, but in a wider 'box' area in the Australian Fishing Zone and Continental Shelf was welcomed by the Indonesian side. A sketch map and coordinates of this 'box' area appears in Annex 1 of this Agreed Minutes.

6. In view of the developments that had occurred since 1974 as highlighted above, Officials considered that to improve the implementation of the MOU, practical guidelines for implementing the MOU as appears in the Annex of these Agreed Minutes were considered necessary.

7. The Indonesian side informed the Australian side on measures that had been and were being taken by the Indonesian authorities to prevent breaches of the MOU. The Indonesian side indicated its willingness to assist in preventing breaches of the MOU and to take necessary steps to inform Indonesian fishermen of the practical guidelines annexed to this Agreed Minutes.

8. The Indonesian and Australian Officials agreed to make arrangements for cooperation in developing alternative income projects in Eastern Indonesia for traditional fishermen traditionally engaged in fishing under the MOU. The Indonesian side indicated they might include mariculture and nucleus fishing enterprise scheme (Perikanan Inti Rakyat or PIR). Both sides mutually decided to discuss the possibility of channelling Australian aid funds to such projects with appropriate authorities in their respective countries.

North West Coast of Australia

9. The Indonesian and Australian Officials discussed matters related to the activities of Indonesian fishing vessels in the Australian Fishing Zone off the coast of North West Australia. They noted that those activities were outside the scope of the MOU and that Australia would take appropriate enforcement action. The Australian side indicated the legal and economic implications of such activities.

10. The Indonesian and Australian Officials felt the need for a long-term solution to the problem. To this end, they agreed to make arrangements for cooperation in projects to provide income alternatives in Eastern Indonesia for Indonesian fishermen engaged in fishing off the coast of North West Australia. The Indonesian side indicated that they might include mariculture and nucleus fishing enterprise scheme (Perikanan Inti Rakyat or PIR). Both sides decided mutually to discuss the possibility of channelling Australian aid funds to such projects with appropriate authorities in their respective countries.

Arafura Sea

11. Indonesian and Australian Officials discussed the activities of Indonesian non-traditional fishing vessels in the Arafura Sea on the Australian side of the provisional fishing line of 1981. Officials agreed that both Governments should take effective measures, including enforcement measures, to prevent Indonesian non-traditional fishing vessels from fishing on the Australian side of the provisional fishing line without the authorisation of the Australian authorities.

12. Officials agreed to make arrangements for cooperation in exchange of information on shared stocks in the Arafura Sea for the purpose of effective management and conservation of the stocks.

Fishing in waters between Christmas Island and Java and other waters

13. The Officials of Indonesia and Australia noted that fisheries delimitation in waters between Christmas Island and Java and in the west of the provisional fishing line remained to be negotiated and agreed. Pending such an agreement, the Officials noted that both Governments would endeavour to avoid incidents in the area of overlapping jurisdictional claims.

Wildlife Cooperation

14. The Indonesian and Australian Officials considered the mutual advantages of the exchange of information on wildlife species populations believed to be common to both countries. It was agreed that each country's nature conservation authorities would exchange information on such wildlife populations and management programs and cooperation in the management of wildlife protected areas. In the first instance Indonesian authorities would be consulted on the management plan for the Ashmore Reef National Nature Reserve.

Consultations

15. The Indonesian and Australian Officials agreed to hold consultations as and when necessary to ensure the effective implementation of the MOU and agreed minutes.

Annex I: Co-ordinates of MOU Area ('The Box')

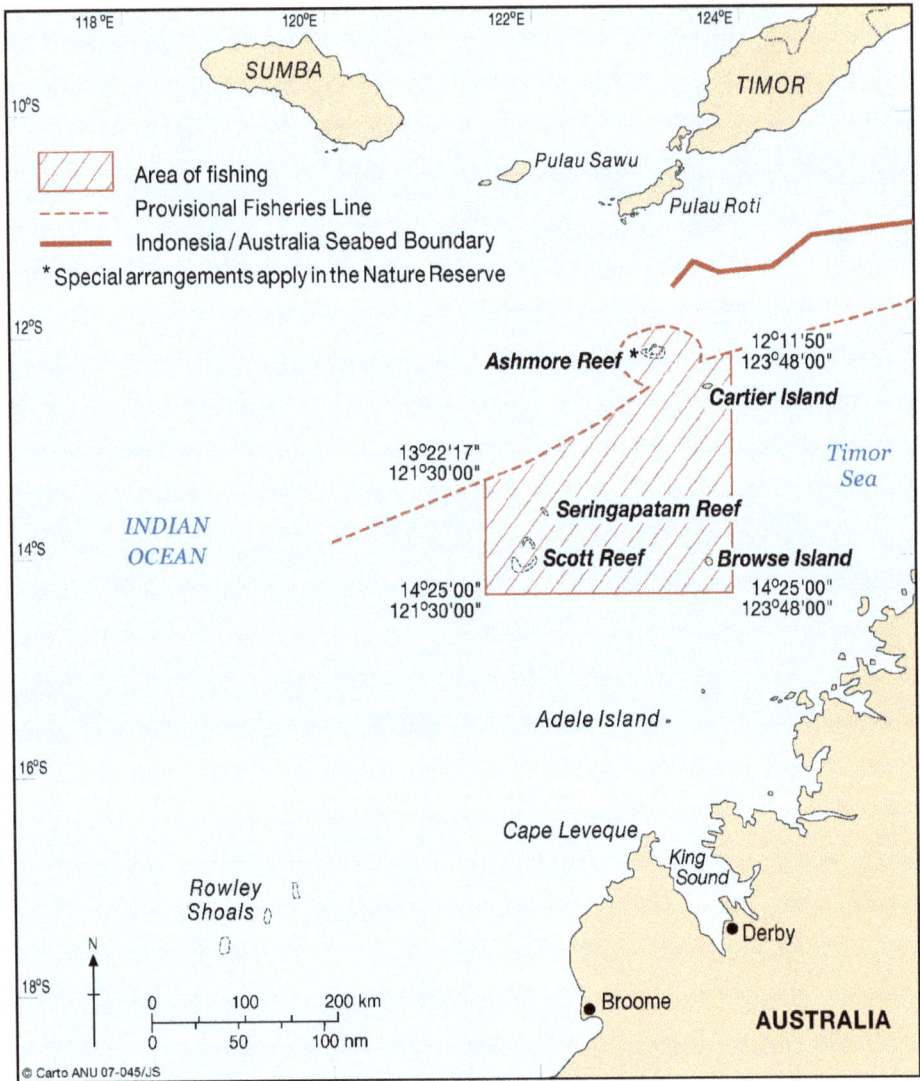

Annex II: Practical Guidelines for Implementing the 1974 MOU

1. Access to the MOU area would continue to be limited to Indonesian traditional fishermen using traditional methods and traditional vessels consistent with the tradition over decades of time, which does not include fishing methods or vessels utilising motors or engines.

2. The Indonesian traditional fishermen would continue to conduct traditional activities under the MOU in the area of the Australian Fishing Zone and the continental shelf adjacent to Ashmore Reef, Cartier Islet, Scott Reef, Seringapatam

Reef and Browse Islet. In addition, Indonesian traditional fishermen would be able to conduct traditional fishing activities in an expanded area as described in the sketch map and coordinates attached to Annex 1 of the Agreed Minutes.

3. To cope with the depletion of certain stocks of fish and sedentary species in the Ashmore Reef area, the Australian Government had prohibited all fishing activities in the Ashmore Reef National Nature Reserve, but was expected soon to adopt a management plan for the Reserve which might allow some subsistence fishing by the Indonesian traditional fishermen. The Australian side indicated that Indonesia would be consulted on the draft plan. Because of the low level of stock, the taking of sedentary species particularly *Trochus nilotocus* in the Reserve would be prohibited at this stage to allow stocks to recover. The possibility of renewed Indonesian traditional fishing of the species would be considered in future reviews of the management plan.

4. As both Australia and Indonesia are parties to CITES, Officials agreed that any taking of protected wildlife including turtles and clams would continue to be prohibited in accordance with CITES.

5. Indonesian traditional fishermen would be permitted to land on West Islet for the purpose of obtaining supplies of fresh water. The Indonesian side indicated its willingness to discourage Indonesian traditional fishermen from landings on East and Middle Islets because of the lack of fresh water on the two islets.

REFERENCES

ABC Radio National, 1995. 'Illegal Indonesian Fishing off North Australia.' Libby Price Show Transcript, 3 February 1995.

Acciaioli, G., 1985. 'Culture as Art: From Practice to Spectacle in Indonesia.' *Canberra Anthropology* 8(1/2): 148–72.

———, 1987. 'Kinship and Debt: The Social Organisation of Bugis Migration and Fish Marketing at Lake Lindu, Central Sulawesi.' Paper presented at the Second International Workshop on Indonesian Studies, Leiden, 2–6 November.

———, 1990. 'How to Win Followers and Influence Spirits: Propitiation and Participation in a Multi-Ethnic Community of Central Sulawesi, Indonesia.' *Anthropological Forum* 6(2): 207–35.

———, 1996. 'Exhibiting the Indigenous: Indonesian Government Representations of the Bajau.' Paper presented at the Asian Studies Association of Australia conference, Melbourne, 8–11 July.

Acheson, J., 1981. 'Anthropology of Fishing.' *Annual Review of Anthropology* 10: 275–316.

AFMA (Australian Fisheries Management Authority), 1995. *Annual Report 1994–1995*. Canberra: AFMA.

Alexander, P., 1982. *Sri Lankan Fishermen: Rural Capitalism and Peasant Society*. Canberra: Australian National University (South Asia Monograph 7).

Ammarell, G., 1995. 'Navigation Practices of the Bugis of South Sulawesi, Indonesia.' In R. Feinburg (ed.), *Seafaring in the Contemporary Pacific Islands: Studies in Continuity and Change*. DeKalb: Northern Illinois University Press.

Anderson, L.P., 1978. The Role of Aboriginal and Asian Labour in the Origin and Development of the Pearling Industry, Broome, Western Australia 1862–1940. Perth: Murdoch University (Honours thesis).

ANPWS (Australian National Parks and Wildlife Service), 1985a. *Annual Report 1983–1984*. Canberra: Australian Government Publishing Service.

———, 1985b. *Annual Report 1984–1985*. Canberra: Australian Government Publishing Service.

———, 1986. *Annual Report 1985–1986*. Canberra: Australian Government Publishing Service.

———, 1987. *Annual Report 1986–1987*. Canberra: Australian Government Publishing Service.

————, 1989. *Ashmore Reef National Nature Reserve Plan of Management.* Canberra: ANPWS.

————, n.d. 'A Tour Guide to West Island, Ashmore Reef National Nature Reserve.' Darwin: ANPWS (unpublished pamphlet).

Asad, T. (ed.), 1973. *Anthropology and the Colonial Encounter.* London: Ithaca Press.

Bach, J.P.S., 1955. *The Pearling Industry of Australia: An Account of its Social and Economic Development.* Canberra: Commonwealth of Australia.

Bailey, C. and C. Zerner, 1992. 'Community-Based Fisheries Management Institutions in Indonesia.' *MAST* 5(1): 1–17.

Bain, M.A., 1982. *Full Fathom Five.* Perth: Artlook Books.

Bergin, A., 1989. 'The Politics of Intrusion: The Case of Ashmore and Cartier Islands.' *Indian Ocean Review* 2(1): 13–19.

Bottignolo, B., 1995. *Celebrations with the Sun: An Overview of Religious Phenomena among the Badjaos.* Quezon City: Ateneo de Manila University Press.

Bottrill, A.M., 1993. 'Some Chronologically Arranged Notes Randomly Garnered from West Australian Sources Concerning Indonesians in Northwest Australia.' Unpublished manuscript.

Burmester, H., 1985. 'Island Outposts of Australia.' In W.S.G. Bateman and M. Ward (eds), *Australia's Offshore Maritime Interests.* Canberra: Australia Centre for Maritime Studies (Occasional Paper in Maritime Affairs 3).

Burningham, N., 1989. 'Four Double-Ended *Perahu Lambo.*' *The Beagle: Records of the Northern Territory Museum of Arts and Sciences* 6(1): 179–93.

————, 1993. 'Bajau Lepa and Sope: A "Seven-Part Canoe" Building Tradition in Indonesia.' *The Beagle: Records of the Northern Territory Museum of Arts and Sciences* 10(1): 193–222.

————, 1996. 'The *Perahu Lambo*: A 20th Century Merchant Sailing Ship.' Unpublished manuscript.

Campbell, B., 1991. The Politics of Exclusion: Indonesian Distant Shore Fisheries and the Expansion of Australia's Maritime Boundaries. Perth: Murdoch University, School of Social Sciences (Honours thesis).

Campbell, B. and B.V.E. Wilson, 1993. *The Politics of Exclusion: Indonesian Fishing in the Australian Fishing Zone.* Perth: Indian Ocean Centre for Peace Studies and Australian Centre for International Agricultural Research.

Cane, S., 1998. 'Aboriginal Fishing on the New South Wales South Coast: A Court Case.' In N. Peterson and B. Rigsby (eds), *Customary Marine Tenure in Australia*. Sydney: University of Sydney (Oceania Monograph 48).

Carrier, J., 1992a. 'Occidentalism: The World Turned Upside-Down.' *American Ethnologist* 19(2): 195–211.

———, 1992b. 'Introduction.' In J. Carrier (ed.), *History and Tradition in Melanesian Anthropology*. Berkeley: University of California Press.

Chou, C., 1997. 'Contesting the Tenure of Territoriality: The Orang Suku Laut.' *Bijdragen Tot de Taal-, Land- en Volkenkunde* 153(4): 605–29.

Collins, G.E.P., 1936. *East Monsoon*. London: Jonathon Cape.

———, 1937. *Makassar Sailing*. London: Jonathon Cape.

Collins, J., 1995. 'Preliminary Notes on the Languages of the Bajo Sangkuang Community of Bacam, East Indonesia.' Paper presented at the 'International Conference on Bajau/Sama Community', Kota Kinabalu, Sabah, 24–28 June.

Commonwealth Ombudsman, 1998. 'Report into Administrative Arrangements for Indonesian Fishermen Detained in Australian Waters.' Canberra: Office of the Australian Commonwealth Ombudsman.

Cordell, J., 1989. 'Introduction: Sea Tenure.' In J. Cordell (ed.), *A Sea of Small Boats*. Cambridge (MA): Cultural Survival.

Cowan, S., C. Mellon and K. Anderson, 1990. 'Fishing a Fine Line — Indonesian Fishing in the AFZ.' *Australian Fisheries* 49(2): 19–23.

Crawford, I., 1969. Late Prehistoric Changes in Aboriginal Cultures in Kimberley, WA. London: University of London (Ph.D. thesis).

———, 2001. *We Won The Victory: Aborigines and Outsiders on the North-West Coast of the Kimberley*. Fremantle: Fremantle Arts Centre Press.

CSIRO (Commonwealth Scientific and Industrial Research Organisation), 1949. 'F.R.V. "Warreen" — Cruise Number 35 (July–November 1949): Biological Log.' Hobart: CSIRO Division of Fisheries (unpublished report).

Darling, J., 1994. 'Below the Wind: Sea Nomads of Indonesia.' Documentary film screened on ABC Television, 13 January.

DFAT (Australian Department of Foreign Affairs and Trade), 1988. 'The Control of Indonesian Traditional Fishing in the Australian Fishing Zone of North-West Australia.' Canberra: DFAT (unpublished report).

———, 1997. Australia-Indonesia Maritime Delimitation Treaty. Canberra: Department of Foreign Affairs and Trade.

Dick, H.W., 1975. 'Perahu Shipping in Eastern Indonesia, Part I.' Bulletin of Indonesian Economic Studies 2(2): 69–107;

Donohue, M., 1994. 'Direction in Tukang Besi.' Paper presented at the Third Maluku Research Conference, Pattimura University, Ambon, 30 June.

———, 1999. A Grammar of Tukang Besi. Berlin: Mouton de Gruyter (Grammar Library 20).

Endicott, K.M., 1970. An Analysis of Malay Magic. Singapore: Oxford University Press.

Environment Australia, 2002. 'Ashmore Reef National Nature Reserve and Cartier Island Marine Reserve (Commonwealth Waters) Management Plans.' Canberra: Environment Australia.

Errington, S., 1983. 'Embodied Sumange' in Luwu.' Journal of Asian Studies 42(3): 545–70.

———, 1989. Meaning and Power in a Southeast Asian Realm. Princeton: Princeton University Press.

Evers, H-D., 1991. 'Traditional Trading Networks of Southeast Asia.' In K.R. Haellquist (ed.), Asian Trade Routes. London: Curzon Press.

Ewins, R., 1998. Changing Their Minds: Tradition and Politics in Contemporary Fiji and Tonga. Christchurch: University of Canterbury, Macmillan Brown Centre for Pacific Studies.

Fabian, J., 1983. Time and the Other: How Anthropology Makes its Object. New York: Columbia University Press.

Fairbridge, R.W., 1948. 'Discoveries in the Timor Sea, North-West Australia.' Journal and Proceedings of the Royal Australian Historical Society 38(4): 193–218.

Flinders, M., 1814. A Voyage to Terra Australis. London: G. and W. Nichol.

Fox, J.J., 1977a. 'Notes on the Southern Voyages and Settlements of the Sama-Bajau.' Bijdragen Tot de Taal-, Land- en Volkenkunde 133(4): 459–65.

———, 1977b. Harvest of the Palm: Ecological Change in Eastern Indonesia. Cambridge (MA): Harvard University Press.

———, 1992. 'Report on Eastern Indonesian Fishermen in Darwin.' In Illegal Entry! Darwin: Northern Territory University, Centre for Southeast Asian Studies (Occasional Paper 1).

———, 1995a. 'Foreword.' In M. Southon, op. cit.

———, 1995b. 'Maritime Communities in the Timor and Arafura Region: Some Historical and Anthropological Perspectives.' Paper presented at the conference on 'Neighbours at Sea: The Shared Interests of Australia and Indonesia in the Timor and Arafura Seas', Darwin, 1–2 November.

————, 1996. 'Fishing Resources and Marine Tenure: The Problems of Eastern Indonesian Fishermen.' In C. Barlow and J. Hardjono (eds), *Indonesia Assessment 1995: Development in Eastern Indonesia*. Canberra: Australian National University, Research School of Pacific and Asian Studies/Singapore: Institute of Southeast Asian Studies.

————, 1998. 'Reefs and Shoals in Australia–Indonesia Relations: Traditional Indonesian Fishermen.' In A. Milner and M. Quilty (eds), *Australia in Asia: Episodes*. Melbourne: Oxford University Press.

Gibson-Hill, C.A., 1950. 'The Indonesian Trading Boats Reaching Singapore.' *Journal of the Malay Branch of the Royal Asiatic Society* 23(1): 108–38.

Handler, R. and J. Linnekin, 1984. 'Tradition, Genuine or Spurious.' *Journal of American Folklore* 97(385): 273–90.

Hancock, D.A., D.C. Smith, A. Grant and J.P. Beumer (eds), 1997. *Developing and Sustaining World Fisheries Resources: The State of the Science and Management*. Collingwood: CSIRO (Proceedings of the Second World Fisheries Congress).

Harvey, B., 1974. Tradition, Islam and Rebellion: South Sulawesi 1950–1965. Ithaca (NY): Cornell University (Ph.D. thesis).

Hawkins, C.W., 1982. *Praus of Indonesia*. London: Nautical Books.

Heersink, C.G., 1994. 'Selayar and the Green Gold: The Development of the Coconut Trade on an Indonesian Island (1820–1950).' *Journal of Southeast Asian Studies* 25(1): 47–69.

Hickey, C.M., 1950. Geography of Fish-Stupefying Plants and Practices in Indonesia. Berkeley: University of California (M.A. thesis).

Hobsbawm, E. and T. Ranger (eds), 1983. *The Invention of Tradition*. Cambridge: Cambridge University Press.

Horridge, A., 1979. *The Lambo or Prahu Bot: A Western Ship in an Eastern Setting*. Greenwich: National Maritime Museum (Maritime Monographs and Reports 39).

————, 1985. *The Prahu: Traditional Sailin g Boat of Indonesia* (2nd edn). Singapore: Oxford University Press.

Hovelsrud-Broda, G., 1997. 'Arctic Seal-Hunting Households and the Anti-Sealing Controversy.' *Research in Economic Anthropology* 18: 17–34.

Howe, H.V., 1952. 'Sea Poaching is a Major Industry.' *Sydney Morning Herald*, 2 February.

Hughes, D., 1984. The Indonesian Cargo Sailing Vessels and the Problem of Technology Choice for Sea Transport in a Developing Country: A Study of the Consequences of *Perahu* Motorisation Policy in the Context of the Economic Regulation of Inter-island Shipping. Cardiff: University of Wales, Department of Maritime Studies (Ph.D. thesis).

Hviding, E., 1996. *Guardians of Marovo Lagoon*. Honolulu: University of Hawaii Press.

———— and G. Baines, 1996. 'Marine Tenure and Fisheries Management: Solomon Islands.' In R. Howitt, J. Connell and P. Hirsch (eds), *Resources, Nations and Indigenous People: Case Studies from Australia, Melanesia and South-East Asia*. Melbourne: Oxford University Press.

Johannes, R.E., 1996. 'A Fisheries Time Warp?' *Australian Marine Science Bulletin* 136: 20–1.

JSCFADT (Australian Joint Standing Committee on Foreign Affairs Defence and Trade), 1993. *Australia's Relations with Indonesia*. Canberra: Australian Government Publishing Service.

JSCT (Australian Joint Standing Committee on Treaties), 1997. *Australia-Indonesia Maritime Delimitation Treaty: 12th Report*. Canberra: Parliament of the Commonwealth of Australia.

Kabupaten Buton, 1994a. 'Kecamatan Wangi Wangi Dalam Angka [Wangi Wangi Sub-District in Figures].' Baubau: Kabupaten Buton, Kantor Statistik [Buton District Statistical Office].

————, 1994b. 'Kecamatan Kaledupa Dalam Angka [Kaledupa Sub-District in Figures].' Baubau: Kabupaten Buton, Kantor Statistik [Buton District Statistical Office].

————, 1994c. 'Kecamatan Tomia Dalam Angka [Tomia Sub-District in Figures].' Baubau: Kabupaten Buton, Kantor Statistik [Buton District Statistical Office].

————, 1994d. 'Kecamatan Binongko Dalam Angka [Binongko Sub-District in Figures].' Baubau: Kabupaten Buton, Kantor Statistik [Buton District Statistical Office].

Kasmin, 1993. Perlawan Suku Bajo Terhadap Bajak Laut Tobelo di Perairan Kepulauan Wakatobi, Buton, Sulawesi Tenggara [Bajo Opposition to Tobelo Pirates in the Waters of the Wakatobi Islands, Buton, Southeast Sulawesi]. Kendari: Haluoleo University, Faculty of Teaching and Education Science (B.Sc. thesis).

Kaye, S., 1995. *Australia's Maritime Boundaries*. Wollongong: University of Wollongong, Centre for Maritime Policy.

Keesing, R. and R. Tonkinson (eds), 1982. 'Reinventing Traditional Culture: The Politics of Kastom in Island Melanesia.' Special Issue 13(4) of *Mankind*.

Kilduff, P. and N. Lofgren, 1996. 'Native Title Fishing Rights in Coastal Waters and Territorial Seas.' *Aboriginal Law Bulletin* 3(81): 16–17.

Kriebel, D.J.C., 1920. 'Het Eiland Bonerate [The Island of Bonerate].' *Bijdragen Tot de Taal-, Land- en Volkenkunde van Nederlandsch-Indie* 76: 202–22.

Lai Ka-Keong, E., 1983. 'Shark Fins — Processing and Marketing in Hong Kong.' *Infofish Marketing Digest* 5: 35–9.

Langdon, R., 1966. 'Our Far Flung Empire.' *New Guinea and Australia, the Pacific and South-East Asia* June/July: 54–8.

Lenhart, L., 1995. 'Recent Research on Southeast Asian Nomads.' *Nomadic Peoples* 36/37: 245–60.

Levinson, D. (ed.), 1993. *Encyclopedia of World Cultures — Volume 5*. New Haven (CT): Human Relations Area Files Press.

Lind, R., 1994. *Cockatoo Island Memories Yampi, Western Australia*. Stuart Hill (WA): R. Lind.

LRC (Australian Law Reform Commission), 1986. *The Recognition of Aboriginal Customary Laws — Volume 2*. Canberra: Australian Government Publishing Service (LRC Report 31).

Mace, P., 1997. 'Developing and Sustaining World Fisheries Resources: The State of the Science and Management.' In D.A. Hancock, D.C. Smith, A. Grant and J.P. Beumer (eds), op. cit.

Macknight, C.C., 1976. *The Voyage to Marege': Macassan Trepangers in Northern Australia*. Carlton: Melbourne University Press.

Marcus, G. and M. Fischer, 1986. *Anthropology as Cultural Critique: An Experimental Moment in the Human Sciences*. Chicago: The University of Chicago Press.

McCarthy, M., 1989. 'Indonesian Divers at Cartier Island.' In *The Flamingo Bay Voyage*. Perth: Western Australian Museum, Department of Maritime Archaeology (Report 45).

McColl, J. and R. Stevens, 1997. 'Australian Fisheries Management Authority: Organizational Structure and Management Philosophy.' In D.A. Hancock, D.C. Smith, A. Grant and J.P. Beumer (eds), op. cit.

McGann, P.J., 1988. 'Malays' as Indentured Labour: Western Australia 1870–1900. Perth: Murdoch University (Honours thesis).

Mellefont, J., 1988. 'The Lete-Lete of Raas: A Report on the Geographic, Economic, Social and Technological Context of the *Lete-Lete* Sekar Aman

Acquired by the Australian National Maritime Museum.' Sydney: Australian National Maritime Museum (unpublished report).

———, 1991a. '*Sekar Aman*: Indonesian Trading *Perahu*.' *Signals* 15: 8.

———, 1991b. 'Between Tradition and Change: An Indonesian *Perahu* in an Australian Collection.' *The Great Circle* 13(2): 97–110.

———, 1997. 'A *Lete-Lete* from Raas.' *Signals* 41: 26–30.

Merlan, F., 1991. 'The Limits of Cultural Constructionism: The Case of Coronation Hill.' *Oceania* 61: 341–52.

———, 1998. *Caging the Rainbow: Places, Politics, and Aborigines in a North Australian Town*. Honolulu: University of Hawaii Press.

Miller, D., 1994. *Modernity: An Ethnographic Approach*. Oxford: Berg.

Mitchell, S., 1994. Culture Contact and Indigenous Economies on the Cobourg Peninsula, Northwestern Arnhem Land. Darwin: Northern Territory University, Faculty of Arts (Ph.D. thesis).

Morwood, M. and D. Hobbs, 1997. 'The Asian Connection: Preliminary Report on Indonesian Trepang Sites on the Kimberley Coast, N.W. Australia.' *Archaeology in Oceania* 32: 197–206.

Nadjmabadi, S., 1992. '"The Sea Belongs to God, the Land Belongs to Us": Resource Management in a Multi-Resource Community in the Persian Gulf.' In M.J. Casimir and A. Rao (eds), *Mobility and Territoriality: Social and Spatial Boundaries among Foragers, Fishers, Pastoralists and Peripatetics*. New York: Berg.

Nagatsu, K., 1995. 'Magambit: Sama's Traditional Fishing Technique and its Change.' *Sama-Bajau Studies Newsletter* May: 7–8.

Naylor, P., 1995. 'Coastwatch: Civil Maritime Surveillance — An Australian Perspective.' Paper presented at the conference on 'Neighbours at Sea: The Shared Interests of Australia and Indonesia in the Timor and Arafura Seas', Darwin, 1–2 November.

Nimmo, H.A., 1990. 'Religious Beliefs of the Tawi-Tawi Bajau.' *Philippine Studies* 38: 166–98.

Noorduyn, J., 1991. *A Critical Survey of Studies on the Languages of Sulawesi*. Leiden: KITLV Press.

Nooteboom, C., 1947. 'The Study of Primitive Sea-Going Craft as an Ethnological Problem.' *Internationales Archiv fur Ethnographie* 45: 216–24.

Pallesen, A.K., 1985. *Culture Contact and Convergence*. Manila: Linguistic Society of the Philippines.

Pannell, S., 1993. '"Circulating Commodities": Reflections on the Movement and Meaning of Shells and Stories in North Australia and Eastern Indonesia.' *Oceania* 64: 57–76.

———, 1996. '*Homo Nullius* or "Where Have All the People Gone"? Refiguring Marine Management and Conservation Approaches.' *Australian Journal of Anthropology* 7(1): 21–42.

Pelras, C., 1972. 'Notes sur Quelques Populations Aquatiques de l'Archipel Nusantarien [Notes on Some Aquatic Populations of the Indonesian Archipelago].' *Archipel* 3: 133–68.

———, 1996. *The Bugis*. Oxford: Blackwell Publishers.

Peterson, N. and B. Rigsby, 1998. 'Introduction.' In N. Peterson and B. Rigsby (eds), *Customary Marine Tenure in Australia*. Sydney: University of Sydney (Oceania Monograph 48).

Pomeroy, R.S., 1994. 'Introduction.' In R.S. Pomeroy (ed.), *Community Management and Common Property of Coastal Fisheries in Asia and the Pacific: Concepts, Methods and Experiences*. Manila: ICLARM.

Reid, A., 1983. 'The Rise of Makassar.' *Review of Indonesian and Malaysian Affairs* 17: 117–60.

———, 1992. 'Indonesian Fishermen Detained in Broome.' In *Illegal Entry!* Darwin: Northern Territory University, Centre for Southeast Asian Studies (Occasional Paper 1).

Ritchie, D., 1999. 'Constructions of Aboriginal Tradition for Public Purpose.' In S. Toussaint and J. Taylor (eds), *Applied Anthropology in Australasia*. Nedlands: University of Western Australia Press.

Roberts, C., 1997. 'Reason for Decision: Mitchell v Nasir, Sahaba, Dona, Dualin and Laduma.' Broome: Court of Petty Sessions (Magistrate's Judgement).

Rose, D.A., 1996. *An Overview of World Trade in Sharks and Other Cartilaginous Fishes*. Cambridge: TRAFFIC International.

Russell, B. and L. Vail, 1988. 'Report on Traditional Indonesian Fishing Activity at Ashmore Reef Nature Reserve.' Darwin: Australian National Parks and Wildlife Service (unpublished report).

Said, E., 1979. *Orientalism*. New York: Random House.

Sather, C.A., 1985. 'Boat Crews and Fishing Fleets: The Social Organisation of Maritime Labour among the Bajau Laut of Southeastern Sabah.' *Contributions to Southeast Asian Ethnography* 4: 165–214.

———, 1993a. 'Samal.' In D. Levinson (ed.), op. cit.

———, 1993b. 'Bajau.' In D. Levinson (ed.), op. cit.

————, 1997. *The Bajau Laut: Adaptation, History and Fate in a Maritime Fishing Society of South-Eastern Sabah*. New York: Oxford University Press.

Schug, D., 1996. 'International Maritime Boundaries and Indigenous People: The Case of the Torres Strait.' *Marine Policy* 20(3): 209–22.

Scott, C., 1993. 'Custom, Tradition, and the Politics of Culture: Aboriginal Self-Government in Canada.' In N. Dyck and J. Waldram (eds), *Anthropology, Public Policy, and Native Peoples in Canada*. Montreal and Kingston: McGill-Queen's University Press.

Scott, N., 1988. *Sekar Aman: An Indonesian Perahu in Australia*. Perth: Scott and Scott.

Serventy, D.L., 1952. 'Indonesian Fishing Activity in Australian Seas.' *Australian Geographer* 6: 13–16.

Sopher, D.E., 1977 (1965). *The Sea Nomads: A Study of the Maritime Boat People of Southeast Asia*. Singapore: National Museum of Singapore.

Southon, M., 1995. *The Navel of the Perahu: Meaning and Values in the Maritime Trading Economy of a Butonese Village*. Canberra: Australian National University, Research School of Pacific and Asian Studies.

Stacey, N., 1992. The *Tujuan*: A Study of the Material Culture of an Indonesian Fishing Vessel held in the Collection of the Northern Territory Museum of Arts and Sciences. Townsville: James Cook University, Material Culture Unit (Grad. Dip. thesis).

————, 1997. 'Points of Encounter: Indonesian Fishing Boats in Australian Museum Collections.' *Proceedings of the 4th National Conference of Museums Australia Inc*. Darwin: Museums Australia, Northern Territory Branch.

Stanzel, K.B. and H. Newman, 1997. 'Operation Wallacea Progress Report on the 1996 Marine Survey of the Tukang Besi (Wakatobi) Archipelago, Southeast Sulawesi, Indonesia.' Unpublished report to Ecosurveys Ltd (United Kingdom) and Wallacea Development Institute (Indonesia).

Stevens, S., 1997. 'Introduction.' In S. Stevens (ed.), *Conservation Through Cultural Survival: Indigenous People and Protected Areas*. Washington (DC): Island Press.

Sutherland, J., 1996. *Fisheries, Aquaculture and Aboriginal and Torres Strait Islander Peoples: Studies, Policies and Legislation*. Canberra: Department of the Environment, Sport and Territories (Report 3).

Teljeur, D., 1990. *The Symbolic System of the Giman of South Halmahera*. Dordrecht: Foris Publications.

Tomascik, T., A.J. Mah, A. Nontji and M.K. Moosa, 1997. *The Ecology of the Indonesian Seas — Volume VIII, Part Two.* Oxford: Oxford University Press.

Tonkinson, R., 1993. 'Understanding "Tradition" — Ten Years On.' *Anthropological Forum* 6(4): 597–606.

———, 1997. 'Anthropology and Aboriginal Tradition: The Hindmarsh Island Bridge Affair and the Politics of Interpretation.' *Oceania* 68(1): 1–26.

Tsamenyi, M., 1995. 'Managing Indonesian Traditional Fishing Activities in Australian Waters: An Australian Perspective.' Paper presented at the conference on 'Neighbours at Sea: The Shared Interests of Australia and Indonesia in the Timor and Arafura Seas', Darwin, 1–2 November.

Van der Spek, K., 1995. Marine Right, Marine Wrong: Bajau Perspectives on Illegal Fishing. Canberra: Australian National University, Department of Archaeology and Anthropology (Honours thesis).

Velthoen, E., 1997. A Historical Perspective on Bajo in Eastern Indonesia. Unpublished paper.

——— and G. Acciaioli, 1993. 'Fluctuating States and Mobile Populations: Shifting Relations of Bajo to Local Rulers and Bugis Traders in Colonial Eastern Sulawesi.' Paper presented at the 'International Seminar on Bajau Communities', Indonesian Institute of Sciences, Jakarta, 22–25 November.

Verheijen, J.A., 1986. *The Sama/Bajau Language in the Lesser Sunda Islands.* Canberra: Australian National University, Research School of Pacific Studies, Department of Linguistics (Pacific Linguistics D70).

Vincent, P., 1997. 'Defendants' Written Submissions: Mitchell v Nasir, Sahaba, Dona, Dualin and Laduma.' Broome: Court of Petty Sessions (Complaint No. 590-5/97).

Wagner, R., 1975. *The Invention of Culture.* Englewood Cliffs (NJ): Prentice-Hall.

Wallner, B. and K. McLoughlin, 1995a. 'Review of Indonesian Fishing in the Australian Fishing Zone.' Canberra: Department of Primary Industries and Energy, Bureau of Rural Sciences (unpublished paper).

———, 1995b. 'Indonesian Fishing in Northern Australia.' In K. McLouglin, B. Wallner and D. Staples (eds), *Fishery Status Reports 1994 — Resource Assessments of Australian Commonwealth Fisheries.* Canberra: Bureau of Rural Sciences.

Warren, C., 1993. *Adat and Dinas: Balinese Communities in the Indonesian State.* Kuala Lumpur: Oxford University Press.

Waterson, R., 1990. *The Living House: An Anthology of Architecture in South-East Asia.* Singapore: Oxford University Press.

White, A.T., L.Z. Hale, Y. Renard and L. Cortesi (eds), 1994. *Collaborative and Community-Based Management of Coral Reefs: Lessons from Experience.* Bloomfield (CT): Kumarian Press.

Wilkinson, R.J., 1901. *A Malay– English Dictionary.* Singapore: Kelly and Walsh.

Wolf, E., 1982. *Europe and the People Without History.* Berkeley: University of California Press.

Woodward, H.P., 1917. 'The Phosphatic Deposits of Western Australia.' *Bulletin of the Geological Survey of Western Australi a* 74: 9–28.

Zacot, F., 1978. 'To Be or Not to Be Badjo — This is our Question.' *Prisma* 10: 17–29.

Zerner, C., 1994. 'Tracking Sasi: The Transformation of a Central Moluccan Reef Management Institution in Indonesia.' In A.T. White, L.Z. Hale, Y. Renard and L. Cortesi (eds), op. cit.

Index

www.ingramcontent.com/pod-product-compliance
Lightning Source LLC
Chambersburg PA
CBHW040247290326

41929CB00054B/3444